CONTENTS

vi   CONTENTS

THE NEUROPSYCHOLOGY OF READING
ABILITY AND DISABILITY: PIECES OF
THE PUZZLE
Raymond L. Ownby   119

STYLES IN EDUCATIONAL RESEARCH
ON TWO SIDES OF THE ATLANTIC
W. Bryan Dockrell   151

LET'S BE TECHNICALLY RIGHT ABOUT
TECHNICAL WRITING
Paul Sorrentino   167

PERSONAL COMPUTERS IN LANGUAGE
AND READING RESEARCH: THREE
VIGNETTES
Daniel W. Kee and Patricia E. Worden   183

RESEARCH ON TEACHER–PUPIL
INTERACTIONS DURING ORAL
READING INSTRUCTION
Jerome A. Niles   207

INDEX   227

ADVANCES IN READING/LANGUAGE RESEARCH

A Research Annual

Editor: BARBARA A. HUTSON
*Division of Curriculum
and Instruction
Virginia Polytechnic Institute
and State University*

VOLUME 3 ● 1985

 JAI PRESS INC.

Greenwich, Connecticut   *London, England*

d642 6.86

LIST OF CONTRIBUTORS

Bertram C. Bruce   Bolt, Beranek and Newman, Inc.,
                                       Cambridge, Massachusetts

W. Bryan Dockrell   Executive Director, Scottish Council
                                       for Research in Education

Eileen B. Entin   Computer Science Department,
                                       Wentworth Institute of Technology

Michael M. Gerber   Graduate School/Special Education,
                                       University of California,
                                       Santa Barbara

Barbara A. Hutson   Northern Virginia Graduate Center,
                                       Virginia Polytechnic Institute and
                                       State University

Daniel W. Kee   Department of Psychology,
                                       California State University,
                                       Fullerton

George R. Klare   College of Education,
                                       Ohio University

Jerome A. Niles   College of Education,
                                       Virginia Polytechnic Institute and
                                       State University

Raymond L. Ownby   Western Reserve Habilitation Center,
                                       Northfield, Ohio

Andee Rubin   Bolt, Beranek and Newman, Inc.,
                                       Cambridge, Massachusetts

Paul Sorrentino	Department of English, Virginia Polytechnic Institute and State University
Francesca Spinelli	Case Western Reserve University, Cleveland, Ohio
Louise Cherry Wilkinson	Graduate School/Educational Psychology, City University of New York
Patricia E. Worden	Department of Psychology, California State University, Fullerton

VIEWING AND REVIEWING READING/LANGUAGE RESEARCH

Barbara A. Hutson

INTRODUCTION

Writers seldom intentionally construct a circular argument, but I hope to do just that. In this brief chapter I will quickly overview the contents, then discuss some aspect (not always the central one) of each chapter in this third volume of the series *Advances in Reading/Language Research*. In the third section I'll try to sketch in quick strokes some ways in which an aspect of each chapter could be projected onto another chapter, providing a new view of the subject and provoking a fuller or better articulated consideration of important topics in reading/language research.

OVERVIEW

As in previous volumes in this series, the chapters range in focus from preschool (Kee and Worden) through adult (Entin and Klare; Sorrentino). It was suggested

Advances in Reading/Language Research, Volume 3, pages 1-8.
Copyright © 1985 by JAI Press Inc.
ISBN: 0-89232-389-2

in Volume 1 (Hutson, 1982) that reading/language research needs to include attention to cognitive, linguistic, social/emotional, and physiological factors. Although cognitive factors are addressed in chapters such as Gerber's and linguistic factors are addressed in chapters such as those by Sorrentino and by Wilkinson and Spinelli (who also deal with social factors), this volume emphasizes more than previous volumes some of the physiological factors (in Ownby's chapter). This volume also gives greater emphasis to use of computers (Kee and Worden; Rubin and Bruce), to writing, and to disabled or poor readers, in chapters by Gerber, by Niles, and by Ownby.

As in the earlier volumes the coverage includes reading (Entin and Klare; Niles), writing (Gerber; Rubin and Bruce; Sorrentino), and oral language (Kee and Worden; Wilkinson and Spinelli), and chapters such as Ownby's and Wilkinson and Spinelli's consider some of the relationships between these aspects. Formats range from reports of clusters of empirical studies (e.g., Entin and Klare; Gerber; Kee and Worden) to review/syntheses of research (e.g., Ownby or Sorrentino) to Dockrell's broad perspective on styles of research. The chapters by Niles and by Wilkinson and Spinelli present results of their programmatic research but give even more emphasis to the conceptual framework within which that work is embedded. Although the chapter by Rubin and Bruce is presented in a nonquantitative manner, their interpretation is informed by an ongoing program of research and evaluation.

Even when authors in this volume address a somewhat similar topic, as do Gerber and Ownby, they emphasize different aspects and bring to bear different theoretical perspectives, as discussed in Hutson (1983). Similarly, Wilkinson and Spinelli, while similar to Niles in this volume and to Pepinsky and DeStefano in Volume 2 (1983) in discussing aspects of classroom interaction, use a perspective different from, but not incompatible with, the frameworks used in those other chapters, though all of these differ from the perspective presented by Tough (1983).

The next section consists of brief comments on each of the chapters in this volume, and the final section will discuss implications that various chapters bear for study of issues covered in other chapters.

VIEWING READING/LANGUAGE RESEARCH

Eileen Entin and George Klare examine the interaction between text features (primarily readability) and reader characteristics such as readers' interest in and prior knowledge of the topic. They not only present results of a series of studies of adults reading expository passages, but speculate about conditions under which readability, usually based on words and sentence length, is sensitive and conditions in which a measure based on higher levels of text structure is required (cf. Harker, Hartley, & Walsh, 1982; Meyer, 1983).

Michael Gerber views spelling patterns in learning-disabled and normally achieving children in terms of developmental cognition: What does this student *understand* about how to spell various sounds he or she hears? Like miscue analysis in reading or error analysis in psychological testing, this approach emphasizes what's right even in an error. This lets us appreciate more fully the fact that although schooling provides input, ultimately the student must construct concepts about the nature of written language.

Louise Cherry Wilkinson and Francesca Spinelli examine the patterns of interaction between students in a classroom during lessons with minimal direct supervision by the teacher. Using a model of the effective speaker, who displays communicative competence in social interactions, they study requests and responses in peer-directed reading groups. The research/theoretical traditions on which they draw include analyses of linguistic form on both the level of the sentence and the broader level of discourse among individuals in a social unit. Wilkinson and Spinelli assess not only the types of requests that students make but the characteristics of requests that are most likely to provoke appropriate responses. In displaying results they effectively integrate text, statistics, graphics, and excerpts from children's discussions.

Andee Rubin and Bertram Bruce describe six linked programs for children's composition on a microcomputer. They discuss integration of computer activities into a classroom context. The six reading/writing programs they discuss are each linked to one of six pedagogical goals: developing skills of planning and critical thinking, integrating reading and writing, making writing public, supporting meaningful communication with real audiences, sharing writing with peers, and facilitating the revision process. These goals for the teaching of composition are certainly congruent with recent descriptions of the writing process in children and adults, and the technology used does not narrow the definition of writing to its minute elements, as much of the software for reading or writing still does.

Ray Ownby examines the neurological bases of dyslexia, drawing both the term and the literature base from neurology and neuropsychology. For the review itself he uses as a frame the categories and models prevalent in those fields, but in his conclusions he draws on conceptions from recent theories of reading and cognitive psychology, and proposes a substantially different organization of the field, a different frame for the puzzle.

Bryan Dockrell, who has had a good view of research on two sides of the Atlantic, believes that the modes of research prevailing in the two regions differ in several ways. The dimensions he discusses are formal hypothesis testing vs. illumination, the influence of broad theory, and degrees of influence from sociology.

Paul Sorrentino frames the study and practice of technical writing in terms of five processed features in Harper's model of human communication: categorization, conceptualization, symbolization, organization, and operationalization. His discussion is enriched by knowledge of classical rhetorical structure, information processing as it has been applied in this area, and direct experience with technical writing.

Daniel Kee and Patricia Worden illustrate the use of computers as means of exploring aspects of language development. In two of the examples instruction is involved, either directly by the computer or by a parent using the computer to help teach a child. The emphasis in this chapter, though, is more on what we can learn about the child's language through use of small personal computers than on what we can teach the child. The discussion could be extended to include on-line gathering of research data or automatic analysis of responses as a basis for differentiated instruction.

Jerry Niles uses teacher decision making as a framework for examining the feedback that teachers provide to students during oral reading. He uses the same framework for organizing his chapter, arranging the review of literature around the various decisions a teacher makes in that situation. The clear structuring of the field invites others to think with him.

REVIEWING READING/LANGUAGE RESEARCH

I promised a circular argument. Rather than attempting to draw together the full circle, I'll organize the chapters into three small circlets, suggesting within each group some mutual implications. By projecting onto one chapter the view used in another it may be possible to review, to see again, the topic. In no sense should this be construed as criticism—first, I am deeply appreciative of the contributions by the authors in this series, and second, the questions provoked by looking at the topic in one chapter from the perspective of another are often different from those emphasized by the authors of either of the chapters.

The first group consists of the chapters by Rubin and Bruce, by Sorrentino, and by Kee and Worden. The chapter by Paul Sorrentino deals with expository writing by skilled adults. In such a group it is safe to assume that the writer has reasonable skill in language and has awareness that readers have differing information needs and viewpoints. The focus is then on developing strategies for manipulating text to achieve those purposes. There is need, however, for more systematic examination of the emergence of technical writing strategies in children and adolescents. To minimize the gap between literacy in school and literacy in the adult world, study of the strands of writing skill considered by Sorrentino could be extended downward to children like those in the chapter by Andee Rubin and Chip Bruce. For example, are there some circumstances under which children display processes such as timebinding, manipulation of media, or adaptation of symbols to social contingencies (as Sorrentino discussed in adults' technical writing)? Could these processes be facilitated by use of well-designed software for microcomputers or word processors? This is not in the least a criticism of either of these chapters, but a suggestion that the juxtaposition of diverse treatments of topics with some underlying similarity can stimulate further thought.

The chapter by Rubin and Bruce in turn has implications for reviewing the topic discussed by Dan Kee and Pat Worden. An attractive feature of Rubin and Bruce's chapter is its organization in terms of a half-dozen pedagogical goals for composition in elementary classrooms. It would be possible for another author to analyze the literacy-related functions or goals of parents of young children, then use such a framework to organize discussion of the ways in which small computers (with or without mediation by adults) can be used to aid or monitor at least some aspects of such learning.

The notion of using computers for analysis of learning or performance, presented by Kee and Worden, is also applicable to the study of the adult writers discussed by Sorrentino. For example, especially with an increasing percentage of technical writing being done on word processors, it is possible to study more precisely the differences between expert and novice technical writers. For example, one can use on-line analysis to ask how expert and novice technical writers differ in modifying text to fit various audiences or various purposes. Do experts, for instance, make major structural changes while novices confine themselves to changes in words or sentence structure? These are not Sorrentino's questions but are some of the questions that would be stimulated if the research strategy from Kee and Worden's chapter were projected on the content of Sorrentino's chapter.

Chapters in the second group share the feature of dealing with students who are to some degree disabled or handicapped in reading. Although most of Ray Ownby's chapter is organized in terms of a sequential process model frequently used in neuropsychological research on dyslexia, he in the end endorses a simultaneous process model that would probably be congruent with Jerry Niles's approach. In fact, Niles's reading teachers may experience a variety of pressures simultaneously, and the exact decision they make about feedback in a given instance may be determined by which pressure has the highest valence at the moment, a consideration influenced by the teacher's previous actions. For now, though, it seems useful to proceed by testing Niles's decision tree as a descriptor, then gathering information about the broad situational and personal factors (in the teacher and in the pupil) that affect those decisions.

The teacher decision-making framework developed by Niles could in turn be applied to the spelling problems studied by Michael Gerber. For example, while Gerber focuses on the student, it would be possible to study teacher feedback during or after students' spelling and to trace the effect of such feedback on changes in spelling "miscues." In addition, it would be possible to design in computer software the capacity to detect spelling errors that at least use an alternative spelling of the correct phoneme and could respond with encouragement but with guidance in finetuning the spelling concepts.

The notion of development of concepts about reading and language in learning-disabled children discussed in Gerber's chapter (see also Ryan & Ledger, 1982, or Yussen, 1982) could also be applied not so much to Ray Ownby's chapter as to some of the research traditions he reviews. For example, one of Ownby's references is called "I don't understand what you mean by comprehension." It is possible that for some appreciable proportion of children who show on tests or in daily performance great difficulty in comprehension or in language use or in some perceptual task, the problem is not so much in their neuropsychological limitations as in their development of concepts about what the task requires and what they need to *do*. Such a finding would bear major implications for instruction.

Three other chapters with less obvious points of similarity also have mutual implications. Bryan Dockrell notes that research in North America is more strongly oriented toward specific hypothesis testing and less oriented toward sociological theory than is British (or European) research. At first glance the chapter by Eileen Entin and George Klare would seem to be a confirmation and the chapter by Wilkinson and Spinelli to be an exception to his conclusions, i.e., Entin and Klare present an "American" empirical study whereas Wilkinson and Spinelli use sociological theory to illuminate educational issues. Yet the long-term, careful scholarship of George Klare and the solid contributions of Eileen Entin are building up a well-grounded theory of multiple factors in text comprehension. Beginning with readability of a given type of text, i.e., factors in the text, they expand to examine the interaction of the text factors with factors in the reader. Any individual study tests only a few specific hypotheses, but the larger research program may illuminate central issues in reading.

The approach taken by Louise Cherry Wilkinson and Francesca Spinelli is clearly rooted in sociological/anthropological issues about interaction, and rather than setting up a researcher-controlled situation (as Entin and Klare do), they study the situation as they find it in the classroom. From the observed patterns they derive categories. But they then quantify and test specific points within and across studies. They transcend the distinctions between qualitative and quantitative research in a research program that examines the nature of peer interaction in classrooms. Some of the publications emanating from that program are technical, some more theoretical integrations, some more applied in communicating findings to teachers and administrators.

Entin and Klare's chapter reminds us that the material used in the peer-directed lessons such as those studied by Wilkinson and Spinelli may differ in readability, familiarity, and interest, perhaps provoking different patterns of peer interaction. In turn, Wilkinson and Spinelli remind us that even adult materials such as those used by Entin and Klare are often read in a social context, in which calling on peers as resources is often a permissible problem-solving strategy.

We can also turn Bryan Dockrell's insights back on his own chapter. In a sense he offers us illuminating observations on which to build grand theory, a sociology of educational research. At the same time he makes specific his thesis (or hypothesis, if you will) and lays out the evidence in a way that makes it possible for others to assess his evidence and to verify or question his interpretations.

This discussion of mutual implications could be extended; the issues of problem solving or concept development or decision making, for example, could be applied to a number of other chapters. And topics, theories, methods, and research strategies of chapters in this volume could be linked to chapters in other volumes.

I hope, however, that this brief discussion will contribute to the reader's active processing and will enhance willingness to read in sometimes unfamiliar topics. Research progresses both by living with a body of work over a long period and by the accidental meeting of ideas—the new insight or new question provoked by the unexpected juxtaposition or serendipitous configuration of familiar elements. Like the turning of a kaleidoscope, some of the views generated by this form of brainstorming may be murky or tiresomely familiar or hard to interpret, but there is always the possibility that a productive new view of a topic will emerge.

REFERENCES

Dockrell, W.B. (1985). Styles in educational research on two sides of the Atlantic. In B.A. Hutson (Ed.), *Advances in reading/language research* (Vol. 3). Greenwich, CT: JAI Press.

Entin, E.B., & Klare, G.R. (1985). Relationships of measures of interest, prior knowledge, and readability to comprehension of expository passages. In B.A. Hutson (Ed.), *Advances in reading/language research* (Vol. 3). Greenwich, CT: JAI Press.

Gerber, M.M. (1985). Spelling as concept-governed problem solving: Learning disabled and normally achieving students. In B.A. Hutson (Ed.), *Advances in reading/language research* (Vol. 3). Greenwich, CT: JAI Press.

Harker, J.O., Hartley, J.T., & Walsh, D.A. (1982). Understanding discourse: A life-span approach. In B.A. Hutson (Ed.), *Advances in reading/language research* (Vol. 1), pp. 155-202. Greenwich, CT: JAI Press.

Hutson, B.A. (1982). The scope of reading/language research. In B.A. Hutson (Ed.), *Advances in reading/language research* (Vol. 1). Greenwich, CT: JAI Press, pp. 1-7.

Hutson, B.A. (1983). Focus and perspective in reading/language research. In B.A. Hutson (Ed.), *Advances in reading/language research* (Vol. 2). Greenwich, CT: JAI Press, pp. 1-7.

Kee, D.W., & Worden, P.E. (1985). Personal computers in language and reading research: Three vignettes. In B.A. Hutson (Ed.), *Advances in reading/language research* (Vol. 3). Greenwich, CT: JAI Press.

Meyer, B.J.F. (1983). Text structure and its use in studying comprehension across the adult life span. In B.A. Hutson (Ed.), *Advances in reading/language research* (Vol. 2). Greenwich, CT: JAI Press, pp. 9-54.

Niles, J.A. (1985). Research on teacher-pupil interactions during oral reading instruction. In B.A. Hutson (Ed.), *Advances in reading/language research* (Vol. 3). Greenwich, CT: JAI Press.

Ownby, R.L. (1985). The neuropsychology of reading ability and disability: Pieces of the puzzle. In B.A. Hutson (Ed.), *Advances in reading/language research* (Vol. 3). Greenwich, CT: JAI Press.

Pepinsky, H.B., & DeStefano, J.S. (1983). Interactive discourse in the classroom as organizational behavior. In B.A. Hutson (Ed.), *Advances in reading/language research* (Vol. 2). Greenwich, CT: JAI Press, pp. 107-137.

Rubin, A., & Bruce, B. (1985). Quill: Reading and writing with a microcomputer. In B.A. Hutson (Ed.), *Advances in reading/language research* (Vol. 3). Greenwich, CT: JAI Press.

Ryan, E.B., & Ledger, G.W. (1982). Assessing sentence processing skills in prereaders. In B.A.

8   BARBARA A. HUTSON

Hutson (Ed.), *Advances in reading/language research* (Vol. 1). Greenwich, CT: JAI Press, pp. 9-50.

Sorrentino, P. (1985). Let's be technically right about technical writing. In B.A. Hutson (Ed.), *Advances in reading/language research* (Vol. 3). Greenwich, CT: JAI Press.

Tough, J. (1983). Learning to represent meaning. In B.A. Hutson (Ed.), *Advances in reading/language research* (Vol. 2). Greenwich, CT: JAI Press, pp. 55-81.

Wilkinson, L.C., & Spinelli, F. (1985). Using requests effectively in peer-directed reading groups. In B.A. Hutson (Ed.), *Advances in reading/language research* (Vol. 3). Greenwich, CT: JAI Press.

Yussen, S.R. (1982). Children's impressions of coherence in narratives. In B.A. Hutson (Ed.), *Advances in reading/language research* (Vol. 1). Greenwich, CT: JAI Press, pp. 245-281.

RELATIONSHIPS OF MEASURES OF INTEREST, PRIOR KNOWLEDGE, AND READABILITY TO COMPREHENSION OF EXPOSITORY PASSAGES

Eileen B. Entin and George R. Klare

INTRODUCTION[1]

Research on comprehension has been approached from two major viewpoints. One approach is to look at the characteristics of the written or spoken message and try to assess what variables tend to make it more or less comprehensible. The other approach is to look at characteristics of readers or listeners which help or hinder them in the process of comprehension.

Recent years have seen a reemphasis of the notion that comprehension is an active or constructive process, not just a matter of decoding spoken or written text. Bransford and Johnson (1972, 1973), Anderson, Reynolds, Schallert, and Goetz (1977), and Pichert and Anderson (1977) have demonstrated that comprehension is affected by variables which readers (or listeners) bring to the situation.

Advances in Reading/Language Research, Volume 3, pages 9-38.
Copyright © 1985 by JAI Press Inc.
ISBN: 0-89232-389-2

Just as some researchers have focused on characteristics which readers bring to the comprehension task, others have looked at characteristics in text which affect comprehension. Frederiksen (1975, 1979), Rumelhart (1977), Mandler (1978), and Meyer (1975, 1977, 1983) have related the structure of text to recall or comprehension. Kintsch (1979; Kintsch & Vipond, 1979) has looked at the complexity of the text, particularly in terms of the number of propositions it contains. Others have used the number of idea units as a variable. (A review of these approaches can be found in Pearson and Campbell, 1981.) Another aspect of the text structure which has occupied considerable attention over the years is the style in which the passage is written. Over 200 readability formulas have been developed to relate stylistic elements of the text to its comprehensibility (Klare, 1963, 1974/75, 1984). Two variables are common to many of the formulas, a semantic or word difficulty variable and a syntactic or sentence difficulty variable. These two variables typically account for well over 50% of the variance when they are regressed against multiple choice or cloze measures of comprehension (Entin & Klare, 1978a).

The research to be described here has included both reader and text variables. The study has focused on two particular reader variables: interest in the topic of the passage and prior knowledge about that topic. Difficulty level, as assessed by a readability formula, has served as the text variable. The two reader characteristics have been related to text readability in terms of their effects on comprehension.

The plan of this chapter is (1) to review the literature and issues related to interest, prior knowledge, readability, and their interaction as factors in comprehension; (2) to present a study (including a cluster of support studies before and during the main study) exploring several of these issues; and (3) to provide a brief discussion of broader issues.

REVIEW OF ISSUES AND FINDINGS ON ADULT COMPREHENSION OF EXPOSITORY PROSE

Independent Variables Affecting Comprehension

Readability

Numerous studies have shown that readability of a text affects its comprehension. In general, when two versions of a given text are several grade levels apart (particularly when above the reader's measured reading grade level), the mean comprehension score on the version written at the lower reading grade level tends to be higher than that for the version at the higher level. Comprehension is measured sometimes by multiple choice tests and sometimes by cloze tests; both measures of comprehension have reflected these differences.

Klare (1976) summarized the results of 36 studies (both published and unpublished) which investigated the effect of readability variables on reading comprehension and/or retention. About half (19 of 36) of these studies reported significant differences between easier and harder readability versions of a text. Six of the studies reported mixed results and the rest were not significant. Since Klare's review was completed, other studies assessing the effect of readability on comprehension and/or retention have appeared (cf. Ewing, Note 1; Greene, Note 2; Kincaid & Gamble, 1977; Swanson, Note 3) with most of them reporting significant results.

Interest

In general, passages on topics of greater interest are comprehended better than those of lesser interest. This relationship was demonstrated in terms of listener comprehension some years ago (Chall & Dial, 1948; Silvey, 1951). More recently, Asher and Markell (1974) found that elementary-aged children's reading comprehension scores (based on cloze tests) were significantly higher on high-interest than on low-interest paragraphs. Asher, Hymel, and Wigfield (1978) reported similar results. Walker (Note 4), who also used elementary school children, found that the high-interest content positively affected comprehension, particularly for average and below-average readers. Allen (Note 5) reported similar findings for college-aged subjects. A review of this area can be found in Asher (1980).

Prior Knowledge

There is a widespread theoretical assumption that prior knowledge affects comprehension, but direct empirical support for this assumption has only appeared recently. Royer and Cunningham (Note 6) assert that "the act of comprehension must entail an interaction between an incoming linguistic message and the reader's world knowledge" (p. 3). They go on to observe that most current tests of reading comprehension use passages which draw upon world knowledge. They conclude from this that some of the variance in reading comprehension test scores can be "attributable to differences in prior knowledge rather than differences in reading skills, *per se*" (p. 44). Entin and Klare (1978b) have presented empirical evidence supporting the idea that many questions on a reading comprehension test may require or permit answering in terms of prior knowledge rather than comprehension of the passage itself (see also Tuinman, 1973/74).

Reder (Note 7; 1980) has also reviewed the literature on comprehension and retention of prose. Like Royer and Cunningham, she reports many suggestions that prior knowledge is intimately related to comprehension of a prose passage but, again, most empirical support is at best indirect (cf. Bower, Note 8; Brown, Smiley, Day, Townsend, & Lawton, 1977; Lantoff, 1978).

A few studies have attempted to assess directly the effects of prior knowledge on comprehension and/or memory. Pearson, Hansen, and Gordon (1979) looked at the effect of background, i.e., prior knowledge about spiders, on the comprehension of a passage about spiders. They found a significant difference between the low- and high-knowledge groups on comprehension. Spilich, Vesonder, Chiesi, and Voss (1979) found that subjects classified as having high prior knowledge about the domain of baseball recalled more pertinent information about a baseball episode than subjects classified as having low prior knowledge of that domain. Chiesi, Spilich, and Voss (1979) found that recognition performance, recall performance, and the anticipation of high-level goal-stated outcomes were all greater for high-knowledge than for low-knowledge subjects. Mutter (Note 9) found that readers' background knowledge of the content of a passage significantly affected comprehension scores. Woern (1977) looked at the effects of readers' real-world knowledge on comprehension of a text. Knowledge of the world, viewed in terms of beliefs about the world, was shown to affect comprehension significantly. Pichert and Anderson (1977) found differences in the kinds of recall displayed by readers cued toward two different sets of knowledge (schemes) before reading.

Readability and Interest

It is interesting that such a simple index as a readability formula score should be able to differentiate reader comprehension levels, but even more interesting to consider the conditions under which these differences are and are not likely to be obtained. Based on his review, Klare (1976) proposed a model suggesting that readability is more important when interest in the topic or some other aspect of motivation is low than when high (and when liberal reading time is available). Studies by Denbow (Note 10) and Fass and Schumacher (1978) support these ideas.

Readability and Prior Knowledge

Klare's (1976) model addresses the question of prior knowledge in terms of the amount of new information gained in reading the passage in relation to information before the passage was read. His ideas suggest that readability is more important when prior knowledge about a topic is low than when it is high. While direct empirical research is lacking, work by Klare, Mabry, and Gustafson (1955) is suggestive. These researchers found that for knowledgeable readers, improving readability had little effect on comprehension, whereas for those whose knowledge was low, comprehension was higher in the more readable version. Similar results were obtained by Funkhouser and Maccoby (Note 11).

Interest and Prior Knowledge

A study by Weber and Ringler (Note 12) looked at the relationship between interest in a particular subject area, the amount of prior knowledge in that area, and reading comprehension. Three different subject areas were studied. In a multiple regression analysis, interest, entered as the first predictor variable, accounted for a significant proportion of the variance. Prior knowledge, entered as a second predictor variable, accounted for a significant proportion of the variance over and above interest. However, when knowledge was entered first, almost all of the variance previously accounted for by interest was accounted for by the knowledge factor alone. According to the Weber and Ringler study, then, it may be that much of the research data involving interest can also be explained by prior knowledge. There is a need to disentangle these factors.

Measurement of the Independent Variables

Readability

Readability as it has been discussed here can be measured by any of a variety of readability formulas. In reviewing the many formulas which are available, Klare (1974/75) concluded that, in general, a two-variable formula, in which one variable is a semantic variable and the other a syntactic variable, gives sufficient predictive validity for most purposes. Research by Entin and Klare (1978a) supports this assertion. The Flesch reading ease formula was chosen to measure readability in this study because it is convenient to apply by hand or by computer and a computer program was available.

Interest

The measurement of interest in a topic typically relies on a subjective estimate made by the prospective reader. One successful interest inventory was devised some years ago by Waples and Tyler (1931). These authors described topics by a brief phrase and asked subjects to rate their interest in each topic using a 3-point scale. With only minor modifications, the Waples and Tyler inventory was later successfully used by Klare, Gustafson, and Mabry (Note 13) with subjects of high-school and college age.

Waples and Tyler (1931) only assessed interests in topics and so did not face the problem of how to find particular prose passages to represent their descriptive phrases. If one needs to link a descriptive phrase about a topic to a particular prose passage, one way to solve the problem is to approach it the other way around, i.e., one can find passages to be assessed and then describe the passages by titles or subtitles used for that passage. For example, one can select passages from an encyclopedia and then use the subtitle headings of the passages as the phrases to be rated in the interest inventory. In this way, one can be more certain that the phrase used to describe the topic is appropriate for the passage actually chosen. Saio (Note 14) used a procedure like this to devise a reading interest inventory for elementary school students.

Shank (Note 15) has suggested a framework specifying factors which make something interesting to individuals. He suggests that several components make something interesting: (1) a life–death situation (or at least a dangerous one); (2) an unexpected event; (3) personal relevance. Shank is basically suggesting that there are parameters by which interest value can be rated and these parameters seem to be generally applicable to a wide range of individuals. Shank's ideas help explain why certain topics are found to be interesting (or uninteresting) from year to year and his framework can be used to help select topics which should be of high interest to readers.

Prior Knowledge

Prior knowledge about a particular topic is the most difficult of the three independent variables to measure. In schema theory, prior knowledge is often used as a very global concept. But when one considers knowledge about a substantive domain rather than knowledge about procedure or form, the meaning of prior knowledge is less clear. Even then, some domains seem easier than others to discuss in terms of prior (or background) knowledge. For example, if one wants to assess how much an individual knows about the game of baseball, one can reasonably ask questions about the terminology, the goals, and the process of playing the game. This is what Chiesi et al. (1979) and Spilich et al. (1979) did.

But in other topic areas the definition of prior knowledge is less clear. Pearson et al. (1979) assessed prior knowledge about spiders with a set of eight questions. They did not specify what the questions were nor how they were chosen. Weber and Ringler (Note 12) used knowledge measures covering detail and conceptual knowledge. They indicated that the questions were made up by "experts" on the subject matter. Mutter (Note 9) used passages from various sources and assessed prior knowledge of the content of the passage by a short-answer survey. Unfortunately, these studies provide little in the way of guidelines for a procedure that can be replicated.

Another perspective on prior knowledge is gained from looking at the textbooks used by the Open University in England. Students enrolled at the Open University do most of their work by correspondence. Many of their textbooks contain a list of terms which students are assumed to know when they begin a course. Knowledge of these terms is assumed to be requisite for understanding the material in the textbook. In other words, prior knowledge is defined and assessed by a list of terms. This conception of prior knowledge is in some ways analogous to the "Given–New" contract discussed by Haviland and Clark (1974).

If one could query the writer of a passage, one could ask what he or she *assumes* the reader already knows. But in terms of an existent passage, there is no systematic way to assess what terms are assumed to be understood by readers before they begin. One possible procedure in that case would be to ask knowledgeable readers to specify what they thought the author assumed. If knowledgeable readers could pick out a common set of terms, these could reasonably be viewed as constituting a test of prior knowledge about the topic.

Assessment of Comprehension as a Dependent Variable

In many studies, comprehension has been inferred from memory measures of recall and/or recognition. In those studies where the focus has been on comprehension, rather than on memory, two techniques were commonly used to assess comprehension. One was the multiple choice test, which is typically given with the passage available rather than after it has been removed. The second technique was the cloze procedure, in which every nth word (usually every fifth word) of the passage is replaced by a blank of standard length. The reader's task is to fill in the missing word. Cloze tests have been scored by both the exact word and synonym scoring methods. The exact word method appears more reliable inasmuch as no judgments need to be made about what an "acceptable" synonym is, and this method is much more commonly used. In any case, the data indicate that the scores obtained from the two methods are highly correlated (Asher, Hymel, & Wigfield, 1978; Rankin, 1978; Weber & Ringler, Note 12). The cloze procedure was chosen as the dependent variable in this study on the following bases.

Simons (1971) argues that "the cloze test is a better measure of reading comprehension than traditional tests. . . . It does not have questions and therefore is not measuring a student's skill in understanding questions. It is not a memory test because a student can continually read and examine the passage." More noteworthy for this research, he goes on to say: "It also does not appear to be measuring a student's familiarity with the content of the passage, at least to the degree that traditional tests do." In other words, Simons is arguing that the cloze test is less subject to the influence of prior knowledge than traditional comprehension tests, i.e., it is closer to being a measure of reading comprehension of the passage at hand. The study by Entin and Klare (1978b) supports this assertion.

Rankin (1978), using an information-processing model of comprehension, also argues that the cloze test provides a valid measure of language comprehension. The College Board (DRP Readability Report, 1982), for these and related reasons, has used a variant of the cloze procedure in its new Degrees of Reading Power reading comprehension tests.

A STUDY OF INTEREST, PRIOR KNOWLEDGE, AND READABILITY IN RELATION TO COMPREHENSION

Hypotheses

The purpose of this research was to study the effects of readability, interest, and prior knowledge on comprehension. The following hypotheses were formulated regarding how these independent variables, taken singly or in combination, would relate to the dependent variable, comprehension.

1. *Readability.*   The mean cloze comprehension scores on passages written at a standard readability level will be significantly higher than those on passages written at a difficult readability level.

2. *Interest.*   The mean cloze comprehension scores on high-interest passages will be significantly higher than those on low-interest passages.

3. *Prior knowledge.*   The mean cloze comprehension scores on the passages about which subjects have high prior knowledge will be significantly higher than those on passages regarding which prior knowledge is low.

4. *Readability with interest and readability with prior knowledge.*   If the effects of both factors in each of these sets are additive, then each of these interaction terms will be nonsignificant. More precisely, the cell which is high on both readability and interest will have a higher comprehension mean score than either of the cells which are high on one factor and low on the other. If readability and prior knowledge are also additive in nature, a similar outcome will occur. On the other hand, the model proposed by Klare (1976) suggests that readability may not be as important when other factors such as interest or prior knowledge are high (and the amount of time given to subjects is liberal) as when other such factors are low. In that case, there will be no significant differences in the means for the cell high on both variables and the cells high on only one variable or the other.

5. *Interest with prior knowledge.*   Weber and Ringler's (Note 15) data suggest that variability in comprehension scores attributable to interest can also be accounted for by prior knowledge. In this case, the interaction involving interest and prior knowledge should be significant. In terms of planned comparisons, when prior knowledge is low, the difference between the mean scores in the high- and low-interest cells should be significant, but when prior knowledge is high, the difference between the high- and low-interest cells should be nonsignificant. This situation would parallel the effects proposed by Klare (1976) for readability, with prior knowledge standing here in place of readability.

6. *Interest, prior knowledge, and readability.*   There are no empirical data from which to draw the hypothesis for the three-way interaction. If each of these independent variables contributes some unique variance to the comprehension scores, then the mean score for the cell high on all three independent variables will be significantly higher than the means for those cells high on only two independent variables. On the other hand, there may be a ceiling effect, i.e., being high on all three independent variables may not contribute anything more to comprehension than being high on two (or even one) of them. In that case, the mean score for the cell high on all three will not be significantly greater than that of the cells in which only two of the independent variables are high.

METHOD

Topics

For this research it was necessary to obtain a set of topics which were interesting to the majority of respondents and another set which were uninteresting. Using the existing literature on interests of students and young adults as a guide, candidate topics were selected from the *World Book Encyclopedia*. The use of an encyclopedia as a source of passages allowed on the one hand for the selection of topics from many diverse subject areas and on the other hand for the selection of topics written in a reasonably similar style. The *World Book* was chosen because extensive work on the readability level had been done by Edgar Dale, a pioneer in this area. In selecting topics, two major guidelines were followed: first, to choose topics which previous research indicated might be of either low or high interest to a college-aged population; second, to select topics for which a suitable passage of about 400 words could be extracted from the *World Book*. In that way, each topic was linked to a particular passage which used that topic title as a heading.

A reading interest inventory, composed of a list of 120 topics, was administered to 532 subjects as part of a summer precollege orientation program at Ohio University. The form of the inventory was based on the Waples and Tyler (1931) Reading Interest Inventory. Subjects rated each topic on a 3-point scale. A topic was said to be of high interest if persons indicated they would read about that topic right away. A topic was said to be of moderate interest if persons indicated they might read about that topic sometime in the future. A topic was considered of low interest if persons would not read about that topic under any circumstance.

Using the results from the 532 subjects, it was possible to obtain mean interest ratings for each topic. The mean was derived by summing the subjects' coded responses (e.g., 1 = interesting; 2 = moderately interesting; 3 = uninteresting) and dividing by the number of respondents. For this research, 12 topics, the six with the lowest and the six with the highest mean scores, were selected as the high- and low-interest topics. The distribution of ratings and mean scores for each of the selected topics is displayed in Table 1. It is clear from that table that there was a higher degree of consensus on the low-interest topics than the high-interest ones, a finding which was also reported by Klare, Gustafson, and Mabry (Note 13).

Comprehension Study

Subjects

Two hundred sixty-six students enrolled in introductory psychology courses at Ohio University served as subjects. The students earned experimental points, which could augment their grade, for participating in the study.

Table 1.   Means and Percentage Distributions for Ratings of Interest
in 12 Selected Topics (Preliminary Study)

Topic	n	Mean	Uninteresting	Moderately Interesting	Interesting
Properties of Aluminum Alloys (Aluminum)[a]	525	2.75[b]	79.8	15.6	4.6
How Cement is Made (Cement)	524	2.72	75.8	20.4	3.8
Basic Properties of Crop Production (Crops)	519	2.66	72.6	20.8	6.6
How Clothes Are Dry-Cleaned (Dry-Clean)	521	2.72	77.5	16.9	5.6
Processes in Meat Packing (Meat)	514	2.69	73.3	22.4	4.3
Rocks as a Hobby (Rocks)	502	2.71	74.9	20.7	4.4
Attitudes About Death (Death)	524	1.62	14.5	32.6	52.9
How Emotions Help and Harm Us (Emotions)	519	1.54	11.9	29.7	58.4
Why We Forget (Forget)	490	1.60	14.3	31.4	54.3
The Nature of Personality (Personality)	500	1.57	14.6	27.8	57.6
Keeping Physically Fit (Physical Fit)	506	1.55	10.7	33.4	55.9
What Happens While We Sleep (Sleep)	495	1.56	12.3	31.1	56.6

Note: This is the only table which refers to results from the Preliminary Study. All subsequent tables refer to the
Comprehension Study.
[a]Key words in parentheses will be used hereafter to refer to these topics.
[b]Higher means reflect lower interest.

Most of the subjects involved in this research were freshmen. During the
summer precollege program, the Nelson–Denny Reading Test (1960) was
routinely administered to incoming students. This test includes both vocabulary
and reading comprehension subsections. The results for incoming students were
made available to the experimenters and were used to provide an index of the
subjects' reading grade level.

Materials

Three instruments were used in this study. Two of them were used to measure
interest and prior knowledge. The third was used to measure comprehension.

1. *Information and Interests Questionnaire.* This instrument was designed to measure the subjects' interest in the selected topics. The 12 selected topics were embedded in a list of 45 topics which each student rated for interest according to a 5-point Likert scale. These interest ratings were used as a check on the ratings obtained in the preliminary study, though the earlier ratings were used in designing the main study.

2. *Prior Knowledge of Terms Questionnaire.* This instrument was designed to obtain measures of the subjects' prior knowledge about the terminology used in the passages. Working from the actual passages to be used, raters were asked to select the terms which they believed it would be necessary for a reader to understand in order to comprehend the passage. These were to be terms which the writer assumed readers would understand before reading the passage, but not terms introduced and explained in the passage itself. Between three and five raters selected terms for each topic, with those picked by a majority used as the "prior knowledge" terms for that topic. Using this procedure, between five and seven terms were obtained for each topic. Altogether, for the 12 topics, there were 72 terms.

For this questionnaire, each term was listed and used in a sample sentence taken from the passage containing the term. Subjects were asked to define or explain the term, or, in a few cases, to give examples of the meaning of that term *as used in the sample sentence.* This measure was used primarily as a covariate and a check on other analyses rather than as a primary design factor.

3. *Comprehension Tests.* Passages of about 400 words were taken from the *World Book Encyclopedia* for each of the 12 selected topics. Each passage was then rewritten to approximately twelfth (standard) and sixteenth (difficult) reading grade levels as measured by the Flesch Reading Ease formula (Flesch, 1948). (These reading grade levels correspond to Flesch scores of about 50 and 30, respectively.) The twelfth-grade level was chosen because it was the approximate average reading grade level of the subjects used in this study. The sixteenth-grade level was above the reading grade level of most of the subjects and so represented difficult material.

After the passages were rewritten, three judges were asked to read both the standard and the difficult versions of each passage and verify that the content of both versions, e.g., what was said, was the same and that they differed only in terms of how the information was stated. The discrepancies pointed out by the judges were resolved to the judges' satisfaction.

With each of the 12 selected passages rewritten at two different readability levels, there were a total of 24 passages. Each passage was prepared as a cloze test. For this test the first 250 words were unaltered. The last 150 words were prepared in a standard cloze form, with every fifth word being replaced by a blank line 15 type spaces long. By leaving the first 250 words unaltered it was possible to clearly identify the topic being discussed and establish the difficulty level of the passage before the subject encountered the mutilated portion of the text.

Each of the 24 different passages was prepared in two different parallel forms of the cloze test, i.e., with two different sets of deleted words. Two deletion forms of each passage were used in order to minimize the possibility of hitting a single unrepresentatively easy or difficult pattern (Klare, Sinaiko, & Stolurow, 1972; Klare, 1982). In total, then, there were 48 different forms (six high-interest and six low-interest topics, each prepared in high- and low-readability versions, with each high- and low-readability version prepared in two forms of the cloze test). Each test form had a total of 30 cloze blanks.

The cloze tests were assembled in booklets comprising four high- and four low-interest passages. Within the high- and low-interest passages, two were written at the standard readability level and two were written at the difficult level. The booklets contained a set of instructions explaining how to do the cloze test, a sample cloze test, and the eight passages. The booklets were assembled in six different random orders.

Procedure

The data were collected in two sessions. The first session was one hour in length and was used to assess interest and prior knowledge. One week later the subjects returned to take the comprehension tests. Two hours was allotted for this portion of the experiment. The subjects were paced through the booklets and worked on each cloze passage for 12 minutes. By keeping the time allocated for each passage constant, subjects were constrained to spend the same amount of time on each passage rather than devoting, for example, more time to the interesting or the uninteresting passages. The remainder of the second session was taken up with an explanation of the task and other administrative details. Following completion of the comprehension tests, subjects were debriefed, thanked for their participation, and dismissed.

RESULTS

Subjects' interest in the 12 selected topics was measured first in the experimental session. The distributions on interest were similar to those obtained in the preliminary study, indicating that the ratings were stable for this population over time (as well as across samples drawn from the population). As was the case in the preliminary study, there was a higher degree of consensus on uninteresting than on interesting topics.

Subjects next defined or explained the terms used in the 12 topics on the prior knowledge of terms questionnaire. The definitions of the terms provided by the subjects were scored on a 3-point scale, whereby a score of 3 meant that the definition was acceptable; a score of 2 meant that the definition was partially

Table 2. Number of Cases, Means, and Standard
Deviations on Prior Knowledge of Terms from
12 Selected Passages

	Objective Score		
Topic	n	Mean	S.D.
Aluminum	230	1.68	.33
Cement	243	1.56	.30
Crops	244	2.26	.43
Dry-Clean	224	1.99	.26
Meat	248	1.91	.34
Rocks	237	1.63	.24
Sum of low-interest topics	200	1.84	.20
Death	234	2.00	.30
Emotions	246	1.58	.43
Forget	229	2.07	.34
Personality	210	1.62	.35
Physical Fit	236	1.84	.38
Sleep	228	1.92	.40
Sum of high-interest topics	176	1.84	.22

acceptable; and, a score of 1 meant that the definition was unacceptable or was not attempted. The 3-point scale was sufficient to discriminate the quality of the subjects' responses and at the same time maintain a reliable scoring system. The individual scores for all the terms on a particular topic were summed and divided by the number of terms associated with that topic to yield a mean score. The means and standard deviations for the 12 topics are presented in Table 2. It can be seen that the mean prior knowledge scores do not differ for the low- and high-interest topics, though scores varied across specific topics within both low- and high-interest categories.

The Nelson–Denny Reading Test (1960) was, as noted, available as a baseline measure of reading skill level. One major purpose of obtaining these test scores was to select a subsample of subjects whose reading grade level was approximately twelfth grade, which corresponds to the readability level of the standard version of the material used in this study. Subjects selected for this subsample were those for whom *both* the vocabulary scores and the reading comprehension scores on the Nelson–Denny fell between grade levels 11 and 13. For these subjects the material written at the standard (twelfth grade) level was approximately at their reading skill level. The material written at the difficult (sixteenth grade) level was somewhat above their measured reading skill level. This subsample of subjects was used to hold reading skill constant in some of the analyses.

Table 3.   Comparisons of Mean Comprehension Scores on
Standard and Difficult Versions of 12 Selected Passages

Passage	Standard Version		Difficult Version		
	n	*Mean*	*n*	*Mean*	*p*[a]
Aluminum	80	14.8	80	12.1	.001
Cement	87	12.8	81	11.3	.003
Crops	77	11.6	70	9.8	.005
Dry-Clean	88	15.4	76	12.6	.001
Meat	76	11.9	91	10.2	.002
Rocks	78	10.7	88	9.2	.002
Death	87	15.8	77	13.8	.001
Emotions	78	14.2	88	13.5	NS
Forget	78	15.3	75	14.7	NS
Personality	80	14.7	88	10.2	.001
Physical Fit	78	14.7	97	13.6	.05
Sleep	73	13.3	73	12.1	.06

[a]Significance level of the difference between the means for the two versions.

Distribution of Scores on the 48 Forms

As noted, each of the cloze passages contained exactly 30 blanks. The number correct ranged from 8.5 to 18.3, or from approximately 30% to 60% correct per passage. In more than half of the 12 pairs yielding 24 different-passage versions, the difference between the two supposedly parallel forms was significant. But by averaging across both forms in all the analyses presented here, any differences that might be attributable solely to having used, by chance, a very easy or very difficult cloze version were minimized.

Comparisons of High- and Low-Readability Versions for the 12 Passages

Mean scores for the high- and low-readability versions of each of the 12 passages are presented in Table 3. Among the low-interest passages, the mean scores on the standard version were significantly higher in all cases than the mean scores on the difficult versions. Among the high-interest passages, the difference between the standard and difficult versions was significant in only about half of the passages.

Interest by Readability Analysis

The 24 passages were used to provide an analysis of the relationship between interest, readability, and comprehension. It will be recalled that each subject read eight passages. Of these, two were low-interest passages written at the standard readability level and two were low-interest passages written at the difficult level. Two were high-interest passages written at the standard readability level and two

Table 4.   Interest by Readability Analysis of Variance
(Within Subjects) on Comprehension Scores

	Total Sample (n = 243)				Subsample (n = 40)	
	Table of Means[a]				Table of Means[a]	
	Readability (R)				Readability (R)	
	Standard	Difficult			Standard	Difficult
Interest (I)				Interest (I)		
Low	25.83	21.70		Low	25.97	22.30
High	29.33	25.86		High	29.38	25.17

	ANOVA Table					ANOVA Table			
Source	MS	df	F	p	Source	MS	df	F	p
Interest	3559.17	1	199.17	.0001	Interest	393.76	1	19.86	.0001
Error	17.87	242			Error	19.83	39		
Readability	3498.14	1	165.40	.0001	Readability	620.15	1	24.65	.0001
Error	21.15	242			Error	25.16	39		
I × R	27.00	1	1.43	NS	I × R	2.76	1	.12	NS
Error	18.87	242			Error	23.29	39		

[a]Mean scores are based on the sum of the scores for the two passages at each interest and readability level.

were high-interest passages written at the difficult level. The cloze scores on the two passages of each type were combined and used in a two-factor within-subjects analysis of variance. The two independent variables were interest (low vs. high) and readability (standard vs. difficult). The dependent variable was the cloze comprehension score. The results of this analysis are presented in Table 4. This and subsequent major analyses were done on two sets of data. One set included the total sample. The other set included the subsample of subjects whose vocabulary and comprehension scores were between grades 11 and 13.

In the total sample, both main effects were significant. The mean score on the high-interest passages was significantly higher than the mean score on the low-interest passages. The mean score on the passages written at the standard readability level was higher than the mean score for the passages written at the difficult level. The interaction was nonsignificant, implying that the difference between the standard and difficult readability versions was not significantly larger in the low-interest passages than in the high-interest passages. In the subsample, the main effects were significant and showed the same mean differences as in the total sample. In the subsample the interaction was again nonsignificant.

Analyses Involving Prior Knowledge

Whereas the levels of readability and interest were set before the data were collected, prior knowledge was empirically determined during the study. Several analyses were performed to assess the effect of prior knowledge on comprehension.

1. *Prior knowledge as a covariate.*   If differences on comprehension scores are in part a reflection of different amounts of prior knowledge, then when this factor is introduced as a covariate into the analysis of variance, the differences due to readability and/or interest should decrease. The results of the analysis of covariance are presented in Table 5.

In the total sample the main effects for interest and readability were still significant. After the means were adjusted to account for prior knowledge as a covariate, the difference between the high- and low-interest cells decreased but was still significant. In the subsample, in which prior knowledge as well as general vocabulary and reading comprehension skills were held constant, readability was significant but interest was no longer significant. In neither the total sample nor the

Table 5.   Interest by Readability Analysis of Covariance
(Within Subjects) on Comprehension Scores

	Total Sample ($n = 204$)		Subsample ($n = 36$)	
	Table of Adjusted Means[a]		Table of Adjusted Means[a]	
	Readability (R)		Readability (R)	
	Standard	Difficult	Standard	Difficult
Interest (I)			Interest (I)	
Low	26.13	22.14	Low 27.35	23.30
High	28.60	25.30	High 27.51	24.34

ANCOVA Table					ANCOVA Table				
Source	MS	df	F	p	Source	MS	df	F	p
Interest	261.20	1	14.46	.0001	Interest	40.27	1	1.38	NS
Cov.	40.81	3	2.26	.08	Cov.	3.67	3	.17	NS
Error	18.06	200			Error	21.44	32		
Readability	2737.11	1	134.83	.0001	Readability	488.55	1	20.16	.0001
Cov.	23.10	3	1.14	NS	Cov.	23.05	3	.95	NS
Error	20.30	200			Error	24.23	32		
I × R	21.88	1	1.19	NS	I × R	10.32	1	.50	NS
Cov.	40.86	3	2.22	.09	Cov.	30.39	3	1.46	NS
Error	18.40	200			Error	20.81	32		

[a]Mean scores are based on the sum of the scores for the two passages at each interest and readability level.

subsample was the interaction significant. In general, then, the effect of holding level of prior knowledge constant was to attenuate or eliminate the differences in comprehension due to the interest level of the passages.

2. *Comparisons on effects of prior knowledge with interest and readabiity held constant.* Another way of measuring the effect of prior knowledge is to view it as an independent variable with comprehension as the dependent variable. For this analysis, the prior knowledge scores for each passage were dichotomized at the mean and subjects were placed into a high- or low-prior knowledge group on each. In addition, subjects were grouped into those who read the standard version of a passage and those who read the difficult version. For each passage, then, it was possible to compute a two-factor between subjects analysis of variance, with prior knowledge and readability as the independent variables and comprehension as the dependent variable. This analysis was similar to the one presented previously involving interest and readability. However, there were two differences. The readability by interest analysis was a within-subjects analysis of variance, whereas the prior knowledge by readability analysis was a between-subjects analysis. Furthermore, in the readability by interest analysis, the dependent variable (comprehension) was derived by summing across two different passages, both of which were of the same level of interest and readability. The prior knowledge by readability analysis, on the other hand, was performed on a single passage so that instead of one analysis there were 12 analyses of variance, or one per passage. Since each subject read 8 of the 12 passages, not all the subjects were involved in each analysis. But since each subject did read 8 of the 12 passages, each of them is involved in 8 of the 12 analyses of variance. This means, of course, that the 12 analyses were not independent of one another. Yet, taken together, they can be informative in that, if particular patterns of results occur, particularly within interest groupings, the conditions under which prior knowledge is or is not important can be elucidated.

The cell means for each passage are presented in Table 6 and the analyses of variance in Table 7. It can be seen that both main effects were significant in almost all the analyses based on the total sample. As in the previous analysis of variance involving interest and readability, the mean scores on the standard version were higher than those on the difficult version. The results were significant in three of the high-interest passages and marginal in a fourth. In the analysis of prior knowledge, subjects whose scores were high had a higher mean comprehension score than subjects whose scores were low. This result was significant in all but three passages. Only one of the 12 analyses showed a significant interaction.

The same analyses based on the subsample could have been used as a way of looking at the effect of prior knowledge, with vocabulary and reading skill held relatively constant. However, due to the small number of subjects in the subsample, these analyses could not be meaningfully interpreted. As another way of estimating the strength of the prior knowledge effect, the analyses for the total

Table 6. Mean Comprehension Scores Broken Down by Readability and Prior Knowledge Scores for 12 Passages

| | Total Sample: Readability | | | | Subsample: Readability | | | |
| | Standard | | Difficult | | Standard | | Difficult | |
Passage[a]	n	Mean	n	Mean	n	Mean	n	Mean
Aluminum								
Low PK	43	13.6	40	11.0	12	13.3	5	11.0
High PK	23	16.0	32	13.5	4	12.0	4	15.0
Cement								
Low PK	37	12.3	29	10.4	6	11.5	4	11.0
High PK	45	13.3	43	11.8	7	13.6	12	12.8
Crops								
Low PK	28	9.7	30	9.0	4	10.5	4	10.6
High PK	38	13.0	35	10.5	5	14.0	7	10.3
Dry-Clean								
Low PK	43	15.3	43	12.1	8	19.0	10	12.0
High PK	32	15.3	26	13.2	6	15.7	4	14.0
Meat								
Low PK	42	10.5	38	9.8	6	10.5	8	9.5
High PK	29	13.8	49	10.5	7	13.4	7	7.9
Rocks								
Low PK	39	10.1	39	8.8	8	9.0	6	11.2
High PK	34	11.7	34	9.7	3	13.0	3	9.3
Death								
Low PK	45	15.6	40	13.6	6	16.5	10	12.8
High PK	39	16.3	23	13.6	7	15.4	4	12.0
Emotions								
Low PK	38	12.7	40	11.8	6	10.8	5	13.4
High PK	35	15.1	42	15.1	6	13.5	5	15.4
Forget								
Low PK	27	14.8	34	13.6	5	14.8	7	13.1
High PK	34	14.9	34	15.5	6	16.0	6	16.0
Personality								
Low PK	28	13.9	41	9.2	4	15.0	8	9.4
High PK	31	15.0	36	11.1	5	15.2	5	10.4
Physical Fit								
Low PK	41	13.3	50	12.3	8	12.1	4	14.3
High PK	34	16.2	31	15.6	7	15.4	5	14.4
Sleep								
Low PK	32	12.3	37	11.2	2	12.5	9	11.0
High PK	34	14.0	28	12.5	6	14.0	4	10.8

[a]PK = prior knowledge.

Table 7.   Summary of Readability by Prior Knowledge Scores:
Analysis of Variance on Comprehension Scores for 12 Passages

	Total Sample				Subsample			
	Significance Level of Effects				*Significance Level of Effects*			
Passage	n	PK[a]	R[b]	PK × R	n	PK[a]	R[b]	PK × R
Aluminum	138	.001	.001	NS	25	NS	NS	NS
Cement	154	.015	.001	NS	29	.10	NS	NS
Crops	131	.001	.001	NS	20	NS	NS	NS
Dry-Clean	144	NS	.001	NS	28	NS	.001	.04
Meat	158	.001	.001	.02	28	NS	.01	.06
Rocks	146	.01	.001	NS	20	NS	NS	.09
Death	147	NS	.004	NS	27	NS	.007	NS
Emotions	155	.001	NS	NS	22	NS	NS	NS
Forget	129	.08	NS	NS	24	NS	NS	NS
Personality	136	.002	.001	NS	22	NS	.001	NS
Physical Fit	156	.001	.105	NS	24	NS	NS	NS
Sleep	131	.012	.007	NS	21	NS	NS	NS

[a]PK = prior knowledge.
[b]R = readability.

sample were recast as analyses of covariance, with vocabulary and reading comprehension scores as the covariates. When these two covariates were included, the main effect for readability became nonsignificant for only two passages. The main effect of prior knowledge for three of the passages became nonsignificant. In other words, when vocabulary and reading comprehension were held constant, the relationship between prior knowledge about and comprehension of a passage was weakened in some cases. It is perhaps more interesting that the effects were maintained in most cases.

3. *Readability by interest by prior knowledge analysis of variance.* To perform this analysis, it was necessary to find a set of subjects whose prior knowledge scores were either low or high for the passages at each combination of interest and readability. As was stated above, each subject read eight passages, two at each of the four possible combinations of high and low interest and high and low readability. If a subject was either high or low in prior knowledge (for one or both passages) at each of the four possible combinations of interest and readability, he or she could be put into the appropriate high or low prior knowledge group. Subjects who were not uniformly high or low on prior knowledge for all the combinations of interest and readability could not be used in the analysis. Furthermore, since the measure of prior knowledge was moderately correlated with reading comprehension, dividing subjects into high and low prior knowledge groups may also incidentally divide them by comprehension skill. In order to circumvent this possibility, the three-way analysis of

Table 8. Interest by Readability by Prior Knowledge Scores:
Analysis of Variance on Comprehension Scores for a Small Subgroup

	Table of Means			
	Low Prior Knowledge (n = 9)		High Prior Knowledge (n = 9)	
	Readability		Readability	
	Standard	Difficult	Standard	Difficult
Interest (I)				
Low	12.56	10.28	14.78	13.44
High	12.94	10.94	16.83	14.28

	ANOVA Table			
Source[a]	MS	df	F	p
Prior Knowledge	178.92	1	8.43	.01
Error	21.23	16		
Interest	17.50	1	3.39	.08
I × PK	3.78	1	.73	NS
Error	5.13	16		
Readability	75.03	1	14.63	.001
R × PK	.17	1	.03	NS
Error	5.13	16		
I × R	1.00	1	.14	NS
I × R × PK	2.53	1	.35	NS
Error	7.14	16		

[a]I = interest; PK = prior knowledge; R = readability.

variance was run only on subjects in the subsample, who were selected for inclusion on the basis of their vocabulary and comprehension scores. From the subsample it was possible to find nine cases in which prior knowledge was low and nine cases in which it was high on one or both passages at each level of interest and readability. In the case where two passages were available for a cell, the average of the two scores was used. Overall, about 40% of the cell entries were based on two passages.

The cell means and the results of the three-factor analysis of variance on this subset of the subsample are presented in Table 8. On the between-subjects factor of prior knowledge, the mean comprehension score for those subjects low in prior knowledge was significantly lower than for subjects high in prior knowledge. Although the mean comprehension score for the high-interest passages was higher than for the low-interest passages, the main effect of interest was only marginal in this analysis (p = .08). The main effect of readability was highly significant, with the mean comprehension score for the passages written at the standard level being significantly higher than that for the passages written at the difficult level. None of the interactions was significant.

DISCUSSION

Methodological Considerations

Generalizability to Various Content Areas

This study looked at the effects of interest, prior knowledge, and readability on the comprehension of expository materials. One advantage of the design used in this study is that the results are based on more than one or two content areas. In many studies only one target passage is used, so that the effects of the independent variables are confounded with the content area. In this study, six different high-interest topics and six different low-interest topics were selected, so that one can at least be confident that the results are generalizable to various content areas. As an aside, one can also note that the high-interest passages seem to contain some of the components, such as personal relevance, which Shank (Note 15) suggests will make a passage interesting.

The Measurement of Prior Knowledge

Whereas the ways of measuring readability and interest are well-established in the literature, the measurement of prior knowledge is more experimental at this time. In the course of this research several approaches were tried, involving both subjective and objective measures. What was found, however, was that subjective measures of prior knowledge about a topic were confounded with interest, i.e., subjects rated their prior knowledge of the interesting topics as high relative to their prior knowledge of the uninteresting topics. Over a range of topics, subjects seemed unable to differentiate these two factors.

The objective approach to measuring prior knowledge used here was to assess the subjects' knowledge of key terms as they were used in a particular passage. (This concept could, of course, be extended to the measurement of key terms assumed to be associated with a particular topic.) These key terms were those assumed to be understood by the reader as opposed to new terms introduced and explained in the passage. The idea of using key terms follows the theoretical orientation offered by Anderson and Freebody (1981, 1983).

A basic question about assessing knowledge of terms involves the selection of the terms. While some passages seemed to involve very topic-specific terms, others did not, and what a rater picked as the important terms were general vocabulary terms. In other words, then, it is not always possible to make a distinction between general vocabulary knowledge and knowledge of terms specific to a passage. But if the concept of prior knowledge is to cover something different from vocabulary strength, one needs to have a measure which is different from a general vocabulary test. It seems that some topics are more likely than others to involve a specialized set of terms, the knowledge of which is not directly tied to general vocabulary knowledge.

One of the reasons for including analyses based on a subsample was to see whether prior knowledge had any effect on comprehension over and above general vocabulary strength. It will be recalled that the subsample was composed of subjects whose vocabulary and comprehension scores were relatively similar. Thus, when subjects in this sample were divided into high- and low-prior knowledge groups, one was not merely separating them into high- and low-vocabulary strength groups. In the three-factor analysis of variance in which the subjects were drawn from the subsample, the main effect for prior knowledge was significant. In fact even when vocabulary was used as a covariate as an extra precaution, the prior knowledge effect was still significant. This analysis offers empirical support for the concept of prior knowledge apart from general vocabulary strength.

Effects of the Independent Variables on Comprehension

Main Effects

The hypotheses concerning the main effects were strongly supported, at least in the cases of readability and interest. Supporting other research findings, mean comprehension scores on interesting passages were significantly higher than mean scores on uninteresting passages. Because a cogent attempt was made to find two sets of passages which were clearly differentiated in terms of their interest value to college-aged students, this result was perhaps not surprising.

Similarly, the mean comprehension scores on the passages written at the standard readability level were significantly higher than mean scores on the passages written at the difficult level. What stood out about these readability differences were their consistency and their strength, i.e., the very strong significance levels. One factor which may have contributed to these strong results is that the difficult and standard versions were as much as four reading grade levels apart. In addition, the standard readability level was *at* and the difficult readability level clearly *above* the reading grade level of most of the subjects in this study. This pattern of relationship between the readability level of the passages and the average reading grade level of the subjects may have led to a stronger main effect on readability than a situation in which the grade level differences were smaller or, in like fashion, in which the easier version was *below* and the harder version *at* the average reading grade level of the subjects—or even in which the easier version was merely somewhat below and the harder version somewhat above the reading grade level of the subjects in the study. In designing studies involving readability, it may be important to set the readability levels of the passages *in conjunction with* the reading grade level of the subjects to be used. This was done by Kincaid and Gamble (1977), who found differences in mean comprehension scores for high-school-aged but not college-aged subjects reading a standard and those reading an easy version of an insurance policy.

The second point to be raised in connection with the readability effect is the nature of the comprehension test. Using a cloze test as a comprehension measure rather than a multiple choice test may have contributed to the strength of the differences between the two versions. In the cloze test, where subjects are required to fill in the missing words, the difference between the two readability levels, which is a direct function of the difficulty level of the words being used, may have stood out more strongly than on a test in which subjects were required instead to answer questions about the passage. Both Bormuth (Note 16) and Rankin (1965) have concluded that the cloze test is probably a more reliable measure of comprehension than a multiple choice test. They point out that in a multiple choice test one can write easy questions about difficult material or difficult questions about easy material. In cloze, the difficulty of the test is more directly tied to the difficulty of the prose, especially when more than one of the five possible cloze versions are used (as was done in this research).

Turning to the main effect for prior knowledge, the analyses of variance involving passage-by-passage readability and prior knowledge indicated significantly higher mean comprehension scores for subjects who were high in prior knowledge than for subjects who were low. When the analyses were recast as analyses of covariance, with Nelson–Denny vocabulary and reading comprehension scores as the covariates, some of the main effects attributable to prior knowledge became nonsignificant, suggesting that when these variables are held constant, the effect of prior knowledge itself on comprehension is reduced. However, in the three-way analysis of variance, the main effect for prior knowledge was significant, with the mean score for subjects whose prior knowledge was high being higher than the mean score for subjects whose prior knowledge was low. In that analysis, it will be recalled, only subjects from the subsample were used, so that general vocabulary strength was controlled.

Taken as a whole, the results indicate that prior knowledge is an important factor in comprehension. The consistency and the strength of these results were not as apparent as for interest and readability. However, as has already been noted, the measurement of prior knowledge about a topic is not as refined as the measurement of readability or as straightforward as the measurement of interest, so that the results are based on an experimental measure. In addition, this variable was not so strongly represented in the design as would be the case if this variable, too, were operationalized at two distinct levels systematically crossed with the other variables.

Interaction Effects

Two different hypotheses were offered concerning interactions between the independent variables. One hypothesis suggested that the effects for each of the independent variables would be additive. In other words, mean scores where values were high on two of the independent variables would be higher than scores where values were high on only one of the independent variables. The other hypothesis, based on a model proposed by Klare (1976), suggested that the independent variables would interact and the effects would not be additive. In other words, being high on two independent variables would not lead to higher mean comprehension scores than being high on only one independent variable. This second hypothesis suggests a significant interaction in a two-factor analysis of variance. The results showed, however, that where values were high on two of the independent variables, mean scores were higher than where values were high on only one. In the three-factor analysis of variance, where values were high for all three independent variables, mean scores were higher than where values were high on two of the three independent variables. In other words, the data in this study clearly suggested that an additive model is a more accurate reflection of the cumulative effects of the three independent variables taken together than a nonadditive model.

There are other studies involving readability and a motivational variable, such as interest or reward (cf. Denbow, Note 10; and Fass & Schumacher, 1978), which offer support for a nonadditive model. One possible explanation for these divergent sets of findings lies in the relationship of the readability level of the prose to the reading ability of the subjects. In this study the standard (or easier) readability level corresponded to the average reading grade level of the subjects. The difficult (or harder) readability level was *above* the reading grade level of most of the subjects in the study. In other studies, however, the readability level of the harder version may have been approximately equivalent to the reading level of the subjects whereas the readability level of the easier version may have been *below* the reading grade level of most of the subjects. It may be that when none of the materials are clearly above the reading grade level of the readers, a nonadditive model is more appropriate. That suggests, for example, that when interest is high, comprehension is *not* improved by writing material below, rather than at, the reading grade level of the readers, whereas when interest is low, comprehension *is* improved by writing the material *below* rather than *at* the reading grade level of the readers. This study does suggest, on the other hand, that when interest is high, as well as when it is low, comprehension is better when materials are written *at*, rather than clearly *above*, the reading grade level of the intended readers. If these speculations are valid, it is extremely important, when considering the effects of various readability levels, to consider them in conjunction with the reading grade level of the individuals who will be using the written materials. This is particularly so when the effect of readability is being considered in combination with other factors such as motivational variables. Regarding motivation, it may be that the effect of an intrinsic motivator, such as the interest variable used in this study, is different from that of an extrinsic motivator such as monetary reward or threat, as used in the Fass and Schumacher (1978) and McLaughlin (1966) studies, respectively. Further research is needed to examine these possibilities more fully.

The interaction between readability and prior knowledge was not as clearly tested in this study as was the readability by interest interaction. The results, such as they were, pointed to an additive model, i.e., each factor has its own effect, not dependent on the others. However, due to the experimental nature of the prior knowledge measure, it does not seem fruitful to speculate at length about the nature of this interaction or about conditions under which a significant interaction between these two factors might have been obtained. Similarly, because of the experimental nature of the prior knowledge measure, it is not possible to say very much about the combined effect of interest and prior knowledge on comprehension. The three-way analysis of variance suggested an additive model. But because most of the other analyses were done on a passage-by-passage basis, it was not possible to test this interaction as thoroughly as the others.

Other Findings

The methodological problems concerning the measurement of prior knowledge have been discussed previously. One point that merits amplification here, though, concerns the relationship between prior knowledge and comprehension. Over a broad range of subjects, scores on reading tests (both vocabulary and comprehension), prior knowledge, and comprehension of passages are all likely to be positively correlated (because they all tap verbal skills). Such correlations were observed in this study. For this reason a subsample with relatively homogeneous vocabulary and reading comprehension scores was used to ensure that any between-subjects effects (particularly those involving prior knowledge) were not merely a function of general verbal ability. But beyond this, it is still important to ensure that the prior knowledge measure is conceptually and empirically different from the comprehension measure. These two measures are often confounded, so that one merely has two measures of comprehension (or two measures of prior knowledge) rather than a measure of prior knowledge and a measure of comprehension. In this study an attempt was made to separate these two measures, both conceptually and methodologically. The prior knowledge scores were derived from subjects' definitions of terms, which were given to them separately (both in form and in time) from the passages. The cloze test, which was the measure of comprehension, required subjects to fill in systematically deleted words. But the subjects did this after they had read an intact portion of the passage which established the nature of the topic being discussed and also served to set the difficulty level of the prose. In other words, in this study prior knowledge and comprehension were assessed by two different techniques and at two different times.

Broader Considerations

The results of this study as a whole support the importance of prior knowledge as a factor in comprehension. These data tie in with much of the recent work which suggests how intimately prior knowledge, as well as interest, is tied to compre-hension. It is consistent with research findings such as those reported by Anderson et al. (1977), who found that subjects with different backgrounds (and thus, presumably, different kinds or degrees of prior knowledge) interpret the same passage differently. It lends support to research by Entin and Klare (1978b, 1980), Pryczak (1972), Tuinman (1973/74), and others whose work suggests that many so-called reading comprehension tests may be to a large extent measuring prior knowledge rather than comprehension. It appears that only when prior knowledge is controlled can a clear measure of comprehension and an under-standing of the relationship between comprehension, interest, and readability, as well as other factors, emerge.

Considering the attention given recently to formal (and formidable) analysis of text structure (cf. Harker, Hartley, & Walsh, 1982; Stone & Crandell, 1982; Meyer, 1983), it is perhaps surprising that such an old fashioned and relatively easily applied measure as readability should capture such a large proportion of the variance in subjects' comprehension. It may be that when the dependent measure of comprehension does not specifically stress the subjects' grasp of the text structure or when the topics are not entirely outside the readers' knowledge, allowing them to infer or construct a structure (and these subjects read at least 250 words on the topic before cloze deletions began), a measure of readability is adequate and efficient for screening text. A measure of readability that includes both syntactic and semantic cues may also indirectly reflect text structure. When, however, the object is not to describe performance but to analyze underlying cognitive processes, or when the structure itself is the primary focus of interest or when the reader is asked (with no prior opportunity to explore the topic) to process difficult and unfamiliar text, explicit measures of text structure may be useful.

Given the intent of the study presented here, a cloze measure of comprehen-sion was both appropriate and efficient. Yet a cloze measure, while reflecting a reader's overall comprehension of the passage, may be particularly sensitive to structural cues at the sentence level rather than the intersentential or text structure levels. If one were to ask largely the same questions asked here but use text structure analysis, it might be useful to include both cloze and measures which assess subjects' recall of high level structure. Although we can arbitrarily separate these levels of language structure, we still need more evidence as to how they are related in readers' functional behavior.

The measure of prior knowledge used here was made on a relatively micro-analytic level, i.e., requiring knowledge of some of the actual terms used in a passage. The findings for prior knowledge, though, are congruent with those in studies of the effects of schema, or background knowledge. Here again, there is a question of whether, for some kinds of research issues, measures of a relatively broad general schema are most useful while for other issues a more detailed and passage-specific measure of prior knowledge is helpful.

In this study interest was used as an independent variable. Reader' interest in various topics was assessed in order to find a set of topics which were either of low or high interest to readers in general. It would be possible to design studies in which interest was used as a dependent variable. As noted earlier, though, questions about the relationships of interest, prior knowledge, readability, and comprehension will require continuing conceptual as well as empirical analysis.

NOTE

1. This paper is based in part on a doctoral dissertation at Ohio University completed by the first author under the second author's direction but incorporating a number of studies prior to that effort, substudies within the dissertation, and continuing developments in the field.

REFERENCE NOTES

1. Ewing, M. J. *A comparison of the effects of readability and time on learning the contents of a state driver's handbook.* Unpublished doctoral dissertation, Florida State University, 1976.
2. Greene, M. T. *Effects of readability and directed stopping on the learning and enjoyment of technical materials.* Unpublished doctoral dissertation, University of North Carolina, 1979.
3. Swanson, C. C. *Readability and top-level structure: Effects on reading comprehension.* Unpublished doctoral dissertation, Arizona State University, 1979.
4. Walker, M. S. *The effects of high and low interest content on instructional levels in informal reading inventories.* Unpublished doctoral dissertation, Auburn University, 1976.
5. Allen, L. L. *The effect of reading preference on reading comprehension of low socioeconomic high school students.* Unpublished doctoral dissertation, North Texas State University, 1979.
6. Royer, J. M., & Cunningham, D. L. *The theory of measurement of reading comprehension.* (Technical Report Number 91) Champaign, Ill.: Center for the Study of Reading, 1978.
7. Reder, L. M. *Comprehension and retention of prose: A literature review.* (Technical Report Number 108) Champaign, Ill.: Center for the Study of Reading, 1978.
8. Bower, G. H. *Comprehending and recalling stories.* Section 3 Presidential Address presented at the meeting of the American Psychological Association, Washington, D. C., September 1976.
9. Mutter, D. W. *A psycholinguistic investigation of the influence of prior knowledge on the oral reading miscues and comprehension of selected high school seniors.* Unpublished doctoral dissertation, University of Massachusetts, 1979.
10. Denbow, C. J. *An experimental study of the effect of a repetition factor on the relationship between readability and listenability.* Unpublished doctoral dissertation, Ohio University, 1973.
11. Funkhouser, G. R., & Maccoby, N. *Study on communicating science information to a lay audience. Phase II.* (Report based on a study funded by the National Science Foundation, NSF GZ-996). Palo Alto, Cal.: Institute for Communication Research, Stanford University, 1971.
12. Weber, C., & Ringler, L. H. *Motivation and knowledge influences on text comprehension.* Paper presented at the annual meeting of the National Reading Conference, San Antonio, Tex. December 1979.
13. Klare, G. R., Gustafson, L. M., & Mabry, J. E. *The reading interests of airmen during basic training.* (Research Bulletin 53-44, Human Resources Research Laboratory) San Antonio, Tex.: Lackland Air Force Base, 1953.
14. Saio, A. L. *The effects of level of interest, achievement and self-concept on the reading comprehension scores of fourth grade boys and girls.* Unpublished doctoral dissertation, University of South Dakota, 1976.

15. Shank, R. *Interestingness: Controlling inferences*. (Research Report No 145, Department of Computer Science) New Haven, Conn.: Yale University, 1978.
16. Bormuth, J. R. *Development of readability analyses*. (Technical Report, U. S. O. E. Project 5-0039) Chicago: University of Chicago, March 1969.

REFERENCES

Anderson, R.C., & Freebody, P. (1981). Vocabulary knowledge. In J.T. Guthrie (Ed.), *Comprehension and teaching: Research reviews*. Newark, DE: International Reading Association, pp. 77-117.

Anderson, R.C., & Freebody, P. (1983). Reading comprehension and the assessment and acquisition of word knowledge. In B.A. Hutson (Ed.), *Advances in reading/language research* (Vol. 2). Greenwich, CT: JAI Press, pp. 231-256.

Anderson, R.C., Reynolds, R.E., Schallert, D.L., & Goetz, E.T. (1977). Frameworks for comprehending discourse. *American Educational Research Journal, 14*, 367-381.

Asher, S.R. (1980). Topic interest and children's reading comprehension. In R.J. Spiro, B.C. Bruce, & W.F. Brewer (Eds.), *Theoretical issues in reading comprehension*. Hillsdale, N.J.: Erlbaum, pp. 525-534.

Asher, S.R., Hymel, S., & Wigfield, A. (1978). Influence of topic interest on children's reading comprehension. *Journal of Reading Behavior, 10*, 35-48.

Asher, S.R., & Markell, B.A. (1974). Sex differences in comprehension on high- and low-interest material. *Journal of Educational Psychology, 66*, 680-687.

Bransford, J.D., & Johnson, M.K. (1972). Contextual prerequisites of understanding: Some investigations of comprehension and recall. *Journal of Verbal Learning and Verbal Behavior, 11*, 717-726.

Bransford, J.D., & Johnson, M.K. (1973). Considerations of some problems of comprehension. In W.G. Chase (Ed.), *Visual information processing*. New York: Academic Press, pp. 383-438.

Brown, A.L., Smiley, S.S., Day, J.D., Townsend, M.A., & Lawton, J.C. (1977). Intrusion of a thematic idea in children's comprehension and retention of stories. *Child Development, 48*, 1454-1466.

Chall, J.S., & Dial, H. (1948). Predicting listener understanding and interest in newscasts. *Educational Research Bulletin, 27*, 141-153, 168.

Chiesi, H.L., Spilich, G.J., & Voss, J.F. (1979). Acquisition of domain-related information in relation to high and low domain knowledge. *Journal of Verbal Learning and Verbal Behavior, 18*, 257-273.

DRP Readability Report, 1982-83. (1982). New York: The College Board.

Entin, E.B., & Klare, G.R. (1978a). Factor analyses of three correlation matrices of readability variables. *Journal of Reading Behavior, 10*, 279-290.

Entin, E.B., & Klare, G.R. (1978b). Some inter-relationships of readability, cloze, and multiple choice scores on a reading comprehension test. *Journal of Reading Behavior, 10*, 417-436.

Entin, E.B., & Klare, G.R. (1980). Components of answers to multiple-choice questions on a published reading comprehension test: An application of the Hanna-Oaster approach. *Reading Research Quarterly, 15*, 228-236.

Fass, W., & Schumacher, G.M. (1978). Effects of motivation, subject activity, and readability on the retention of prose materials. *Journal of Educational Psychology 70* 803-808.

Flesch, R.F. (1948). A new readability yardstick. *Journal of Applied Psychology, 32*, 221-233.

Fredericksen, C.H. (1975). Representing logical and semantic structure of knowledge acquired from discourse. *Cognitive Psychology, 7*, 371-458.

Frederiksen, C.H. (1979). Discourse comprehension and early reading. In L.B. Resnick & P.A. Weaver (Eds.), *Theory and practice of early reading* (Vol. 1). Hillsdale, N.J.: Erlbaum, pp. 155-186.

Harker, J.O., Hartley, J.T., & Walsh, D.A. (1982). Understanding discourse: A lifespan developmental approach. In B.A. Hutson (Ed.), *Advances in reading/language research* (Vol. 1). Greenwich, CT: JAI Press, pp. 155-202.

Haviland, S.E., & Clark, H.H. (1974). What's New? Acquiring new information as a process in comprehension. *Journal of Verbal Learning and Verbal Behavior, 13*, 515-521.

Kincaid, J.P., & Gamble, L.G. (1977). Ease of comprehension of standard and readable insurance policies as a function of reading ability. *Journal of Reading Behavior, 9*, 85-87.

Kintsch, W. (1979). On modeling comprehension. *Educational Psychologist, 14*, 3-14.

Kintsch, W., & Vipond, D. (1979). Reading comprehension and readability in educational practice and psychological theory. In L. Nilsson (Ed.), *Perspectives on memory research*. Hillsdale, N.J.: Erlbaum, pp. 329-365.

Klare, G.R. (1963). *The measurement of readability*. Ames, IA: Iowa State University Press.

Klare, G.R. (1974/75). Assessing readability. *Reading Research Quarterly, 10*, 62-102.

Klare, G.R. (1976). A second look at the validity of readability formulas. *Journal of Reading Behavior, 8*, 129-152.

Klare, G.R. (1982). Readability. In H.E. Mitzel (Ed.), *Encyclopedia of Educational Research* (5th ed.). New York: The Free Press, pp. 1520-1531.

Klare, G.R. (1984). Readability. In P.D. Pearson (Ed.), *Handbook of research in reading*. New York: Longman, pp. 681-744.

Klare, G.R., Mabry, J.E., & Gustafson, L.H. (1955). The relationship of style difficulty to immediate retention and to acceptability of technical material. *Journal of Educational Psychology, 46*, 287-295.

Klare, G.R., Sinaiko, H.W., & Stolurow, L. (1972). The cloze procedure: A convenient readability test for training materials and translations. *International Review of Applied Psychology, 21*, 77-108.

Lantoff, R.E. (1978). Two factors affecting text recall. In P.D. Pearson & J. Hansen (Eds.), *Reading: Disciplined inquiry in process and practice*. 27th Yearbook of the National Reading Conference, Clemson SC: National Reading Conference, pp. 93-98.

Mandler, J.M. (1978). A code in the node: The use of a story schema in retrieval. *Discourse Processes, 1*, 14-35.

McLaughlin, G.H. (1966). Comparing styles of presenting technical information, *Ergonomics, 9*, 257-259.

Meyer, B.J.F. (1975). *The organization of prose and its effects on memory*. Amsterdam: North-Holland Publishing Company.

Meyer, B.J.F. (1977). The structure of prose: Effects on learning and memory and implications for educational practice. In R.C. Anderson, R.J. Spiro, & W.E. Montague (Eds.), *Schooling and the acquisition of knowledge*. Hillsdale, N.J.: Erlbaum, pp. 179-200.

Meyer, B.J.F. (1983). Text structure and its use in studying comprehension across the adult life span. In B.A. Hutson (Ed.), *Advances in reading/language research* (Vol. 2). Greenwich, CT: JAI Press, pp. 9-54.

Nelson, M.J., & Denny, E.C. (1960). *The Nelson-Denny Reading Test*. Boston: Houghton Mifflin.

Pearson, P.D., & Campbell, K. (1981). Comprehension of text structures. In J.T. Guthrie (Ed.), *Comprehension and teaching: Research reviews*. Newark, DE: International Reading Association, pp. 27-55.

Pearson, P.D., Hansen, J., & Gordon, C. (1979). The effect of background knowledge on young children's comprehension of explicit and implicit information. *Journal of Reading Behavior, 11*, 201-209.

Pichert, J.W., & Anderson, R.C. (1977). Taking different perspectives on a story. *Journal of Educational Psychology, 69*, 309-315.

Pyrczak, F. (1972). Objective evaluation of the quality of multiple-choice test items designed to measure comprehension of reading passages. *Reading Research Quarterly, 8*, 62-71.

Rankin, E.F. (1965). The cloze procedure—a survey of research. In E.L. Thurston and L.E. Hafner

(Eds.), *The philosophical and sociological bases of reading*. 14th Yearbook of the National Reading Conference. Milwaukee, WI: National Reading Conference, pp. 133-150.

Rankin, E.F. (1978). Characteristics of the cloze procedure as a research tool in the study of language. In P.D. Pearson & J. Hansen (Eds.), *Reading: Disciplined inquiry in process and practice*. 27th Yearbook of the National Reading Conference. Clemson, SC: National Reading Conference.

Reder, L.M. (1980). The role of elaboration in the comprehension and retention of prose. *Review of Educational Research, 50*, 5-53.

Rumelhart, D.E. (1977). Understanding and summarizing brief stories. In D. LaBerge & S.J. Samuels (Eds.), *Basic processes in reading perception and comprehension*. Hillsdale, NJ: Erlbaum, pp. 265-304.

Silvey, R. (1951). The intelligibility of broadcast talks. *Public Opinion Quarterly, 15*, 299-304.

Simons, H.D. (1971). Reading Comprehension: The need for a new perspective. *Reading Research Quarterly, 6*, 338-363.

Spilich, G.J., Vesonder, G.T., Chiesi, H.L., & Voss, J.F. (1979). Text processing of domain-related information for individuals with high and low domain knowledge. *Journal of Verbal Learning and Verbal Behavior, 18*, 275-290.

Stone, D.E., & Crandall, T.L. (1982). Relationships of illustrations and text in reading technical material. In B.A. Hutson (Ed.), *Adcvances in reading/language research* (Vol. 1). Greenwich, Conn.: JAI Press, pp. 283-307.

Tuinman, J.J. (1973/74). Determining the passage dependency of comprehension questions in 5 major tests. *Reading Research Quarterly, 9*, 206-223.

Waples, D., & Tyler, R.W. (1931). *What people want to read about*. Chicago: University of Chicago Press.

Woern, Y. (1977). On the relationship between knowledge of the world and comprehension of texts: Assimilation and accommodation effects related to belief structures. *Scandinavian Journal of Psychology, 18*, 130-139.

SPELLING AS CONCEPT-GOVERNED PROBLEM SOLVING:

LEARNING-DISABLED AND
NORMALLY ACHIEVING STUDENTS

Michael M. Gerber

INTRODUCTION

Recently, I had the opportunity to be a spectator during the final rounds of a local school district's "spelldown." The final three contestants were reduced to two by the misspelling of ALLUMINUM/aluminum. One of the last two was a young Vietnamese–American, who a few years earlier could speak no English whatsoever. As I watched the young immigrant agonize over "ensnare" and "orient," and ultimately fail on QUINNINE/quinine in the 53rd round of competition, my "researcher" demeanor was temporarily forgotten and I, too, was filled with admiration for her accomplishment. In honesty, I had already lost to her several rounds before by mentally misspelling "yacht" (I thought there was

Advances in Reading/Language Research, Volume 3, pages 39-75.
Copyright © 1985 by JAI Press Inc.
All rights of reproduction in any form reserved.
ISBN: 0-89232-389-2

a 'g' somewhere), "chili" (I thought there were two 'l's'), and others which a Ph.D., not to mention a spelling researcher, might be expected to spell correctly.

How was it that these children, whose first language was so different in its phonology, syntax, and orthography, had so well mastered American–English spelling? For that matter, how does *any* child master the complex skill of spelling? Most of us would acknowledge an unwritten list of spelling "demons" which individually and/or collectively we can only spell with difficulty. Even well educated adults continue to produce a low rate of spelling errors when they write (Hoptopf, 1980; Wing & Baddeley, 1980). The most frequent writing error produced by remedial college freshmen is misspelling (Higgins, 1975). In one recent study, 84% of all written compositions contained misspellings. The discrepancy between actual and expected spelling achievement increases steadily as students with 'learning disabilities' (LDs) progress through school (Poplin, Gray, Larsen, Banikowski, & Mehring, 1980). Why is it that these and other children never seem to achieve mastery of this important skill?

Upon closely scrutinizing the 'spelldown', especially individual behavior while spelling, it was readily observed that each child approached new words in a distinct manner. Characteristic differences in spelling behavior were apparent even though each child was, in a sense, equally "expert" as a speller. For example, the girl mentioned above took a great deal of *time*, i.e., about 3 minutes on "ensnare" and about as long on "orient," reflecting on certain words before she would commit herself to an attempt. However, the boy with whom she was competing tended to spell quickly, nodding his head while the caller read each word and illustrative sentence. Moreover, despite these durable general characteristics, each child also displayed subtle differences for different words. In fact, all the children varied somewhat in their response style—sometimes reflecting at length before attempting a response, sometimes pausing during an attempt, sometimes spelling rapidly without any hesitation whatsoever. In short, there were certain qualitative as well as quantitative differences both between and within spellers, all of whom spelled most words correctly. That is, although these were school champions representing the top 1% of their age group, not every child spelled the same way as his or her peers or even the same way for each word.

A tentative hypothesis can be formed from these unsystematic observations and might be framed as follows: In the face of response uncertainty, skilled spellers can be better characterized by their flexible, strategic, and efficient problem-solving behavior than by the number of words they can spell correctly. A corollary of this position might be as follows: Poor or unskilled spellers *lack* specific word knowledge and also have difficulty acquiring that knowledge because they lack flexible, strategic, and efficient problem-solving repertoires. Thus, just as variability in skilled spelling performance leads us to appreciate the subtlety of processes which produce correct spellings, similar variability in errors and error-making behavior should warn against uncritical assumptions that poor spellers are cognitively deviant.

The point to be made here is that spelling performance by both skilled and unskilled spellers can be interpreted both too casually and too dogmatically. Researchers and practitioners might benefit from greater appreciation for normal variability in individual learners attempting to spell. Central to such appreciation is recognition of cognitive components and information-processing systems which contribute to typical as well as atypical acquisition of spelling skill.

This chapter will discuss how these issues have been addressed by an ongoing program of research. In so doing, it will be argued that beyond its obvious importance as a tool skill by which written composition and expression are facilitated, spelling represents an interesting example of subtlety and fluency of emerging cognitive abilities in children attempting to master elemental academic skills. Moreover, variability in performance and concomitant behaviors of children learning to spell provides excellent potential models for studying the effects of individual differences on success and failure in acquiring academic skills. This latter point is underscored by the fact that difficulties in spelling appear to persist even after reading skills have improved in children who were regarded as reading-disabled (Carpenter & Miller, 1982; Rutter & Yule, 1973), learning-disabled (Poplin et al., 1980), or dyslexic (Boder, 1971).

Paradigm for Research

The theoretical perspective taken by research presented in this chapter derives from an information-processing research paradigm (Lachman, Lachman, & Butterfield, 1979). Over the past decade this paradigm has fostered important advances in conceptualization and practice regarding LD children (cf. Hall, 1980; Lloyd, Hallahan, & Kaufman, 1981; Torgesen & Kail, 1980). Recently, the information-processing paradigm has influenced a resurgence of interest in spelling as cognitive process rather than merely as a topic of curriculum subservient to reading (e.g., see Farnham-Diggory & Simon, 1975; Frith, 1980; Simon & Simon, 1973).

Therefore, this chapter will review a growing body of evidence that young students and cognitively delayed, i.e., "learning-disabled," older students develop and learn in a similar manner to use special adaptations of general problem-solving ability when they learn to spell. In presenting this research, alternative approaches which have assumed brain damage or brain difference are intentionally excluded (e.g., for discussions from a neuropsychological perspective, see Boder, 1971; Kinsbourne & Warrington, 1964; Nelson & Warrington, 1974; Ownby, 1985; Rourke, 1983; Rourke & Orr, 1977; Sweeney & Rourke, 1981; Warrington, 1967). The emphasis, rather, will be on development of spelling ability from early dependence on stimulus-driven task management to more mature, concept-driven problem solving.

Advantages of a Problem-Solving Perspective

It is reasonable to ask, what is the advantage, either for practitioners or researchers, in viewing spelling acquisition as problem solving rather than rote learning of defined sequences of word types and rules? One advantage is that our sights are raised above traditional concern for behavioral concomitants of specific academic skills to greater awareness of and appreciation for the overarching importance of knowledge, self-regulation, and judgment as hallmarks of what we regard as competent human behavior. A second advantage is that framing questions about acquisition in terms of problem solving helps center our attention on problem solvers as agents. Viewing children as having competence as 'problem solvers' forces researchers as well as practitioners to be concerned about how children attempt to do the things we require of them rather than what they are not able to do. If acquisition of elemental academic skills, such as spelling, is defined as a concentric array of increasingly complex problems to be solved by children, emphasis is placed on how children become active, self-managing, and cognitively engaged rather than on behaviors which are often interpreted to show passivity, need for environmental manipulation, and detachment. A problem-solving perspective on spelling acquisition encourages researchers and teachers to approach students as active and inventive organizers, integrators, and managers of their experience during instruction, not as passive receptacles to be filled or blank memory banks to be programmed.

It is useful, therefore, for research to explore what distinction can be made between learning how to spell particular words, i.e., achievement, and learning how the spelling system works, what its ambiguities and utilities are, how to manage task demands, and how one goes about using the system effectively to produce written communication, i.e., ability. After teachers carefully impart facts, rules, and mnemonics, after they provide response opportunities, corrective feedback, and ample practice opportunities, students must learn to use this complex array of information in a flexible, strategic, and deliberate manner. In effect, they must use each spelling problem encountered to gradually develop *generalizable* solutions and strategies.

In simplest terms, spelling may be considered a problem whenever would-be spellers are uncertain about how to represent words they wish to write. Uncertainty, in this sense, need not be equivalent to conscious doubt. It merely implies that search, retrieval, and encoding processes which are necessary for accurate responding are not 'automatic' for that learner. Attention must be shared among various competing mental operations and task demands. The array of potentially useful information possessed even by very young preschool children (cf. Read, 1975) confronted with spelling problems is stored in some organized structure or "map." The effort required to search this array efficiently and the accuracy of retrieval and encoding depend on at least four factors:

1. Motivation of students to 'solve' spelling problems
2. Sufficiency and relevance of stored information
3. Organization and integration of spelling-related knowledge
4. Efficiency with which attention is controlled and allocated

Moreover, these factors probably interact in critical ways during problem solving. For example, motivation may depend in part on conscious evaluation of one's chances for solving a problem. Furthermore, evaluation of solution likelihood may depend on organization of relevant knowledge, i.e., although spellers may be aware that problems are soluble, they may also be aware that, as a function of past experience and poorly organized knowledge, excessive effort would be required to reach acceptable solutions in contrast to perceived importance and desirability of problem solutions. Similarly, if individuals have difficulty controlling and focusing attention, the knowledge they possess, however adequate, cannot be searched efficiently. Finally, inadequate control of attention or lack of motivation may impede acquisition and organization of relevant spelling information, as a result of which future search and retrieval, even under highly motivated conditions, will be less fruitful.

If the above sketch of factors contributing to spelling acquisition and performance is to be believed, it is first necessary to demonstrate that error making, even by so-called 'learning-disabled' children, reveals something about the developing interplay among these factors. Despite the relatively minor attention given to spelling in the modern curriculum and by researchers, there is nevertheless a long and interesting scholarly history (e.g., see Cahen, Craun, & Johnson, 1971; Fitzsimmons & Loomer, 1977; Cates & Russell, 1954) of attempts to determine what factors contribute to poor spelling and what instructional interventions will be most effective with those who have failed to develop adequate spelling ability. With regard to children considered to be 'learning-disabled' (LD), inspection, categorization, and interpretation of spelling errors has historically played an important, even pivotal, role in conceptualization and clinical diagnosis of learning problems (Boder, 1971).

While practitioners (and many researchers) have tended to weigh spelling ability directly on the basis of the number of errorless spellings an individual produces, there is increasing support for the position that such achievement evaluations discard potentially valuable data about typical and atypical development of specific information-processing abilities and, particularly, how these abilities influence competence in using written language (Gerber & Hall, 1982). Although there is no doubt that achievement represents some "ability," there is reason to believe that data based on *numbers* of correctly spelled words are not perfect 'windows' through which teachers and researchers have an unobstructed view of all that constitutes *spelling* ability. (For discussion of measurement issues in spelling assessment, see Croft, 1982; Gerber & Cohen, in press; Shores & Yee, 1973). Nor are spelling errors less opaque than correctly spelled words as

44   MICHAEL M. GERBER

'windows' into cognitive ability. Rather, spelling errors will be viewed here as products of a process which, at different times and for different purposes, evokes several distinct cognitive abilities, none of which in itself constitute a "pure" *spelling* ability. Data presented in this chapter have been interpreted to support the hypothesis that spelling attempts by novice spellers are often special cases of concept-driven problem solving. As such, spelling errors might be interpreted as reflections of attempts by children to use limited knowledge to derive solutions to orthographic problems. If this interpretation is supported by empirical evidence, errors made by atypical learners, such as LD students, might be more profitably (and parsimoniously) studied as products of suboptimal information *processes* rather than subnormal mental *structures*, i.e., neurological deficiencies of anomalies.

PRELIMINARY STUDIES

Background

Researchers at the Learning Disabilities Research Institute (LDRI) at the University of Virginia began a series of studies in 1978 to investigate acquisition of spelling skills in LD students characterized by attentional difficulties (Gerber & Hall, 1979, 1980, 1981, 1982). These studies were stimulated by experimental findings indicating that at least a sizable subgroup of LD students were characteristically impulsive and distractible (Hallahan & Reeve, 1980; Tarver, Hallahan, Kauffman, & Ball, 1976) and relatively passive in task performance (Torgesen, 1977, 1983). It was hypothesized that attentional problems might interfere with acquisition of basic academic skills as well as with research/clinical task performance. Research findings appeared increasingly to support the inference that inefficient task performance by LD students was attributable to "maturational lag" in development of various cognitive abilities, such as selective attention and memory (Hallahan & Reever, 1980; Tarver et al., 1976; Torgesen & Kail, 1980) rather than neuropsychological deviance or damage (see also Rourke, 1976 for a neuropsychological viewpoint).

The ensuing early studies of development of spelling ability began with the observation that skilled spellers are able to spell most words even though they have received direct instruction and test feedback in spelling only a few thousand specific words. Average fourth-grade students are more able spellers than a computer programmed with hundreds of specific phoneme–grapheme translation algorithms (Simon & Simon, 1973). Thus, competence in spelling implies a generalized "ability," acquired over time and experience, which extends beyond knowledge of specific words or explicit rules.

Measurement Considerations

Consider the 24 *different* misspellings of "cathedral" produced by 44 sixth-grade spelling contest semifinalists presented in Table 1. Compare these

Table 1. Variety of Spelling Errors Produced by
Learning Disabled and Normally Achieving Students

Normally Achieving Sixth Graders[a]	Learning Disabled Fourth and Fifth Graders[b]
Word: CATHEDRAL	Word: PEEKED
kafedro	pecked
cafetol	peket
caves	peekt
cafigrel	peeged
cathedril	peeckt
catedro	peakt
cl	peek
corcedro	pecked
corthedath	pecated
kaveatel	peted
cafedo	peed
covitrel	peekt
cons	peet
cafeetre	pect
cafedro	piet
cavedrow	pened
cafegcle	peck
cafidral	pick
cathrndro	qeet
cathedrie	qeeb
cathidral	qiedt
cafedrele	beetd
cathetro	pte
cathfdo	pe

[a]Six of 50 normally achieving students spelled this word correctly.
[b]One of 47 learning disabled students spelled this word correctly.

'incorrect' spelling attempts to those of 47 attention-disordered, learning-disabled spellers, similar in tested achievement and intelligence, whose 24 different misspellings of "peeked" are also shown in Table 1. It is unlikely that the specific words "cathedral" and "peeked" have orthographic properties which *induce* so many different misspellings. More probably, these observations might best be interpreted to mean that, despite age and level of achievement, spelling is a generative, inventive, and perhaps idiosyncratic process for novice spellers. However these examples are interpreted, they illustrate the potential size of the "problem space" created by attempts to spell new words. Uncertainty increases as a function of alternatives judged by spellers to be plausible.

In planning our research, one thing seemed clear. Error making was not random, though there was normal variability in production of both correct and incorrect spellings. It was important to devise a measurement system which was sensitive to this variability. Dichotomous systems of assessment would ignore and waste information embedded in observed variability of individual performance. However, error classification systems typically employed in learning disabilities research have frequently replaced the correct-incorrect dichotomy with an equally questionable trichotomy—correct, good phonetic equivalent, poor phonetic equivalent (e.g., see Boder, 1971; Nelson & Warrington, 1976; for data contradicting these classification systems, see also Holmes & Peper, 1977). Interpretation of what constitutes a "good" phonetic equivalent is intuitive and is usually based on judgments made by skilled adults about the readability of each spelling attempt. Specific errors or patterns of errors are interpreted (within these systems) to reflect an essentially passive system which produces errors because of specific abnormalities or anomalies. Variations within classifications of incorrect spellings are viewed as essentially random.

From a different perspective, however, LD students' error making results from immature cognitive control processes (e.g., selective attention, Hallahan & Reeve, 1980; verbal encoding, Vellutino, 1977; and intentional recall, Torgesen & Kail, 1980), indicative of information processing that is more typical of younger, normally achieving students. Therefore, appropriate measurement of spelling attempts should reveal organization and integration of emerging cognitive components of spelling ability. Errors by LD students, as with their younger, normally achieving peers, would be expected to reflect insufficient *automaticity* in processing of stimulus information, cumulative deficiency in task-relevant knowledge, and failure to spontaneously monitor and attempt correction of incorrect responses.

Spelling Error and Development

Based on seminal work by Read (1971, 1975) and extensive research with normally achieving children conducted by Henderson and his colleagues (e.g., Gentry, 1977; Henderson & Beers, 1980), we have attempted over the past years to develop systematically the empirical basis for a developmental, information-processing model of spelling ability in normally achieving and learning-disabled students (Gerber & Hall, 1980, 1981, 1982; Nulman & Gerber, 1983; Varnhagen & Gerber, 1984). Research has been directed toward delineating inadequacies due to immaturity in cognitive self-control and their manifestation in error making and low rates of achievement.

Read's (1975) work first drew our attention to the active, inventive nature of spelling for preschoolers experimenting with written expression. Read argued persuasively that early attempts to spell were reflective of different, not deviant, systems of phonetic categorization. That is, spelling errors could be interpreted to show how children attempted to parse phonemic strings and use knowledge of the alphabet to create (or, in Read's terms, "invent") a reasonable system of sound-symbol representation. On the basis of this approach to attempted spelling, Henderson and his colleagues (e.g., Henderson & Beers, 1980) have carefully documented the cognitive–developmental aspects of spelling systems generated by children in primary grades.

Two conclusions from work by Read and Henderson and colleagues were striking. First, attempted spellings for words containing specific phonetic features, e.g., tense and lax vowels; consonant doubling; nasalized consonants; schwa sounds in unstressed syllables such as the *a* in "about"; past tense marking; etc.) appeared to follow a relatively fixed sequence of developmental stages during early primary education. Moreover, Henderson et al. found that much of this sequence reflected development of a concept for "word." Better understanding and amalgamation (Ehri, 1980) of the many identities possessed by words induces changing abilities to comprehend, remember, and use conventional orthography *independent* of specific instruction. Thus, rule learning and knowledge of specific words alone could not account for the predictability of children's attempt to spell certain phonetic features. Second, this body of work from studies of normally developing children highlighted the active, inventive effort required by children trying to solve the puzzle of English orthography. Essentially, early spellers must continually reinvent spellings they have already attempted while more skilled spellers have established stable, organized routines which facilitate reliable responding with reduced need for conscious attention. Read's (1975) and Henderson's (Henderson & Beers, 1980) work helps to explain the stimulus-driven, i.e., bottom-up, nature of immature spelling attempts. Deciding how to spell a word on one trial does not yet reliably predict how novice spellers will solve the same spelling problems on the next occasion. Each situation creates a spelling problem anew. Over time misspellings are characterized by horizontal (i.e., nonrandom, within-individual differences in problem resolution across occasions) as well vertical (i.e., successive approximations to conventional spelling across time) changes. From this perspective, spelling ability appears to develop as changes in both organization of information and efficiency of cognitive manipulation of this information occur. Ultimately, these qualitative changes would be expected to produce quantitative differences in the size of each individual's corpus of known spellings.

A similarly *qualitative* perspective on changes observable in spelling attempts by LD students, both cross-sectionally across age groups and longitudinally over time, was adopted in conducting the research reviewed in the remainder of this chapter. For purposes of analysis, "qualitative" changes include changes in letter representation of phonemes and syllables, spelling speed, declarative spelling knowledge, and overt behavior during spelling. These "qualitative" changes in spelling are to be contrasted with changes in N-gram structure, i.e., the number of correct letters in a correct sequence, of spelling attempts. The purpose of examining qualitative change is to gauge whether, even when errors are still present, they are "better" errors, reflecting the development of generalizable concepts about spelling, rather than memorization of specific words.

We have found that spelling quality ratings (SQRs), based on the fidelity of phonemic representation as well as number of correct bigram sequences (e.g., see Deno, Mirkin, Lowry, & Kuehnle, 1980) were both predictive of relative rank of student performance on standardized spelling tests (Gerber & Hall, 1982). However, when these two methods for evaluating spelling attempts were used to rank misspellings of specific words, such as the LD students' misspellings of "peeked" in Table 1, different rank orders resulted (Gerber & Hall, 1982). For example, of the misspellings of "peeked" shown in Table 1, "peakt" is rated as superior to "peek" if phonological completeness is of concern because all of the sounds are represented in some manner, whereas "peek" is rated as superior when orthographic completeness, i.e., correct letter sequence, is emphasized. Analyses of quality judgments made by teachers showed that improved numbers of correct letters in proper sequence and improved phonemic representation are distinct, though mutually interactive, factors influencing judgments of quality of spelling attempts by novice spellers (Gerber, 1983). Because these two factors influence pronounceability, and thus readability, for adults, it is clear that spelling attempts tend to be judged most deviant when phonological and orthographic completeness most diverge. Thus, "jsg" is a relatively complete representation of phonemes in "dressing," but may be judged as deviant by adults who are unable to reconstruct the spelling logic applied by immature spellers.

The following sections will describe a series of studies of spelling in learning-disabled and normal children. The studies, which used a variety of techniques, each answered some questions and raised others about the development of concepts in spelling.

Spelling Quality and Acquisition

Our first studies were planned to discover whether spelling acquisition by children thought to be learning-disabled, especially those characterized as having attention problems, was different from that of their normally achieving peers. In carrying out our various studies, we have focused on quality of spelling performance as a plausible indicator of underlying cognitive structure and processes. Thus, studies were designed to investigate how spellings were produced, what underlying strategies could be inferred, how these strategies were organized and reorganized across children at different ages and over time by the same individuals, and what self-reported behaviors could be observed concurrently with attempts to spell. Attention to quality of performance marked a major departure from other researchers' concern for "phonetic accuracy" as part of a trichotomous system (i.e., correct, incorrect but phonetically accurate, and incorrect/inaccurate) for deducing degree of cognitive maturity or disability (e.g., Boder, 1971; Sweeney & Rourke, 1978). Moreover, in differentiating our work from laboratory studies of problem solving by LD students (e.g., Mckinney & Haskins, 1980), we hoped that these data from applied spelling tasks might lead to informed inferences about problem solving by LD students during acquisition of basic academic skills (Kirk, 1983, pp. 6–7).

Study 1

Using a modification of error classification schemes developed by Gentry (1977) and Zutell (1978), we found in our first study (Gerber & Hall, 1979) that virtually none of the errors produced by fifth- and sixth-grade LD students with attention problems were unclassifiable or interpretable as "deviant" from those anticipated from studies of younger, normally achieving spellers. Although specific errors varied across individuals, as seen in Table 1, general error *types* were categorized and described as follows:

Preliterate. These attempts were unintelligible symbol strings, mixed letters and nonletters, and were interpreted as showing lack of basic knowledge of alphabet, or insufficient concept of writing in general or written words as units in particular. In the absence of convergent evidence, it would seem premature to describe these spellings as 'deviant'. Only three spellings meeting this definition were produced by upper elementary LD subjects out of 658 spelling attempts.

Example: 8T for "eighty"

Prephonetic. These attempts were characterized by plausible alphabetical representation of one or more, but not all, phonemes, and were interpreted to indicate uncertainty in (1) deciding where to "place" phoneme boundaries, i.e., "parsing" phonemic strings, (2) deciding on plausible alphabetical representation, and/or (3) maintaining acoustical stimulus in working memory long enough to extract relevant information.

Example: UM or UN for "human"

Phonetic. These attempts included representation for every phoneme in the stimulus, but representation which systematically used articulation of letter names as a basis for deciding on grapheme–phoneme relationships, i.e., the letter *name* is used as its sound. These spellings were interpreted as evidence of students' compensatory decisions when faced with limited knowledge about conventional rules of sound–symbol relationships in English orthography.

Example: HIKT for "hiked"; or ATE for "eighty"

Transitional. These spelling attempts are readable, pronounceable, and recognizable by adults as approximations to conventional spelling. Characteristically, these spellings (1) do not violate rules governing legal letter sequence, (2) use legal, though incorrect, letter combinations to represent phonemes, and (3) demonstrate consistent use of orthographic marking conventions, e.g., silent *e*, vowel doubling, consonant doubling, past tense *ed*). Transitional spellings were interpreted as showing systematic knowledge of simple phonics and orthographic rules pertaining to syntax, but lack of relatively abstract knowledge pertaining to semantic information, such as word units and/or inability to spontaneously recognize or use phonetic, syntactic, or semantic analogies from a corpus of known words.

Example: PEAKED for "peeked"; ELEVATER for "elevator"

Correct. These attempts yielded a conventional spelling for intended words, but were interpreted as including subclassifications suggested by variability in spelling speed, and overt spelling behavior, such as verbalization and self-correction rates.

Examples: YOU (pause, rewrite U)NITED (pause, change I to E, pause) for "united"; UNITED (no pause or changes) for "united"

Data analysis clearly indicated that LD students' spelling attempts varied as a function of student age, with older LD students producing errors which were orthographically and phonetically more similar to correct spellings than errors produced by younger LD students. Moreover, and most important, the preponderance of errors produced by LD students were similar to those expected of normally achieving children who were 3–5 years younger.

For example, subject 223 (chronological age [CA] = 8-5; verbal intelligence quotient [VIQ] = 78) produced UIT for "united," HT for "hiked," AT for "eighty," and FR for "flipper." Spelling attempts like these were interpreted as showing that LD students were able to make reasonable letter choices to represent some, but not all, of the intended phoneme string. In some cases, students left blank spaces in the middle of their spellings and verbally indicated that, although they knew "something" should be written, they were not sure *what* to write. As observed with younger, normally achieving children, fifth- and sixth-grade LD students had difficulty deciding where to assign phonemic boundaries (Liberman, Liberman, Shankweiler, & Mattingly, 1980) and what letters were appropriate for representing each bounded speech unit thus perceived (Gentry, 1977; Henderson & Beers, 1980; Read, 1975).

Another, older student (subject 224: CA = 9-7, VIQ = 81) was able to produce DRESING for "dressing," EGEL for "eagle," PEKED for "peeked," and TRAEDID for "traded." Spelling attempts like these revealed an ability to represent plausibly all conventionally perceived speech sounds as well as to select legal letter strings from among plausible alternatives for this purpose. The most common type of spelling errors produced by all LD students in our sample fell somewhere between these extremes. Predominantly, LD students' errors revealed evidence of a "phonetic" strategy, i.e., letters were selected because the articulation of their *names* was perceived as being approximately the same as articulation of speech sounds which the students intended to represent. Errors of this type have been shown to be typical in early spelling attempts of first-grade, normally achieving children (Henderson & Beers, 1980). Nevertheless, it is striking that in all cases, without exception, LD spellers were observed to apply logical, albeit limited, knowledge and strategies for solving spelling "problems."

Study 2

We replicated these findings with a new, similarly described sample of LD students, but also examined longitudinal changes in errors on the same words within a subsample of subjects from study 1 (Gerber & Hall, 1980). Analysis of longitudinal data revealed that LD subjects, over a 7-month interval during which no specific spelling instruction was received, produced qualitatively better spelling attempts. Although spelling attempts were mostly incorrect, as expected, they showed clear qualitative shifts toward conventional orthography. For example, subject 223, whose earlier spelling attempts were illustrated above, now produced UNATT for "united," HEEK for "hiked," ATE for "eighty," and FAPR for "flipper." Subject 224, whose earlier spellings had been classified as transitional, now produced correct spellings for "united," "dressing," and "traded." Although some students did not present evidence of categorical shift in error quality, no student's spellings revealed general regression to less mature error types.

These data added support for inferences drawn from our cross-sectional analyses in study 1, and increased our confidence that the evidence, taken as a whole, supported developmental delay rather than deficit explanations of LD students' difficulties in acquiring spelling skills. However, these data raised several new questions. Specifically, what accounted for the correlation between age and quality of spelling attempt in the absence of—one is tempted to say, in spite of—specific instruction? More important, did developmental shifts in error quality represent generalized or idiosyncratic changes? That is, were students better able to spell difficult and unknown words in general, or only those words which were employed in study 1 and repeated in study 2?

RECENT STUDIES

Instructional Pragmatism and Individual Differences

To answer these questions, we carefully reviewed empirical studies relating aspects of spelling instruction and performance. Not surprisingly, strict instructional pragmatism has dominated research on spelling instruction. For example, Fitzsimmons and Loomer (1980) concluded that the use of test/self-correction/

retest procedures is the approach best supported by empirical evidence. More recent work by behavioral technologists has emphasized the importance of various contingency arrangements for increasing levels of spelling performance (e.g., Dineen, Clark, & Risley, 1977; Foxx & Jones, 1978; Neef, Iwata, & Page, 1980; Kauffman, Hallahan, Haas, Brame, & Boren, 1978). However, consistent with Fitzsimmons and Loomer's conclusions, one common denominator in all effective instructional techniques appears to be inclusion of some corrective feedback condition which permits students to compare and contrast their spelling attempts with correct models.

From an information-processing perspective, corrective feedback may not only strengthen particular, targeted spelling responses, but might also serve to control attention to important information within a 'problem space'. Moreover, by influencing selective attention to salient portions of spellings, corrective feedback may also assist individuals in accommodating existing knowledge structures and spelling operations to new information or in reorganizing knowledge and related processes. We hypothesized that corrective spelling feedback during instruction may provide with more potency for LD students what incidental encounters with written language appear to provide for young nondisabled learners, namely, a mechanism for establishing efficient, concept-driven, i.e., "top-down," spelling strategies.

Unfortunately, available research was of limited assistance. Instructional pragmatists and behavioral engineers have been less interested in understanding individual differences in acquisition of spelling ability per se than in demonstrating the relative power of instructional interventions to produce correct spellings of specifically targeted word lists. From a pragmatist's perspective, spelling attempts are either correct or incorrect. That is, all spelling attempts which result in expected, conventional letter order are equally correct, and all attempts which do not correspond with this expectation are equal in their 'incorrectness'. Thus, a third-grade student whose behavior while spelling "trade" is as follows:

TER (stops, erases E) T RAD (pauses) T RAD E

is assumed to be equal in ability to the sixth-grade student who writes the same word immediately and without hesitation,

TRADE.

Similarly, students who produced the following variants of "elevator" would simply be scored as "wrong," despite evidence, such as was generated by our early studies, that such variation probably reflects differences in cognitive maturity.

L   R
LUVTR
ELVATR
ELIVATER
ELEVATER

Just as quality of error could be interpreted as evidence of cognitive status, shifts in quality of error over instructional trials might be interpretable as evidence for spontaneous reorganization of cognitive structures and processes pertinent to spelling acquisition.

To investigate this speculation, we wished to consider a simple, straight-forward, and empirically valid method of correcting spelling error during instruction. Our attention was drawn to studies done by Jobes (1975) which demonstrated that modeling correct spelling with contingent corrective feedback not only was successful in improving the spelling performance of target LD students but also influenced the performance of LD students who passively observed effects of training procedures on target subjects. From her analysis it was impossible to conclude with certainty whether modeling or feedback procedures or some other variable was responsible for observed effects. Likewise, it could not be concluded unequivocally, as Jobes did, that spelling performance improved merely as a result of experimentally induced discrimination learning. It is equally plausible that training imposed organization on task-relevant infor-mation, which facilitated remembering and production of both words and orthographic features within words. Moreover, because her analysis focused on correctly spelled words, Jobes was unable to address whether training and feedback had impact on "ability" in a general sense. For example, if subjects spelled words incorrectly but had learned how and when to represent a specific phonetic element, this would indicate that effects of training and feedback extend beyond single word lists.

In another behaviorally oriented study, Kauffman, Hallahan, Haas, Brame, & Boren (1978) showed that a system of contingent imitation of error followed by modeling of correct response improved spelling performance of mildly handi-capped students. Kauffman et al. (1978), like Jobes (1975), sought to explain their results as evidence for effects of contingent imitation/modeling on dis-crimination or concept learning. It was further speculated that in some way this procedure directed student attention to features which discriminated modeled (correct) from imitated (incorrect) spellings. Remarkably, both investigations also provided some evidence that LD students' spelling of particular lists could be markedly improved by fairly minimal instruction. Neither investigation included overt, specific teaching of phonics, linguistic analysis, or orthographic rules. In fact, Kauffman et al. (1978) provided some evidence that contingent imitation/ modeling was *superior* to normally provided teaching.

In pondering these results, it is recalled that in our longitudinal study we had already demonstrated that error quality of spelling attempts improved over time without word-specific instruction. One implication from these various findings was that new spelling skill principles could be incidentally acquired and productively applied by LD students through naturally occurring environmental feedback. Although LD students are usually thought to require very direct and intensive instruction, results from Jobes and Kauffman et al. seemed to show that

LD students could be self-organizing when given repeated learning trials accompanied by simple corrective procedures. Thus, in a new series of studies, we wished to study more directly how explicit feedback influences selective attention to and memory for critical orthographic features.

It is important to consider, however, that efficient control of attention during problem solving can be both a cause and an effect of previously inefficient learning, depending on whether attention is driven by existing knowledge organization. Failure of LD students to spontaneously generate appropriate problem-solving and task management strategies might also be a residual effect of enduring inefficiencies in selective attention which, during previous learning, resulted in inadequate development of pertinent, task-relevant knowledge and strategies. These students may not know enough to know what to attend to. In hypothesizing about LD student performance on dictation spelling under conditions of contingent imitation and modeling, we felt that if subjects failed to transfer learning to new, similar words, it would be reasonable to conclude that their control over attention during spelling is not influenced by previous spelling experiences. In a similar vein, Read (1975) observed preschool children reinvent spellings for words which, at a previous time, they had already attempted using different spellings. Such lack of stability in attempting spellings by immature learners compared with highly reliable spelling in mature spellers, serves to illustrate how attention control gradually shifts from stimulus salience to routines based on previously learned and organized knowledge structures.

Effects of Feedback on General Spelling Ability

Using Kauffman and associates' (1978) within-subject instructional design, we observed spelling attempts of an 8½-year-old LD boy ("Joe") who had exhibited severe difficulty in learning to spell despite above-average ability, i.e., PPVT standard score = 130. Our research departed from the Kauffman et al. paradigm in three significant ways (Nulman & Gerber, 1982).

Mastery Learning Criterion

First, rather than terminating contingent imitation/modeling procedures after numbers of correctly spelled words were observed to increase, we contined to apply corrective procedures until the entire list of 10 words was spelled correctly. In so doing, we recognized that the number of trials needed by students to spell a word list correctly was probably *not* incidental to their need to integrate and reorganize new and old spelling information (e.g., for discussion of "time to learn" as a predictor of achievement, see Gettinger & White, 1979). Even when they can spell it correctly, some students may need more practice and feedback to gain fluency and automaticity.

Observation of Qualitative Shift

Second, we observed and analyzed *qualitative* changes in spelling errors across trials as well as changes in numbers of correctly spelled words. We hypothesized that if trying to spell during acquisition stages of learning was a special case of problem solving, then each new spelling experience must contribute to automatic, dynamic reorganization of knowledge structure and associated cognitive strategies for spelling. Unless new spelling knowledge could be acquired and made available in this way, it would be difficult to account for qualitative improvements in spelling performance observed in our longitudinal sample of uninstructed LD students. Thus, we expected that imitation/modeling promoted improvements in spelling attempts by prompting learners not only to attend to specific errors, but also to actively consider plans for phonological representation and retrieval of correct letter sequence.

Generalization Probes

Our third departure from the Kauffman et al. (1978) paradigm was to probe for generalization. It was believed that if successive spelling attempts did reveal focal improvements in specific orthographic *features*, reflecting growth in concepts rather than simple incrementing of letters, correct retention of some or all improvements on a new list of words would constitute evidence of generalization. We reasoned that such improvement on a second list could be interpreted to mean that spelling attempts require a mental activity that is similar, and perhaps identical, to general problem solving. Moreover, such results would indicate that acquisition of spelling 'skills', by LD as well as normally achieving learners involves gradual but spontaneous generalization of knowledge, not merely accumulation of known spellings by rote memorization. Consequently, after he reached the criterion on list 1 we presented our subject with a second list, containing words which, except for changes in initial consonant, blend, or digraph, were identical to those on the first list in spelling and pronunciation.

Results showed that the subject spelled all words correctly after eight trials. Although the subject made about as many errors on the second list i.e., eight on list 1, seven on list 2, the "quality" of errors was markedly improved, i.e., orthographic elements and features which were misspelled on list 1 were often spelled correctly, or more plausibly and obviously related to conventional representation, on list 2. The clear implication from this study was that progress toward learning target lists using imitation/modeling procedures occurs by 'leaps' in understanding rather than by rote memorization for successively larger N–grams. For example, Table 2 shows a comparison of his first spelling attempts on each list. In particular, it is notable that specific features in list 1 were spontaneously generalized in his attempts to spell list 2, such as "-sh" in "wish-dish," "-mp" in "bump-lump," "-s" in "stars-bars," "-k" in "dark-bark," "-unch" in "lunch-hunch," and "-ope" in "hope-dope."

Table 2.   Comparison of First Spelling Attempts by an
LD Boy on Similar Spelling Lists Presented Before and After
Use of Contingent Imitation/Modeling

	Before Use of Imitation/Modeling: List 1		After Use of Imitation/Modeling: List 2	
Word	Attempt	No. of Trials	Word	Attempt
game	GAME	1	name	NAME
hide	HIDE	1	side	SIADE
grass	GASS	4	lass	LACS
wish	WITH	4	dish	DASH
bump	DOPP	6	lump	LAMP
stars	STHRE	7	bars	BRASS
dark	DRACK	7	bark	BRAK
river	RIVRE	6	liver	LRIVRE
lunch	LATHE	7	hunch	HUNCH
hope	HOPPE	7	dope	DOPE

To systematically replicate these results, we studied 11 additional LD students identified as having severe problems in acquiring spelling skills (Gerber, 1984). In this set of experiments,[1] three lists which varied only in initial consonant, blend, or digraph were presented to each student. During presentation of list 1, trainers were instructed to imitate errors and then to model correct spellings. Trainers were instructed to acknowledge correct spellings without delivering social praise. List 2 served as a probe for spontaneous generalization. Before list 3 was administered, however, trainers explained the similarity among the lists and pointed out that spellings of previous lists would be useful in attempting words in list 3. Summary data from these experiments are presented in Table 3.

Table 3 indicates that 10 of 11 subjects reached criterion performance in fewer than 11 trials, i.e., days. Subject 6 was the only student who failed to reach criterion by trial 11, and further trials were terminated. Two further conclusions can be drawn from Table 3: (1) subjects generally reached criterion in fewer trials for each successive list, and (2) percentage of correctly spelled words and possible bigrams on first trials of each list also tended to increase for each successive list. Moreover, although performance on list 3, the prompted generalization condition, was almost universally better for all subjects than performance on list 1, performance on list 2, the unprompted generalization probe, was also better than performance on list 1. Thus, in the absence of additional information, traditional spelling instruction, or specific instructions to use what had been learned, most LD students were *spontaneously* able to transfer orthographic information obtained on list 1 to similar words.

Table 3. Summary Results: Use of Imitation/Modeling to Improve Spelling Performance of 11 LD Elementary School Students[a, b, c]

			First Trial (% correct words)			First Trial (% correct bigrams)			Trials to Criterion			
Subject	Age	Grade	L1	L2	L3	L1	L2	L3	L1	L2	L3	Total
1	13	6	60	90	70	86	96	88	5	6	4	15
2	7	1	0	40	90	60	72	94	7	6	2	15
3	12	6	0	30	50	50	50	71	4	3	3	10
4	10	5	0	90	70	49	97	87	9	4	4	17
5	13	6	30	100	70	78	100	98	5	2	4	11
6[b]	10	4	0	(→	50)	40	(→	68)	12	—	—	—
7[c]	9	3	0	—	90	61	—	92	10	—	—	—
8	11-6	6	40	50	90	73	80	93	5	5	3	13
9	19	6	0	20	70	55	59	85	7	3	3	15
10	7	1	20	60	80	64	84	92	6	3	3	12
11	15	9	20	20	90	65	63	98	10	7	2	19

[a]L1, L2, L3 = first trials on List 1, 2, and 3, respectively.
[b]Subject 6 failed to reach criterion after 12 trials; table values reflect improvement on Trial 12.
[c]List 2 was not administered to Subject 7; table values reflect performance on Lists 1 and 3 (i.e., with instructional cue).

To illustrate, consider the performances of subjects 2 and 9 presented in Figures 1 and 2, respectively. Subject 2 misspelled 10 words on the first trial of list 1, 6 words on the first trial of list 2, and only 2 words on the first trial of list 3. Subject 9, similarly, missed 10 words on list 1, 7 words on list 2, and 3 words on the first trial of list 3. More important, however, inspection of misspellings by both subjects, both across trials and across lists, reveals much evidence of active decision making and strategic attempts to recall information received from corrective feedback, and not much evidence to support inferences that learning correct spellings results from rote memorization. First, it can be observed that certain "phonetic" solutions to spelling problems persisted, even in the face of repeated corrective feedback, e.g., TOR for "tar," GOD for "good," and FRAT for "freight." These spelling attempts result from a strategy which satisfactorily solves the "problem" for immature spellers. Only after a relatively large number of trials was this strategy abandoned in an attempt to organize information obtained from corrective feedback into a new solution. However, Figures 1 and 2 show that phonetic spellings are largely abandoned after the first trial. Second, spelling attempts reveal a variety of different solutions to spelling specific features over trials. It is unlikely that this variety reflects simple, random guessing. In most cases, choices are limited to one feature at a time and are logical, given the evidence for nonconventional strategies discussed previously. Finally, these attempts show that specific, identifiable orthographic features were central to problem solving and once "solved" were often maintained across trials and lists even while whole words may have been incorrect.

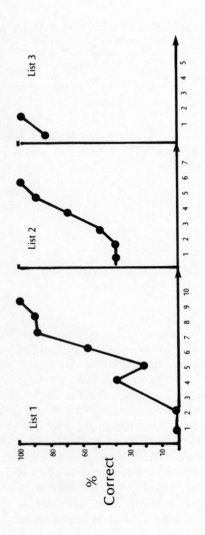

Number of Trials

% Correct

List 1

Word	1	2	3	4	5	6	7	8	9	10
mice	mise	nise								
went	wet	weat	wot	whet	wet	whet				
good	god	gad	gad	god	god	god				
saw	sel	soo	swo	sou	suo	stou		sa		
car	cror	cre	core	crar	cor	croe				
found	fond	fan	fand		fuound					
like	lice	lik	licke		lice					
lots	los	llos	looce	lace	lace	lats	lats			
sacks	sackx	sack	sax	sace	sace					
face	fase	fase								

List 2

Word	1	2	3	4	5	6	7	8	9	10
rice										
bent	bat	bint	bint							
hood		hod	hid	haud						
paw	pa	poow	poo	how						
tar	tor	tre	tor	tor	tor					
sound	soud	soun								
bike										
dots		bost	bost							
tacks	tats									
race	rase									

List 3

Word	1	2	3	4	5	6	7	8	9	10
nice										
sent	stent									
wood										
law										
far										
pound										
hike										
pots										
backs	pack									
pace										

Figure 1. Effects of imitation-modeling: spelling performance of LD students—subject 2.

59

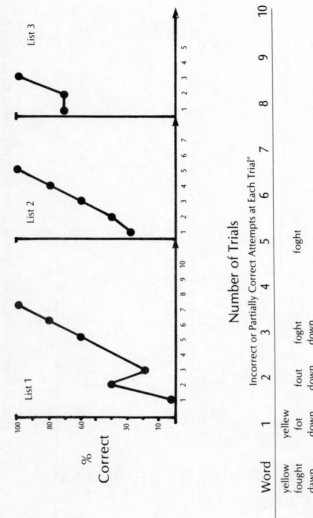

List 3 List 2 List 1

% Correct

Number of Trials

Number of Trials

Incorrect or Partially Correct Attempts at Each Trial[a]

List 1	Word	1	2	3	4	5	6
	yellow	yellew					
	fought	fot	fout	foght		foght	
	dawn	down	down	down			
	weight	weit	wat	wignt			
	tough	tof		tof	togn	togh	
	gruel	grall	grall	groll	groul	group	group
	sneeze	sraezz	seenz	seenze			
	sour	souer					
	crawl	croll		calw	crowl		
	bridge	brige	brigh	drig	brig	brige	bridg

60

List 2	Word	1	2	3	4	5	6	7	8	9	10
	mellow										
	bought	bot	boght	bout	borght						
	lawn										
	freight	frat	frat	frat	frat						
	rough	ruf	rouf								
	duel	dool	dowl	dowl							
	breeze										
	flour	flawer	four								
	brawl	brall									
	fridge	frige	fige	friege							

List 3	Word	1	2	3	4	5	6	7	8	9	10
	fellow										
	sought										
	fawn										
	eight										
	enough	engh	enogh								
	fuel										
	freeze										
	hour	hor									
	drawl		dawl								
	ridge	righg	ridgh								

Figure 2. Effects of imitation-modeling: spelling performance of LD students—subject 9.

[a]Trials were continued for an individual only until he/she achieved one fully correct trial. A blank on a trial indicates that the word was correctly spelled.

For example, subject 2 failed to learn the correct spelling for -NT until trial 7 on list 1 but recalled this spelling pattern without cues from the trainer on the second trial of list 2. Five different spelling attempts were made to spell the vowel in "went"; only two alternatives were tried while spelling "bent" on list 2. Such variety can be interpreted as "search" behavior, part of any problem-solving routine, and not as either random behavior or failure of simple rote recall. In another example, subject 9 struggled first with spellings for two phonemes in the word "fought"—OU and GHT. Correct spellings were mastered after five trials, but the pattern of attempts reveals how attention to discrete features was allocated, finally organized into memory, and then shifted to remaining features.

Early trials on lists 1 and 2 often elicited a number of 'phonetic' spellings, displaying a typical, economic strategy of selecting the least number of letters, based on similarity of letter name to intended speech sound, in order to represent the phonemic string, e.g., FOT/BOT for "fought"/"bought," WAT/FRAT for "weight"/"freight." Let's look at successive attempts to spell "fought," then "bought." On trial 2, OU was recalled, but not GHT, producing the attempt FOUT. Trial 3 showed recall of GHT, but loss of OU, i.e., FOGHT. The target word was correctly spelled on trial 4, but apparently not yet *learned* because the word was again misspelled on trial 5, i.e., FOHGT. On list 2, the same student reproduced the error from list 1 over the first three trials, except that on this list GHT appeared before OU. After a problem in recalling the correct vowel structure, i.e., OR for "ou" on trial 4, the spelling was mastered. When subject 9 was cued to use what he had learned on list 2 in attempting list 3, OU and GHT were spelled correctly on the first trial. Similar learning patterns can be discerned in subject 9's attempts to spell "tough," "rough," and "enough." In these cases, OU and GH must be mapped onto phonemes (sounds) different from those found in "fought," "bought," and "sought." Nevertheless, subject 2 revealed similar, feature-by-feature, incremental patterns of acquisition for these words.

In summary, these data can be interpreted to show that, as problem solving was induced with list 2, relevant information concerning specific orthographic features was more rapidly accessed (i.e., fewer trials to criterion) and successfully applied (i.e., both percent correct and numbers of higher quality errors) than on list 1. Although it was not totally clear whether instructions to use previous information facilitated further improvements on list 3 or whether improvements represented a natural, ongoing process of generalization, these data clearly indicate that LD students characterized as having severe problems in acquiring spelling skills are capable of spontaneously organizing and applying task-relevant information after receiving no further instruction than what is provided by repeated exposure to imitations of their errors and to models of correct responses.

These findings raise intriguing questions about how the learning 'disabilities' of these subjects interfere with spelling skill acquisition. Apparently, these students were able to organize new information about sound–symbol relationships in

English orthography so that it could be applied to similar spelling problems on list 2 without specific instructions to do so. If LD students fail to generalize from spelling experiences, it might be because natural encounters, including classroom instruction, either (1) do not afford LD students sufficient time to 'master' particular spellings or (2) do not provide corrective feedback in a manner which supports efficient control of selective attention processes.

When insufficient time to learn obtains, students may employ strategies which facilitate rote memorization, say for a weekly test, but may not be able to integrate whatever new information is embedded in a particular spelling with preexisting spelling knowledge. On the other hand, the 'time to learn' needed may itself be a function of how efficiently attention is controlled during problem solving. In this case, new information would be processed in an inefficient or chaotic manner, leaving students with disorganized knowledge which would be difficult to search, retrieve, and relate to new problems. If LD spellers have difficulty controlling attention and consequently are slow in selecting what internally accessible (e.g., a corpus of known spellings) or externally provided (e.g., speech sounds) information will most likely reduce response uncertainty, additional allotment of learning time will not suffice by itself to assure increased rates of acquisition.

LD students, such as those we have studied, appear to face fundamental barriers to normal rates of acquisition because of the contingent relationships among attention control, search and retrieval, and formation of knowledge structures as new information is manipulated, used, and evaluated. If the dynamic interdependency among these processes is disturbed at early stages of acquisition, initial difficulties are severely compounded over time. In essence, demands for greater speed and accuracy are increasingly made of a system which is characterized by a relatively decreasing capacity to respond. As a consequence, LD students develop a limited word corpus, have difficulty relating past learning to new problems, are less able to resolve uncertainty, and probably spell too slowly and laboriously to subordinate spelling to the larger problem of expository writing (Poplin et al., 1980).

Preliminary Studies of Automaticity

The general problem facing novice spellers is how to obtain greater accuracy *and* greater speed. Results from studies of imitation/modeling only addressed issues of accuracy. Although it is desirable to spell correctly, spelling achieves its greatest tool value when it occurs rapidly, without conscious direction or attention. From an information-processing perspective, it would be expected that cognitive systems underlying spelling performance tend, at some point in development, to trade increased accuracy against increased speed. For normally achieving children, this may mean that (1) environmental or self-generated demands for faster spelling result in some basal rate of incorrect responses or (2) continued concern for accuracy may result in slower decision making, slower spelling speeds, and, therefore, slower composing of written ideas. The aim of development of spelling ability is reliably accurate spellings produced at a rapid rate. Ultimately, skilled spellers need to allocate very little attention to spelling, but instead can attend to problems of exposition, theme, vocabulary, and intent. This implies that to obtain optimal performance at each level of development, a dynamic equilibrium must exist between accuracy and speed, whereby successively more efficient organization and retrieval of spelling-relevant information permits successively faster spelling speeds. Simply stated, spellers spell as fast as they can, given both motor limitations and information-processing constraints imposed by prior knowledge, fluency of attention, encoding and memory control mechanisms, and decision making.

Ideally, complete automaticity of spelling occurs whenever spelling speed approaches maximum handwriting speed, allowing for legibility. Investigations of mature, presumably skilled spellers, i.e., college students, have shown that there is apparently a "normal," though low (approximately 1.5% of written words) error rate (Hotopf, 1980; Wing & Baddeley, 1980). Wing and Baddeley (1980) have interpreted this basal rate of error making as evidence of two distinct processes. Errors by mature, skilled spellers, according to these authors, occur either because spellings are unknown, i.e., unlearned, or because of lapses of attention during writing, i.e., "slips."

Clearly, understanding the development of spelling ability is made more complex by the fact that the various motor encoding components which influence writing speed are also subject to maturational changes. A near-linear relationship relates grade level to writing speed, i.e., average number of letters per minute. For example, average second graders can write about 31–33 letters per minute whereas average eighth graders write about 73–82 letters per minute (Freeman, 1916; Green & Petty, 1975). Advanced college students produce about 43.8 syllables per minute, or approximately 131 letters per minute (Hotopf, 1980, p. 296).

Despite changes in handwriting technology (paper, writing instruments, manuscript and cursive letter styles), early estimates of writing speed conducted by Freeman (1916) compare favorably with those made more recently by Green and Petty (1975). Freeman's data are also interesting in that they include estimates for students at different grades by ability. His data showed that handwriting speeds for lower ability students developed at about the same rate, but were 10–17 letters per minute slower than for higher ability students between second and eighth grades.[2] Thus, at least with regard to motor encoding of letters, there appears to be a similar developmental trend for both higher and lower ability students. However, there is no evidence that the 'lag' displayed by low-ability students, i.e., in cross-sectional data, disappears. These normative data may be interpreted as suggesting that at least some portion of processing capacity is unavailable for either spelling-related or text composition decisions in lower ability students because it must be allocated to motor encoding routines, the actual writing of the letter. With higher ability students, faster writing time appears to reflect the availability of processing capacity for other writing purposes besides generation of letter forms. As a consequence it would be expected that, independent of specific spelling task demands, lower ability students also do not or cannot achieve the spelling speeds obtainable by higher ability students. The questions of interest would then be: Are LD students slower spellers because of slower handwriting speeds, slower spelling decision processes, or both? Also, does the inability to achieve faster spelling speeds interfere with quality of spelling attempts?

Decision Speed During Spelling by LD Students

A simplified model of spelling decision would posit at least two component processes. First, spellers must search for a letter or letters to represent perceived phonemes. (In conditions of high uncertainty, this component might include searching for a useful search strategy!) After selecting letters, spellers must then encode their choices in a form which matches response requirements implied by particular tasks, e.g., speaking, writing, touching. The organization of appropriate response implies a second sort of search—this time spellers search for the elements or routines which are essential for responding.

LD children or a significant subgroup thereof may have difficulty searching memory for information relevant to their spelling problems. They may also have great difficulty organizing appropriate responses, even when they have selected, i.e., remembered, appropriate letter representations. In this latter case, encoding their choices in appropriate motor routines for drawing letters may defeat them. For example, most letter reversals and inversions, such as "bekt" for "peeked," may represent difficulties in remembering how to draw intended letters, not necessarily difficulties in spelling. The validity of this inference can be checked by asking spellers who produce reversals or inversions, while they are writing, what letters they intend to produce. In general, extended search times may be interpreted to mean not only that certain responses are not automatic, i.e., overlearned, but also that significant amounts of attention must be allocated to search processes and are therefore unavailable for other purposes. In this perspective, obtainable rates of acquisition are tied to and must await development of automaticity in critical search and retrieval processes.

Two preliminary experiments were performed to investigate these issues. In the first study, subjects were low-achieving, regular grade (RG) third graders ($\overline{X}$ = 9 years, 2 months; S.D. = 6 months) who were compared with older, learning-handicapped (i.e., LH, or "mildly handicapped") students ($\overline{X}$ = 11 years, 5 months; S.D. = 1 year, 2 months) placed in a self-contained special education classroom. Both groups were administered computerized and handwritten versions of a standardized, dictation-style spelling test (Varnhagen & Gerber, 1984).

Table 4. Comparison of Learning Handicapped and Regular Grade Students
on Computer Administered and Handwritten Versions
of a Standardized Spelling Dictation Test
(words per minute)

	Computer Version		Handwritten Version	
	X̄	S.D.	X̄	S.D.
RG class	19.39	12.74	21.22	12.22
LH class	12.56	6.64	13.78	6.22

It was reasoned that if motor encoding of handwritten spelling attempts rather than letter selection and decision accounted for most of the variance in spelling speeds, performance might be improved if letter choice on typewriterlike keyboards was offered as an alternative mode of response. Results showed that LH students produced fewer correct spellings than RG peers regardless of test medium assessed and, surprisingly, both groups of students performed better on handwritten, not computer-administered tests (see Table 5). Upon closer analysis it was determined that higher error rates on the computer administered version could be attributed to unintentionally striking incorrect keys. Evidently, therefore, lack of keyboard familiarity contributed to *increased* probability of error for both groups.[3]

Some support for this interpretation was obtained by comparing alphabet typing speeds before and after administration of the computerized test. Alphabet typing times were expected to decrease as a function of keyboard exposure during spelling. Results indicated that both RG and LH students took from 40 to 45 seconds less to find and type in the alphabet after the computer-administered spelling test. Table 5 presents summary statistics for alphabet typing and writing times.

Did lack of keyboard familiarity contribute to decreased numbers of correct spellings? Table 5 shows that RG and LH students had approximately the same alphabet typing speeds following their computerized spelling task. Nevertheless, younger RG students tended to spell more words correctly than older LH students. Any increase in attention to letter search on the keyboard induced by testing on computers did not impede either speed or accuracy of phoneme representation decisions. On the other hand, LH students, although locating letters as quickly following testing, produced many more errors than RG students on both types of test. It can be inferred, therefore, that encoding responses on computers was not as difficult as deciding which letters should be selected to represent perceived phonemes.

Analysis of handwritten performance revealed that LH students on the average required 8.89 seconds (S.D. = 3.7) to complete each spelling attempt, while younger RG students on the average took 6.77 seconds (S.D. = 2.03) per

Table 5. Alphabet Typing and Writing Speeds
for Regular Grade and Learning Handicapped Students[a]

Subjects	On Computer		Handwritten
	Before	*After*	
Regular grade	116.5	78.1	47.2
(S.D.)	(33.8)	(33.7)	(13.3)
Learning handicapped	122.7	75.3	82.8
(S.D.)	(55.0)	(30.0)	(97.1)

[a]in seconds

attempt. Analyzing spelling times in terms of the number of phonemes in each word, RG students were found to be about half a second faster than LH students in deciding on representations for each phoneme as well as being more often accurate in their choice. It is reasonable to infer that greater automaticity in spelling decision processes resulted in decreased spelling times for the young, regular grade students. Unless handwriting speeds alone can account for differences in time required to produce spelling attempts, it is plausible that LH students lack automaticity in determining what letters best represent target phonemes.

While comparison of mean alphabet writing speeds appears to show that LH students were much slower, i.e., mean times = 82.8 vs. 47.2 seconds, than regular grade peers, it must be noted that considerable variability in alphabet writing speeds was observed, leaving it somewhat unclear as to how generally valid inferences from these estimates can be. It is recalled that these subjects were a heterogeneous group of school-identified "learning-handicapped," a generic classification for students whose mild learning problems may result from a variety of causes. However, it seems safe to infer from these data that LH students in general are slower in producing written alphabets, although we cannot state with precision how much slower.

Upon subject-by-subject inspection of the data, it was not only noted that LH students wrote alphabet letters at a slower rate than regular grade peers, but also that LH students made twice as many errors as younger RG students and often could not produce the entire alphabet. This latter observation seems significant in light of the fact that failure to produce the alphabet as instructed was not necessarily correlated with alphabet knowledge; LH students were able to produce many letters during spelling attempts which were omitted during the alphabet-writing task. Thus there is evidence that alphabet writing and spelling speed may not be highly correlated for many LH students. Rather, failure to perform adequately on this type of confrontational recall task is compatible with findings reported by other researchers who have investigated carefully defined subgroups of problem learners.

For example, Denckla, Rudel, and Broman (1981) found that confrontation naming tasks (tasks in which they were explicitly asked to name something, rather than indirectly displaying such knowledge) elicited much slower rates of responding from clearly defined "dyslexic" than from "other" learning-disabled boys. Similarly, Torgesen and Houck (1980) found that a specific subgroup of LD students who performed poorly on the digit-span test had extreme difficulty in establishing mnemonic codes for stimulus material which was highly familiar. Thus, it is likely that this LH sample included students whose difficulties in selecting appropriate representations of perceived phonemes were exacerbated by difficulty in encoding letters motorically.

Whereas low-achieving third graders took about 1.82 seconds per letter to write the alphabet, which is approximately the rate predicted for second graders from Green and Petty's (1975) normative data, LH students were quite a bit slower—approaching 3 seconds per letter (depending on how one chooses to deal with outlying scores). However, searching for and typing letters on the computer was as fast for LH students as "internal" search for and manual production of letters. Thus, internal letter search for LH students for making symbol representation, not motor-encoding, decisions was already so slow that being unfamiliar with the keyboard did not add a significant attention burden to spelling attempts. We conclude, therefore, that difficulty in making decisions about how to represent speech sounds, not difficulty in writing letters, is primarily responsible for slow spelling speeds in this group of LH children.

Automaticity and Awareness

In a second experiment to investigate the relationship between slow spelling speeds and spelling quality, students who met a stricter, discrepancy definition of learning disabilities (WISC-R Full-Scale IQ: $\overline{X} = 93.3$, S.D. $= 10.03$; reading achievement standard score: $\overline{X} = 7.6$, S.D. $= 5.33$; age: $\overline{X} = 10$ years, 5 months; S.D. $= 1$ year) were studied. In addition to academic underachievement, all students had been identified by teachers as having significant attention problems during instruction. Subjects were administered the same dictation-style spelling test used in studies of error quality. Dependent measures were alphabet-writing speeds, spelling speeds, spelling quality rating, and spelling confidence. One objective of this experiment was to estimate a rough 'decision' residual by subtracting alphabet letter-writing speed from spelling speed. Results indicated that average time per letter in alphabet production was *greater* than time per letter measures of decision speed for about 40% of these LD subjects. Although measurement error could possibly explain these findings, it is more likely that, as seen in the previously described experiment, instructions to write the alphabet, as with other confrontation naming tasks, elicited markedly slower responding from some subgroup of LD students than would be predicted from level of knowledge about the stimuli in question, as demonstrated by these students in other circumstances.

Table 6. Correlation of Decision Time, IQ, Self-Confidence Ratings, and Error Quality in Spelling Performance of Learning Disabled Students

	Decision Time[a]	Pre-spelling Confidence	Post-spelling Confidence	SQR2[b]	FSIQ[c]	Mean (S.D.)
Decision Time	–	−.77**	−.26	−.63†	−.30	2.27 (1.21)
Pre-Spelling Confidence		–	−.10	.71*	.04	2.07 (.18)
Post-Spelling Confidence			–	.07	.04	2.08 (.23)
SQR2				–	.23	2.98 (.57)
FSIQ					–	93.3 (10.0)

[a]Decision Time = average seconds per letter.
[b]SQR2 = average quality rating (1-5) per phoneme representation.
[c]FSIQ = WISC-R full-scale IQ.
†p < .06.; *p < .05; **p < .02.

In an attempt to influence attention, students were asked to rate on a 3-point scale their confidence in their ability to produce a correct spelling. The scale was presented as a series of "faces" immediately before and after spaces on which spellings were to be attempted. A 'sad' face indicated certainty that a word would be misspelled. A 'smiling' face indicated certainty that a word would be spelled correctly. A face with neutral expression was to indicate uncertainty, i.e., $p = .50$ that spelling would be either correct or incorrect. Before attempting to spell a word, students were asked to mark a face to indicate their level of confidence. This was a prediction rating. Following each attempt, students were instructed to proofread, make corrections, and again indicate confidence. This was an error detection rating. Final spelling attempts were assigned a spelling quality rating (SQR2) indicating the average rated quality of each phoneme-representation decision. The SQR2 used, on a phoneme-by-phoneme basis, the same general criteria which had been applied to entire words in our first two studies. Table 6 is the correlation matrix showing relationships among these various measures.

Results indicated that average spelling speed was 2.24 seconds per letter (S.D. = 1.21), or 26.8 letters per minute of spelling. This is approximately the same as phoneme-writing speed (2.10 seconds per phoneme) of LH students in the previous experiment. Referring back to normative handwriting speeds reported by Green and Petty (1975) and Freeman (1916), these LD students needed approximately 0.8 second additional time per letter than would be expected from a typical third grader whose spellings were produced at handwriting speed, i.e., 1.38 seconds per letter, and over half a second longer than would be expected from a *low-achieving* third grader, i.e., 1.60 seconds per letter. Further, these LD students required about 1 second longer than would be expected from similarly aged, low-achieving peers (Freeman, 1916). If we assume that motor encoding by LD students is approximately as difficult as it is for other low achievers, then these data may be interpreted to mean that these LD students with attention problems required on the average about 1 second to make representation decisions for each letter during spelling attempts.

However, decision speed may not necessarily be correlated with accuracy. Presumably, immature, normally achieving spellers are capable of rapid 'decisions' which produce inaccurate spellings. This means that mature, skilled spellers must be capable of not only very rapid decisions, but also decisions which incorporate self-monitoring routines that increase the probability of accuracy. Spontaneous self-correction is an observable manifestation of this ability. Therefore, it was expected that students who were confident, i.e., had low initial uncertainty, would spell faster and qualitatively better.

LD students' spelling quality and their ability to predict or detect error were correlated with spelling times. Results showed that self-confidence ratings made before spelling attempts were good predictors of both spelling time ($r = -.77$; $p < .02$) and spelling quality ($r = .71$; $p < .05$). Spelling time and spelling quality were therefore related ($r = .63$; $p < .05$). Self-confidence ratings completed after spelling were not strongly correlated with either spelling time or quality, indicating perhaps that spelling and word recognition processes are not necessarily symmetrical in cognitively immature learners. Intelligence (Full-Scale IQ) also was not a strong correlate of either spelling time or quality. This finding is reasonable in light of the fact that LD students, by definition, have average intelligence but discrepant achievement levels which are not predicted on the basis of tested intelligence.

Therefore, it can be inferred that decreased decision times, i.e., spelling speeds, are strongly associated with initially low uncertainty (indicated by predictive self-confidence ratings) and increased quality of spelling attempts, i.e., spelling quality ratings. We may only speculate about the direction of causality in this relationship, but it is intuitively sensible, and supported by our other studies taken as a whole, that developing spelling ability in learning-disabled as well as normally achieving students is manifested by decreases in time necessary to make letter representation decisions. It is likely that decision speed is in turn influenced by successively better organization of spelling-relevant information. Moreover, increasing ability involves increasing meta-cognitive awareness of the relative ease or difficulty inherent in each problem and general appreciation for what cognitive-managerial resources are likely to be available for attacking spelling problems. When LD students are unable to direct their attention efficiently to task-relevant information, decision making is more difficult, speed of processing decreases, and quality of spelling attempt declines.

SUMMARY

This chapter has briefly summarized an ongoing program of research which approaches spelling underachievement in learning-disabled students from an information-processing rather than a neuropsychological or behavioral perspective. In summarizing our research on spelling acquisition and ability in learning-disabled and normally achieving children, the following useful generalizations can be made:

1. Spelling ability is reflected in, but not synonymous with, spelling achievement. Rather, spelling ability develops in tandem with general cognitive skills with which children learn to solve problems. As in other problem-solving tasks, immature spellers are stimulus driven, while older, more mature spellers display more concept-driven spelling behavior. Thus, good spelling ability is marked by an increasing number of words which can be spelled, but also by an increased general competence in managing cognitive resources necessary for skilled spelling.

2. LD students produce spellings attempts which, in qualitative terms, resemble those expected from younger, normally achieving peers. There is little evidence that spellings reflect deviant psychological processes. Rather, LD students appear to be developmentally delayed in critical cognitive processes which contribute to successively more skilled spelling.

3. Spelling attempts by LD children, as by their normally achieving peers, represent a special case of problem solving in which attention must be dynamically and strategically deployed, memory must be searched for task-relevant information, and decisions must be made which have the highest probability of reducing response uncertainty.

4. Much of the development of spelling depends on individuals' abilities to organize and rapidly access previously learned information, routines, and knowledge. LD students are capable of spontaneously generalizing spelling principles gained from study problems to similar problems if they (a) receive sufficient time to master exemplars and (b) receive corrective feedback which assists them in directing attention to critical contrasts between their spelling attempts and conventional spellings.

5. LD students are significantly slower spellers than even younger, low-achieving peers, requiring as much as half a second longer per letter than would be expected from developmentally similar, younger children. It is likely that slowness in deciding on letter representations of speech sounds begins a sequence of mutually deleterious effects which result in observed slower than expected rates of acquisition. However, as spelling information gradually becomes better organized and more extensive, there is evidence that decision speed increases, as does spelling quality. Moreover, with increased ability, LD students acquire increased awareness of the likelihood of spelling words correctly.

72   MICHAEL M. GERBER

NOTES

1. The author gratefully acknowledges the assistance of J. Bertoldi, K. Marberger, S. O'Brien, K. Hawkins, B. Lieuwen, A. Biskner, D. Terry, O. Romero, L. Beckon, S. Flores, and B. Johnson, who collected and helped interpret these data.
2. Analysis by grade level may also distort the developmental picture for learning-disabled students because those with most difficulty in written language may be retained one or more times during their school career.
3. With more opportunity to become familiar with the keyboard, it is possible that one or both groups would become faster on the keyboard than in handwriting. Informal observations, for example, suggest appreciable benefits for learning-disabled students in using word processors for composition.

REFERENCES

Boder, E. (1971). Developmental dyslexia: Prevailing diagnostic concepts and a new diagnostic approach. In H. Myklebust (Ed.), *Progress in learning disabilities*. Vol. 2. New York: Grune & Stratton, pp. 293-321.

Cahen, L.S., Craun, M.J., & Johnson, S.K. (1971). Spelling difficulty: Survey of the research. *Review of Educational Research*, *41*, 281-301.

Carpenter, D., & Miller, L. (1982). Spelling ability of reading disabled LD students and able readers. *Learning Disability Quarterly*, *5*, 65-72.

Croft, A.C. (1982). Do spelling tests measure the ability to spell? *Educational and Psychological Measurement*, *42*, 715-723.

Denckla, M.B., Rudel, R.G., & Broman, M. (1981). Tests that discriminate between dyslexic and other learning-disabled boys. *Brain and Language*, *13*, 118-129.

Deno, S.L., Mirkin, P.K., Lowry, L., & Kuehnle, K. (1980). *Relationships among simple measures of spelling and performance on standardized achievement tests* (Research Report No. 21). University of Minnesota, Institute for Research on Learning Disabilities.

Dineen, J.P., Clark, H.B., & Risley, T.R. (1977). Peer tutoring among elementary students: Educational benefits to the tutor. *Journal of Applied Behavior Analysis*, *10*, 231-238.

Ehri, L. (1980). The development of orthographic images. In U. Frith (Ed.), *Cognitive processes in spelling*. London: Academic Press, pp. 311-338.

Farnham-Diggory, S., & Simon, H.A. (1975). Retention of visually presented information in children's spelling. *Memory and Cognition*, *3*, 599-608.

Fitzsimmons, R.J., & Loomer, B.M. (1977). *Spelling: Learning and instruction—Research and practice*. Iowa City, IA: University of Iowa.

Freeman, F.N. (1916). Handwriting. In *Fourteenth Yearbook of the National Society for the Study of Education*, Part I.

Frith, U. (Ed.) (1980). *Cognitive processes in spelling*. London: Academic Press.

Foxx, R.M., & Jones, J.R. (1978). A remediation program for increasing the spelling achievement of elementary and junior high school students. *Behavior Modification*, *2*, 211-230.

Gates, A.I., & Russell, D.H. (1954). *Diagnostic and remedial spelling manual*. New York: Bureau of Publications, Teachers College, Columbia University.

Gentry, J. (1977). *A study of the orthographic strategies of beginning readers*. Unpublished doctoral dissertation, University of Virginia.

Gerber, M.J. (1984 April). *Promoting generalized spelling ability in LD students using a contingent imitation and modeling procedure*. Paper presented at the annual meeting of the American Educational Research Association, New Orleans.

Gerber, M.M. (1984). Orthographic problem-solving ability of learning disabled and normally achieving students. *Learning Disability Quarterly, 17*, 157-164.

Gerber, M.M. (1982). *Effects of self-monitoring training on the spelling performance of learning disabled and normally achieving students.* Paper presented at the annual meeting of the American Educational Research Association, New York City, March.

Gerber, M.M., & Cohen, S. (1985). Assessment of spelling Skills. In A.R. Rotatori, & R. Fox (Eds.), *Teacher assessment in special and regular education: A case study format.* Austin, Texas: Pro Ed, 249-278.

Gerber, M.M., & Hall, R.J. (1979/80). *Spelling errors and cognitive strategies in attentionally disordered learning disabled children* (Technical Report). Charlottesville, VA: University of Virginia, Learning Disabilities Research Institute.

Gerber, M.M., & Hall, R.J. (1981). *The development of orthographic problem solving strategies in learning disabled children.* Paper presented to the annual meeting of the American Educational Research Association, Los Angeles, CA, April.

Gerber, M.M., & Hall, R.J. (1985). *Development of spelling in learning disabled and normally achieving children.* Unpublished Monograph.

Gettinger, M., & White, M.A. (1979). Which is the stronger correlate of school learning? Time to learn or measured intelligence? *Journal of Educational Psychology, 71*, 405-412.

Green, H.A., & Petty, W.T. (1975). *Developing language skills in the elementary schools.* Boston: Allyn & Bacon.

Hall, R.J. (1980). An information processing approach to the study of learning disabled and mildly retarded children. In B. Keogh (Ed.), *Advances in special education* (Vol. 2). Greenwich, CT: JAI Press, pp. 79-110.

Hallahan, D.P., & Reeve, R. (1980). Selective attention and distractibility. In B. Keogh (Ed.), *Advances in special education* (Vol. 1). Greenwich, CT: JAI Press, pp. 141-181.

Henderson, E.H., & Beers, J.W. (Eds.) (1980). *Developmental and cognitive aspects of learning to spell—A reflection of word knowledge.* Newark, DE: International Reading Association.

Higgins, J.A. (1975). Remedial students' needs vs. emphasis on text-workbooks. *College Composition and Communication, 24*, 188-193.

Holmes, D.L., & Peper, R.J. (1977). An evaluation of the use of spelling error analysis in the diagnosis of reading disabilities. *Child Development, 48*, 1708-1711.

Hotopf, N. (1980). Slips of the pen. In U. Frith (Ed.), *Cognitive processes in spelling.* London: Academic Press, pp. 287-307.

Jobes, N.K. (1975). *The acquisition and retention of spelling through imitation training and observational learning with and without feedback.* Unpublished doctoral dissertation, George Peabody College for Teachers.

Kauffman, J.M., Hallahan, D.P., Haas, K., Brame, T., & Boren, R. (1978). Imitating children's errors can improve their ability to spell. *Journal of Learning Disabilities, 11*, 217-222.

Kinsbourne, M., & Warrington, E.K. (1964). Disorders of spelling. *Journal of Neurology, Neurosurgery, and Psychiatry, 27*, 224-228.

Kirk, U. (1983). Introduction: Toward an understanding of the neuropsychology of language, reading, and spelling. In U. Kirk (Ed.), *Neuropsychology of language, reading, and spelling.* New York: Academic Press, pp. 3-31.

Lachman, R., Lachman, J.L., & Butterfield, E. (1979). *Cognitive psychology and information processing.* Hillsdale, NJ: Erlbaum.

Liberman, I.V., Liberman, A.M., Mattingly, I.G., & Shankweiler, D.P. (1980). Orthography and the beginning reader. In J.F. Kavanaugh & R.L. Venezky (Eds.), *Orthography, reading, and dyslexia.* Baltimore, MD: University Park Press.

Lloyd, J., Hallahan, D., & Kauffman, J. (1981). Learning disabilities: A review of selected topics. In L. Mann & D. Sabatino (Eds.), *The fourth review of special education.* Philadelphia, PA: JSE Press.

McKinney, J.D., & Haskins, R. (1980). Cognitive training and the development of problem-solving strategies. *Exceptional Education Quarterly*, *1*, 41-51.

Neef, N.A., Iwata, B.A., & Page, T.J. (1980). The effects of interspersal training versus high density reinforcement on spelling acquisition and retention. *Journal of Applied Behavior Analysis*, *13*, 153-158.

Nelson, E.H., & Warrington, E.K. (1976). Developmental spelling retardation. In R.M. Knights & D.J. Bakker (Eds.), *Neuropsychology of learning disorders—theoretical approaches*. Baltimore, MD: University Park Press, pp. 325-332.

Nelson, H.E., & Warrington, E.K. (1974). Developmental spelling retardation and its relation to other cognitive abilities. *British Journal of Psychology*, *65*, 265-274.

Nulman, J.H., & Gerber, M.M. (1984). Improving spelling performance by imitating a child's errors. *Journal of Learning Disabilities*, *17*, 328-333.

Ownby, R.L. (1985). The neuropsychology of reading ability and disability: Pieces of the puzzle. In B.A. Hutson (Ed)., *Advances in reading/language research* (Vol. 3). Greenwich, CT: JAI Press, pp. 119-149.

Poplin, M., Gray, R., Larsen, S., Banikowski, A., & Mehring, T. (1980). A comparison of components of written expression abilities in learning disabled and non-learning disabled students at three grade levels. *Learning Disability Quarterly*, *3*, 46-55.

Read, C. (1975). *Children's categorization of speech sounds in English*. Urbana, IL: National Council of Teachers of English.

Read, C. (1971). Preschool children's knowledge of English phonology. *Harvard Educational Review*, *41*, 1-34.

Rourke, B.P. (1976). Reading retardation in children: Developmental lag or deficit? In R.M. Knights & D.J. Bakker (Eds.), *Neuropsychology of learning disorders: Theoretical approaches*. Baltimore, MD: University Park Press, pp. 125-137.

Rourke, B.P. (1983). Reading and spelling disabilities: A developmental neuropsychological perspective. In U. Kirk (Ed.), *Neuropsychology of language, reading, and spelling*. New York: Academic Press, pp. 209-232.

Rourke, B.P., & Orr, R.R. (1977). Prediction of the reading and spelling performances of normal and retarded readers: A 4-year follow-up. *Journal of Abnormal Child Psychology*, *5*, 9-20.

Rutter, M., & Yule, W. (1973). Specific reading retardation. In L. Mann & D. Sabatino (Eds.), *The first review of special education*. Philadelphia, PA: Buttonwood Farms, pp. 1-50.

Shores, J.H., & Yee, A.H. (1973). Spelling achievement tests: What is available and needed. *Journal of Special Education*, *7*, 301-309.

Simon, D.P., & Simon, H.A. (1973). Alternative uses of phonemic information in spelling. *Review of Educational Research*, *43*, 115-137.

Sweeney, J.E., & Rourke, B.P. (1978). Neuropsychological significance of phonetically accurate and phonetically inaccurate spelling errors in younger and older retarded spellers. *Brain and Language*, *6*, 212-225.

Tarver, S.G., Hallahan, D.P., Kauffman, J.M., & Ball, D.W. (1976). Verbal rehearsal and selective attention in children with learning disabilities: A developmental lag. *Journal of Experimental Child Psychology*, *22*, 375-385.

Torgesen, J.K. (1977). The role of nonspecific factors in the task performance of learning disabled children: A theoretical assessment. *Journal of Learning Disabilities*, *10*, 27-35.

Torgesen, J.K. (1983). The learning disabled child as an inactive learner: Educational implications. *Topics in Learning & Learning Disabilities*, *2*, 45-52.

Torgesen, J.K., & Houck, D.G. (1980). Processing deficiencies of learning-disabled children who perform poorly on the digit span test. *Journal of Educational Psychology*, *72*, 141-160.

Torgesen, J.K., & Kail, (1980). Memory processes in exceptional children. In B. Keogh (Ed.), *Advances in Special Education*, Vol. 1. Greenwich, Conn.: JAI Press, pp. 55-99.

Varnhagen, S., & Gerber, M.M. (1984). Microcomputers and spelling assessment: Reasons to be cautious. *Learning Disability Quarterly*, *7*, 266-270.

Vellutino, F.R. (1977). Alternative conceptualizations of dyslexia: Evidence in support of a verbal deficit hypothesis. *Harvard Educational Review*, *47*, 334-354.

Warrington, E.K. (1967). The incidence of verbal disability associated with reading retardation. *Neuropsychologia*, *5*, 175-179.

Wing, A.M., & Baddeley, A.D. (1980). Spelling errors in handwriting: A corpus and a distributional analysis. In U. Frith (Ed.), *Cognitive processes in spelling*. London: Academic Press, pp. 251-285.

Zutell, J. (1978). *Spelling strategies of primary school children in relation to the Piagetian concept of decentration*. Unpublished doctoral dissertation, University of Virginia.

USING REQUESTS EFFECTIVELY IN PEER-DIRECTED READING GROUPS

Louise Cherry Wilkinson and Francesca Spinelli

INTRODUCTION

In this chapter, we examine elementary school students' use of requests and responses in their reading groups. Although grouping students for instruction is a common practice in elementary school classrooms, research on the processes of interaction which may support and maintain different outcomes, such as achievement, has been a neglected topic, particularly in the naturalistic setting of the classroom. There has been some research on teacher–student interactional processes in reading ability groups (Eder, 1982; Weinstein, 1976) but very little on all-student, peer-directed interaction (Webb, 1980; Wilkinson & Calculator, 1982a; Wilkinson & Spinelli, in press).

Advances in Reading/Language Research, Volume 3, pages 77-96.
Copyright © 1985 by JAI Press Inc.
All rights of reproduction in any form reserved.
ISBN: 0-89232-389-2

No previous research examines students' use of requests and responses in peer-directed reading groups. Making requests and receiving adequate responses is central to teaching and learning in small groups. Requests are used by children to exchange information and regulate their interpersonal behavior. Requests are very prevalent in classroom situations, accounting for two-thirds of the teachers' speech to students (Mehan, 1978; Sinclair & Coulthard, 1975). There are few data available on the frequency of requests in student–student interaction, although the study of Cazden (1976) suggests that the requests are also common in these interactional contexts.

Using language to influence the actions of other people is an aspect of communicative competence that shows continuity from the preschool through the school years. In this chapter, we introduce the model of the *effective speaker*, who displays communicative competence in social interaction, i.e., one who uses knowledge of language forms, functions, and contexts to achieve communicative goals. Elsewhere we have proposed a model of the effective speaker that characterizes the use of requests and responses by school-age children; this model has been tested and received support from data on first-grade students in reading groups (Wilkinson & Calculator, 1982a, 1982b; Wilkinson & Spinelli, in press). In this chapter, we extend our model by testing it in a new situation, third-grade students' peer-directed reading groups. We are concerned with the generalizability of the model to older students' interactions in instructional groups. Both quantitative and qualitative data are presented. A rich description of the variation and complexity of school-age children's use of requests to peers complements the results of quantitative analysis.

The present chapter includes a discussion of the background and theoretical perspective that motivated the work, including a summary of the model of the effective speaker's use of requests. Presentation of information about the methods of collection and analysis is followed by the quantitative results of the study and the qualitative description of the variety and complexity of third-grade children's use of requests and responses in their peer-directed reading groups.

THE EFFECTIVE SPEAKER

Effective speakers use their knowledge of language forms, functions, and contexts to achieve communicative goals. For example, in the case of requests, effective speakers are successful in obtaining responses for their requests from listeners. The theoretical work of Labov and Fanshel (1977) has been useful in our development of the model of effective speakers' use of requests.

Labov and Fanshel (1977) believe that the direct imperative form underlies all requests for action, e.g. "Give me that book." They have formulated a general "rule of requests" that specifies the preconditions of sincerity under which a listener will understand a speaker's utterance as a request for action: the need for action, the need for the request, the ability of the listener to comply, the obligation or willingness of the listener to comply, and the right of the speaker to make the request. They have formulated the "rule for indirect requests" by which a request for action is conveyed without use of the direct imperative form. Indirect requests are accomplished frequently by reference to one or more of the preconditions of the rule of requests, as well as by reference to the existential status of the action and the consequences or time of performing the action. For example, an indirect request can be made by referring to the precondition of ability, as in the following: "Can you pick up the children?" Even though there is no direct imperative form used here, the intention of the request for action is expressed. Similarly, by saying, "The children need to be picked up," a speaker makes a reference to the first precondition, the need for action, which in this case would be interpreted as a request that the listener take action to remedy the situation.

Speakers use requests for information to obtain information from listeners. Labov and Fanshel (1977) believe that requests for information are related closely to requests for action. In the latter type of request, the speaker may say "Give me X," whereas in the former, the speaker may say, "Give me information about X." In the rule of requests for information, Labov and Fanshel claim that the following two preconditions hold for all valid and sincere requests for information: the speaker believes that the listener has the information requested, and the speaker does not have that information.

In adult conversations, requests for action and information typically do *not* take the direct form, the interrogative form, such as the wh-, yes/no, or tag question forms, or the imperative form. Labov and Fanshel (1977) claim that indirect requests are used frequently because they can be mitigated or aggravated. Mitigation refers to the softening of requests in order to avoid creating offense whereas aggravation refers to increasing the force of the request in order to make it more powerful, such as by repeating the same request many times. Mitigation can be accomplished by the use of such expressions as "please" or "if you don't mind," or by using one of the direct interrogative forms, such as want/need statements ("I need your pen"); embedded imperative form ("Can I have a book?"); declarative statement with a request intention ("That piece of pie sure looks good"); or intonational questions ("It's four o'clock already?"). Labov and Fanshel believe that mitigation is crucial for the maintenance of smooth social interaction because a mitigated request often allows the listener additional options for responding to the speaker beyond simply complying with the request. A request that has been aggravated often takes a direct form and does not give the listener a choice of responses in compliance.

THE EFFECTIVE SPEAKER'S USE OF REQUESTS

We have introduced a model of the effective speaker (Wilkinson & Calculator, 1982a). This model characterizes the use of requests and responses by young students. The model identifies the following characteristics of requests that predict obtaining appropriate responses from listeners. First of all, speakers may express acts clearly and directly in an attempt to minimize ambiguity and multiple interpretations of the same utterance. For example, speakers may use direct forms and specifically designate them to one particular listener when making a request. Second, in the classroom, requests that are on-task, i.e., those that refer to the shared activities in the teaching–learning situation, are most likely to be understood by the listeners and thus these types of requests are most likely to be successful in obtaining compliance from listeners. Third, requests that are understood by listeners as sincere are most likely to result in obtaining responses, according to Labov and Fanshel (1977). Finally, effective speakers are flexible in producing their requests, e.g., speakers should revise their initial request when appropriate responses from listeners are not obtained. They must make judicious use of the techniques of mitigation and aggravation, when revising their initial requests, in order to be successful in eventually obtaining appropriate responses from listeners.

RECENT RESEARCH ON CHILDREN'S USE OF REQUESTS AND RESPONSES

Previous research by the first author on first-grade children provides support for the model of the effective speaker (Wilkinson & Calculator, 1982a, 1982b). Data collected on 30 subjects interacting in their peer groups (a data base of more than 1,025 requests and their responses) show that first-grade students are, on the whole, effective speakers because they obtained appropriate responses to their requests for action and information about two-thirds of the time. The typical child usually produced requests that were direct, sincere, on-task, and designated to a particular listener. In cases when the listener did not comply with the speaker's request, children revised their requests two-fifths of the time. Figure 1 shows the characteristics of requests and appropriate responses (adapted from Wilkinson & Calculator, 1982a). The data show individual differences in the characteristics of direct forms, revisions, and appropriate responses.

Further analyses of the data set provided strong evidence for the predictive nature of the model. A hierarchy of log linear models was used to fit the data. The model that best fits the data assumed that there were associations among the five characteristics identified (direct, sincere, on-task, designated, revised), whether the request obtained compliance and whether the request referred to action or information. The major conclusions from the analysis were that the characteristics of requests are correlated and that whether a request obtains compliance depends on all of the other six characteristics identified by the model.

Some of the most interesting results to emerge from the quantitative analysis of the first-grade data concern differences between the two types of requests and

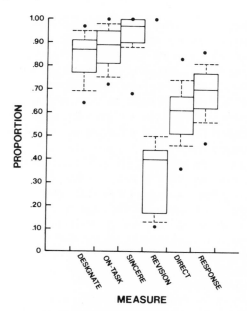

Figure 1. Characteristics of requests and appropriate responses: first grade.

individual differences among the children in usage. The data show that requests for information, in comparison with requests for action, are used more frequently (57% vs. 43%), are twice as likely to take the direct form (88% vs. 42%), and are more likely to receive compliance from listeners (82% vs. 61%). The children showed the greatest individual differences in three of the characteristics: directness of the form of the request; whether the request, if initially unsuccessful, was revised; and rate of compliance to the requests. These results suggested that it may be worthwhile to examine the variety and complexity of children's use of directness and revision of requests and their consequences for obtaining responses from listeners.

The results of several other studies are relevant to directness and revisions of requests in young children; however, there is a noticeable gap in the research literature on the use of requests by school-age children. No previous research has examined the spontaneous production of requests for action and information in instructional groups.

Garvey (1975) in a study of nursery school children's spontaneous speech found that younger children used fewer indirect requests compared with the older children; however, direct forms predominated. Garvey reported the frequent occurrence of her subjects explaining or justifying the need for their direct requests by using adjuncts that refer to the sincerity conditions of their requests.

These adjuncts usually took the form of explaining the need for the action to be performed, citing reasons for their producing the requests, and inquiring as to the listener's willingness to perform the action, usually accomplished by appending the tag "okay?" at the end of the request. Garvey found that the children refused on occasion to comply, and they used two types of refusals: outright refusals, and responses in which compliance appears to be postponed. Labov and Fanshel (1977) refer to this type of response as "putting off a request" and they emphasize the importance of an adult listener's providing the speaker with a reasonable accounting for noncompliance.

Montes (1978) also reported the greater use of adjuncts by older school-age children. She used an experimental task in which speakers were required to produce requests in order to obtain their own objects which were in the possession of another child. Older children, in comparison to younger children, tended to use more indirect requests, those that did not overtly refer to the action or outcome desired, but rather called attention to the speakers' rights and reasonableness. Montes attributes the observed developmental differences to the older children's greater understanding and acceptance of the adult norms of politeness and cooperativeness.

Read and Cherry (1978) provide evidence that older and younger preschool children are both capable of using a variety of direct and indirect forms for requests for action and revisions. They observed developmental differences in the greater tendency of older children to accomplish indirectness through the use of language itself, in contrast with the greater tendency of younger children to rely on gesture and paralinguistic actions to accomplish indirectness. This finding supports Garvey's (1975) position that during the course of development, children learn how to accomplish actions with words that they had accomplished previously with gestures.

In summary, previous research documents that young children use requests to obtain appropriate responses at an early age. Although they tend to produce direct requests initially, their verbal requests become increasingly indirect as they get older.

THE PRESENT STUDY

In the present study, third-grade students in peer-directed reading groups were observed throughout the academic year. Audio and video recordings of interaction were collected and transcribed so that requests and responses could be identified and described. The following questions were addressed: (1) Are students effective in their use of requests for action and information in their peer reading groups? (2) Are there individual differences in their use of requests and responses, and are the differences stable over the year? (3) Do particular aspects of requests predict whether appropriate responses will be obtained? (4) Is there a relationship between reading and using requests and responses?

METHODS

Subjects

The subjects were 35 third-grade students who comprised seven reading groups in the third grade of one school. The reading groups were determined by the teachers prior to the study and there were three to six subjects per group. According to the teachers, the students' reading skills at the beginning of the school year differed among the groups, even though no formal assessment of these skills had been given. All of the students were Caucasian, native speakers of English, and from middle-class families, and they ranged in age from 7 to 8 years. There were no students who were diagnosed to have learning disabilities or any language disorders. There were 16 boys and 19 girls.

Individual Assessment

Information concerning each student's language ability and reading achievement was collected by individual testing in the fall and in the spring. The assessments typically lasted for 45 minutes; they included a speech sample, a test of grammatical comprehension, and a test of reading achievement.

The speech sample consisted of approximately 50 spontaneous utterances from each student. It was obtained during an informal conversation in which an experimenter posed open-ended questions regarding topics presumed to be of interest to the children, such as television and friends. Grammatical complexity (production) was assessed by segmenting each student's transcript into a series of communication units, then computing the average number of words per unit using a procedure based on that of Loban (1976). Thirty communication units were used as an index of the Loban score.

Students' grammatical comprehension was assessed by their performance on the Miller–Yoder Test of Grammatical Comprehension (Miller & Yoder, 1975). This test, which consists of 84 items, requires the student to point to the picture, given a choice of four pictures, that depicts the meaning of each utterance read by the experimenter. Various syntactic structures are tested, including prepositions, subject and object pronouns, possessives, and tenses. Reading achievement was assessed by the Metropolitan Reading Achievement Test (McGauvran & Nurss, 1976).

Data Collection

Recording the Reading Event

Reading activities were the units of sample for data collection. Reading activity typically began at 9:00 A.M. and lasted until approximately 9:40 A.M. in each of the classrooms. Teachers announced both the beginning and the end of the activity. Students chose their seats at the reading tables designated by the teacher. The teachers often provided instructions for the reading groups when the students were in the whole-group formation; however, some of the teachers provided instructions after the students had formed their small reading groups. In both situations, the completion of the instructions marked the beginning of the reading event.

All of the groups were similar in their organization and structure, such as the way that activities were initiated, maintained, and terminated. Initially, assignments and instructions were presented by the teachers; the teacher then left the reading group and the students functioned as a group in order to accomplish the individual tasks. In all cases, the task was the same for all of the members of the group for that particular reading activity, e.g., a worksheet or a workbook page. The final phase of the reading group included another teacher-directed period that occurred shortly before the groups disbanded, when the teacher often provided evaluation.

All of the groups were seated at small tables that also contained other groups of students. Background noise and general environmental characteristics appeared to be comparable among the groups, and all of the groups performed one or more activities requiring a written response, such as completing worksheets, drawing a picture of events that the students had read about, or printing sentences from the stories that they had read.

The reading activities were audio- and videotaped in the classrooms for each of the reading groups. Data were collected in the fall, for 3½ weeks at the end of October and beginning of November, and then again in the spring for 3½ weeks in April. There were three separate tapings for each reading group in each session for a total of six samples for each group; there were approximately 42 hours of recordings.

Two portable video cameras (Sony Portapak) were used to record the reading activity of each group; cameras were visible to the students and were positioned across from one another so that nearly full-face views of all of the students would be recorded on one or the other camera. Two microphones (Electra Voice 635A) were placed in the middle of each group's table.

Prior to, during, and following the recording, two observers prepared descriptions of the ongoing events in the group in order to supplement the recordings with relevant contextual information which might not have been included on the tapes. There were four adults in addition to the students, teachers, and school staff in the classrooms. The subjects were familiar with the presence of several adults in the classroom in addition to the teachers; these included parents, aids, and others. According to the principal, videotaping of both teachers and students was common in these classrooms.

Transcription of Tapes

The videotapes collected for each group were transcribed by a member of the research team who had been present during data collection. A relatively long segment of all-student interaction for each group was chosen for detailed analysis in this study (10–30 minutes). During this segment, the teacher was not present in the group; typically, he or she was in the classroom assisting other students. Transcripts were rechecked against both of the tapes. Percentage agreement on these data had been established for word and utterance boundaries, and they exceeded 80%. Following transcription, the videotapes were viewed for relevant nonverbal and spatial information which then was included on the transcripts.

Two transcripts—one coded previously by the same observer, the second by an associate—were randomly selected and recoded by the second author. Interobserver agreement, represented as the number of coding agreements divided by the number of agreements plus disagreements, was then computed with respect to each of the variables included in the study. Agreement ranged from 80 to 100% for each coding category.

Coding. The samples of data selected for analysis were coded according to the following categories:

Utterance—A string of words communicating one idea.
Requests for action or directives—Attempts by speakers to get listeners to perform actions.
Requests for information or questions—Attempts by speakers to obtain information from listeners.

All requests were coded into the following categories:

On-task/off-task—An on-task request is related to the academic content, procedures, and/or materials of the assignment. Examples of on-task requests for information are: "Kara, what's that word?" "How do you do this page?" "Where can we get a dictionary?" Examples of on-task requests for action are: "Sit down and get back to work." "When can we get a dictionary?" An off-task request is unrelated to the task, such as "Did you watch that show about the magician last night?" "Where'd you get that T shirt?"
Designated/nondesignated—A designated request is directed to a specific listener. The intended listener may be overtly signaled by behaviors such as naming, e.g., "Susie, give me the pen," or gaze, or may not be overtly signaled by the speaker at all. Nondesignated requests are directed to two or more listeners.
Sincere/insincere—A sincere request for information is a request in which the speaker seeks information from a listener expected to have the desired information when the speaker does not have it, e.g., "What is the answer to number two?" A sincere request for action is a request which the speaker wants carried out, cannot or does not want to perform herself, and is directed to a listener capable of complying (Labov & Fanshel, 1977). Insincere requests for information and action violate the definitions for sincere requests; an example of an

insincere request for information is one child saying to another about the latter's drawing, "That's a pig?" "Go ask the chalk" is an example of an insincere request for action, which was given in response to the request, "How do you spell chalk?"

Direct/indirect—For requests for action, direct forms include imperatives ("Give me that eraser"); direct requests for information include "wh" questions ("How do you spell think?"), yes/no questions ("Is can spelled c-a-n?"), and tag questions ("We're supposed to do this page, aren't we?). All other forms were coded as indirect requests and included commonly occurring forms of embedded requests ("Can I borrow your eraser?"), declarative statements ("I need help"), intonational questions ("Can is spelled c-a-n?"), and nonlexical requests ("Whaa?").

Revision/nonrevision—A revised request is the reinitiation of the same request made previously by the same speaker to the same listener within three turns of the initial request. (A turn equals all speech by one speaker until another speaker speaks.) Revisions may or may not be elicited by the listener. Examples include the following:

Jim: What's this supposed to be?
Tim: Huh?
Jim: What's this supposed to be?

Sue: You should put your books away.
         (no response)
         We should put our books away.

Nonrevisions are all requests that do not qualify as reinitiations as defined.

Appropriate/inappropriate responses—Responses to requests were coded as appropriate if the requested action or information was provided or if a reason was given for the lack of compliance, as illustrated by the following examples:

Jay: Jeff, can I borrow your eraser?
Jeff: I don't have an eraser.

Jay: What goes here?
Tim: Huh? Oh, a bird.

Inappropriate responses included responses by which the listener refused outright to comply ("No, I won't tell you"), nonresponses, postponements ("I'll tell you later"), irrelevant responses ("Doo-de-doo-de-doo"), and indications that the listener does not know the appropriate answer ("Uh, I'm not sure...").

Measures

For each subject, the quantity of speech was computed as the number of utterances produced. In addition, the following proportional scores were computed: all requests divided by all utterances; appropriate responses divided by all requests; direct forms of requests divided by all requests; on-task requests divided by all requests; designated requests divided by all requests; sincere requests divided by all requests; revised requests divided by all requests which failed to elicit responses.

RESULTS

The data base included 11,915 utterances, of which 2,650 (22%) were requests, with 878 requests for action and 1,772 requests for information.

Differences in Initial Reading Achievement and Language Ability

One standard score was computed for reading achievement from the two tests administered in the fall and spring. Kruskal–Wallis analyses revealed that there were significant differences in ability among the seven groups $[\chi^2(6) = 12,89; p < .05]$. Further analyses revealed that the fall reading achievement was positively related to the spring achievement (tau = .53; $p < .01$). The groups differed significantly in reading achievement in the spring $[\chi^2(6) = 14.93; p\ p < .01]$ but not in the fall $[\chi^2(6) = 5.90]$.

One standard score for language knowledge was calculated based on the score from the two separate assessments in the fall and spring. Kruskal–Wallis analyses for overall language ability revealed that there were no significant differences among the groups.

Question 1:   Are Third Graders Effective in Their Use of Requests?

The data for the characteristics of requests and appropriate responses are displayed in Figure 2. These displays are an adaptation of Tukey's (1977) "box and whisker" diagram, which has the advantage of displaying all the data and their variability. The following information is given for each variable: the lowest value in the sample (black circle), the 10th percentile (dash bar), the 25th percentile (solid bar), and the median (solid bar), the 75th percentile (solid bar), the 90th percentile (dash bar), and the highest value in the sample (black circle). The "box" represents the interquartile range, or middle half of the sample.

There seem to be two kinds of variables represented in Figure 2. One group of variables, represented on the extreme left-hand side of the figure, shows high medians and moderate interquartile ranges (.04–0.16) indicating low spread, and ceiling effects. This group of variables, which includes designated listener, on-task, and sincere requests, suggests a common competence among the children on these aspects of their communication. The second group of variables, which can be seen on the extreme right-hand side of the figure, shows medians in the middle range with moderate interquartile ranges (0.10–0.15) indicating medium

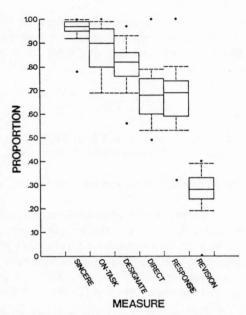

Figure 2.   Characteristics of requests and appropriate responses: third grade.

spread. These variables, which include directness, revisions, and appropriate responses to requests, show enough variation among the children to suggest genuine individual differences.

Overall, the data showed that this group of third graders were effective in obtaining appropriate responses to their requests for action and information more than two-thirds of the time. The typical child usually made requests that were direct, sincere, on-task, and directed to a designated listener. When the listener did not respond appropriately, the typical child tried again only one-third of the time.

Question 2:   Are There Individual Differences in Requests and Responses?

Group Data.   With some exceptions, the patterns concerning both requests for information and requests for action were stable from fall to spring. Wilcoxon matched pairs signed ranks tests were used to examine the significance of differences between fall and spring, and between the two types of requests. There was only one significant difference between seasons. Designated requests ($z = 2.48; p < .01$) were used by the children more often in the spring than the fall.

There were several differences between the two types of requests. Requests for action were more likely to be sincere ($z = 2.30; p < .02$) and to be designated to a particular listener ($z = 3.44; p < .010$). Requests for information were more likely to occur (rate of requests, $z = 4.87$; $p = .01$), to be revised when initially unsuccessful ($z = 3.43$; $p < .01$), to be direct in form ($z < 4.57$; $p < .01$), and to receive an appropriate response ($z = 4.88$; $p < .01$).

This pattern of differential language usage for requests for information and action reflects increasing sophistication in language usage, including the differential uses of both types of request. In contrast, adults' requests for information typically do not take a direct form, which is considered to be rude and impolite. For the children in this study, the probability of listener understanding may be increased by use of the characteristics of designated listener and by reference to the topic at hand. On the other hand, the probability of listener understanding and compliance seems to be increased by the use of sincere requests of a direct form.

Individual Differences.   Overall, individual differences among children are shown in Figure 2. In this section we consider selected examples of children who are effective and ineffective speakers, including references to quantitative (see Figure 3) and qualitative data.

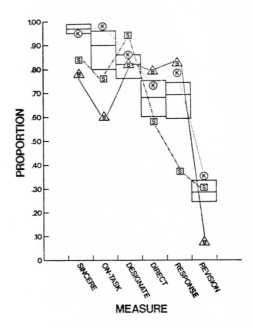

Figure 3.   Individual differences in characteristics of requests and appropriate responses.

Child K is a good example of an effective and appropriate speaker. Karen designates her listeners, uses direct forms, and revises her unsuccessful requests at above-average levels. Her performance on the sincere and on-task variables suggest that she speaks appropriately. Several factors may contribute to her high level of success in obtaining appropriate responses. She frequently obtains her listeners' attention in a direct manner by using names or tapping rather than just looking at them. Her requests are specific; for example, she may ask her listeners to confirm her choice or to select one of two alternatives. She also tends to revise rather than repeat her requests. Although Karen frequently reinitiates when her requests are unsuccessful initially, she appears able to determine when a reinitiation will be unsuccessful and does not persist. Furthermore, this speaker makes relatively few requests; they are usually successful.

In the following exchange Karen's requests to Diane demonstrate some of these behaviors:

Karen:	Diane (touches), does this say "fazed, faced?"
Diane:	Faced. I'm done with my first page.
Karen:	None of them rhymes with blazed.
Diane:	Fazed, faced, that's what I put down.
Karen:	Diane (taps), I don't get this.
Diane:	It's a siren.
Karen:	I know but (reads) siren, lemon, siren, liken.
Diane:	(circles correct answer on Karen's page)
Karen:	(tapping) I don't get this.
Diane:	(ignores)
Karen:	Hey (looks at Diane), this could be "hermit," couldn't it?
Diane:	Yeah.
Karen:	(smiles) Hermant.

Scott, shown as S in Figure 3, is an example of an unsuccessful speaker. His success in obtaining appropriate responses is below the tenth percentile. He tends to make fewer direct and sincere requests than his peers and is off-task more often than other children. Not only are Scott's direct requests less frequent than those of his peers, they are more aggravated, i.e., stronger (Labov & Fanshell, 1977). Scott initiates or is drawn into arguments readily. These result in numerous unsuccessful requests. In the following example, Ben and Scott have been arguing over the possession of a pencil; Ben is taunting Scott in order to continue the argument:

Ben:	Tell me more about it Scott. Big Scott boy.
Scott:	Stop that or you're gonna get beat up outside at recess.
Ben:	Gonna make me?
Scott:	Yeah, outside for recess.
Ben:	Big Scott boy.
Scott:	You two be out there.

The inappropriateness of the content of Scott's talk and the apparent insincerity may also contribute to his lack of success in obtaining responses. In the following example, Scott's attempt to guide the group back on-task is not interpreted sincerely by group members, e.g., Donald:

Donald: Scott, can't you ever stop laughing and making jokes?
Scott: Now let's all be serious.
Donald: How can you be serious, Scott?
Scott: I don't know. It's hard.

Bob, shown as B in Figure 3, is an inappropriate yet effective speaker. He exhibits low scores on sincerity and on-taskness, but his compliance rate is very high (.82). He makes many direct requests and designates his listeners (.82). In addition to specifying his listeners by name, he makes frequent use of attention getters such as "hey," "oh-oh," "see," and "y'know something?" as in the following example:

Bob: Oh-oh, Tim, lookit what's behind you.
Tim: (looks)

Bob's off-task comments may contribute to his high rate of obtaining responses, in contrast to Scott's. Although the children in the group do sometimes comment on the frequency of Bob's off-task behaviors, they often are interested in them. One reason is that Bob successfully uses these comments to entertain his peers as the following example illustrates.

Bob: Wanna see my funny hat?
Tim: Okay.
Bob: Da-da. (places book on his head)

Bob has learned that he can sometimes control the behavior of his peers by controlling their attention. When the children in his group threaten to report his actions to the teacher, he distracts them by making attention-getting statements and requests for information. The children often respond to these requests, perhaps because they are already attending to him and because they know the answers. This tactic is occasionally successful. In the first example, Bob has taken Tim's notebook. He distracts Tim for a while but is unsuccessful in obtaining an appropriate response from his peer. In the second example, Cindy reprimands Bob for talking about and touching the experimenter's microphone. His distraction attempt is successful:

Tim: Gimme that.
Bob: Watch this. (plays with the notebook)
Tim? Don't! C'mon. I'm telling. I'm telling.
Bob: There. Two and two is four. Ain't I smart?

Tim: I'm telling.
Bob: Two times two is four.
Tim: I'm telling.
Bob: What's two times two?
Tim: It's four you dumb——— . (expletive deleted).
Bob: Two? Two twos?
Tim: I know, it's three, ya big dummy.
Bob: You think two times two is three, hey?
Tim: No, it's three ya dip. (expletive deleted)
Bob: Three times two are four. Four times four are eight. (singing)
Tim: Better erase that 'cause I'm telling the teacher.
Bob: 28 times 28 is 30, is 65, 65 times 65 is 232.
Tim: I'm going to tell. (leaves)
Cindy: Bob, I'm telling on you.
Bob: What'd I do?
Cindy: You're talking and you're not supposed to talk about that stuff.
Bob: What stuff? Okay, I'll get working. Ouch, my eyeball.
Cindy: Tell on you anyhow.
Bob: Tell on me, I'll tell on you.
Cindy: What am I doing?
Tim? You're crying.
Cindy: I'm not crying.
Bob: Well you were, so there.
(Children resume working)

Many of Bob's utterances suggest that he is an attentive listener. He frequently helps to maintain topics by requesting clarification and elaboration and by adding new information, as can be seen in the following examples:

Tim: Oh-Oh, we're in trouble.
Bob: I know, I know, I know.
Tim: We better say our prayers. You know, my ma, when she saw my report card, she smacked me.
Bob: (giggle) How did she smack you?
Tim: She saw the report card and she went, she went (imitates nagging). And she went (imitates nagging, slap). Ooh!
Bob: You know what? Last year my mother saw my report card, said I went to Unit 3, and she goes (slaps self) and then she goes, I go, What's your big problem—You're in Unit 3, why'nt you stay in Kindergarten?

Lisa: I don't get this.
Bob: What don't you get?

Question 3: Do Aspects of Responses Predict Whether Appropriate Responses to Requests Will Be Obtained?

An analysis was conducted to address the question, "Do selected characteristics of requests predict whether an appropriate response will be obtained?" This question was addressed by classifying the requests in a multidimensional contingency table defined by the following dimensions: response, direct form, designated listener, on-task, sincere, revision, and request for action/information. Log linear models were fit to this table in an effort to find the simplest model that adequately predicted the frequencies that were observed in the table (Bishop, Fienberg, & Holland, 1975).

In the simplest model, it was assumed that the six characteristics of requests were completely independent of one another. This model was rejected, $\chi^2(120) = 378.32$, $p < .01$. In a more complex model, it was assumed that appropriate responses depended on the other characteristics but that these other characteristics did not depend on each other. This model was rejected, $\chi^2(114) = 265.59$, $p < .01$, but it was a significant improvement over the first model, $\chi^2(6) = 112.73$, $p < .01$. In a still more complex model, it was assumed that there were associations between every pair of characteristics but no higher order associations. This model did fit the data, $\chi^2(99) = 94.44$. Moreover, it fit better than the preceding model in which it was assumed that only appropriate response was associated with other characteristics, $\chi^2(15) = 171.15$, $p < .01$. Finally, this model fit better than the one in which it was assumed that all pairs of characteristics were associated except the pairs involving appropriate responses, $\chi^2(6) = 97.97$, $p < .01$. The major conclusions, therefore, are (1) that characteristics of requests are correlated and (2) that whether a request received an appropriate response depended on the other characteristics of the request. This latter effect received support from two sources: the goodness of fit improved when the effect was added to the model and worsened when it was removed.

Because the observations are dependent, the significance levels which were obtained are not completely trustworthy. One solution to this problem is to select a statistic which measures an effect of interest and to jackknife that statistic by groups (Mosteller & Tukey, 1977).[1] The log linear effect of each characteristic on appropriate responses was computed and jackknifed by groups. The results suggested that all characteristics predicted appropriate responses. Requests were more likely to obtain appropriate responses if they were for information than action, $t(6) = 15.17$, $p < .01$; if they were of direct form, $t(6) = 4.23$, $p < .0$; and if they were revised (after initial attempt), $t(6) = 4.08$, $p < .01$. These results confirm the validity of the model.

Question 4: Is There a Relation Between Reading Achievement and Requests?

Analyses were conducted to examine whether students' requests and appropriate responses differed in ability groups, which may affect reading achievement. The relationship between characteristics of requests and reading achievement was examined. Appropriate responses to requests are predicted by characteristics of requests (action/information, direct form, designated listener, revision, on-task, sincere). Because the content of these requests usually refers directly to some aspect of the reading assignment, selected aspects of requests were expected to show relationships to reading achievement.

Rank order correlations were computed between these variables and a standardized score for overall reading achievement. Rank order correlations were used because they are as powerful as Pearson correlations but are less likely to be biased by extreme cases, which occurred occasionally in these data.[2] It was expected that the measures of the appropriate response, direct form, and revision were likely to show a relationship with reading achievement, but the other measures were not likely to yield high correlations for purely statistical reasons of lack of variability in the measures showing ceiling effects.

The correlation between direct forms and reading achievement was .23 ($p <$ .03). One interpretation of this finding is that children who are direct in expressing their wants are securing appropriate responses to their on-task requests, which may contribute to their knowledge of reading. Another possible intereptation of the data is that the better readers are more sophisticated in their use of language and aware of multiple ways to obtain appropriate responses.

CONCLUSION

The results of this study have shown that third-grade students are effective speakers in their peer reading groups, since they obtained appropriate responses to their requests for action and information most of the time. The data confirm our model of the effective speaker's use of requests. The typical child produced requests that were direct, sincere, on-task, and designated to a particular listener. The use of language by these school-age children places a premium on explicitness, directness, and assertiveness. This pattern is consistent with findings reported by Ervin-Tripp (1976), Read and Cherry (1978), Garvey (1975), and Montes (1978). The pattern contrasts with that typically associated with adults, who express cooperation and politeness in requests through their use of indirect forms (Ervin-Tripp, 1976; Lakoff, 1973). Individual differences emerge in both characteristics of requests and effectiveness of obtaining appropriate responses. The data reported here support the model of the effective speaker, as proposed in the Introduction.

The results also suggest the possible causes of the maintenance of differences in achievement in reading groups throughout the year that are not actively directed by the teacher. Initial differences among students' reading achievement and effective use of language may be maintained by differences in communicative processes within groups. Thus the positive correlation between requests and reading achievement may reflect the true association between them. This association may be either a direct or an indirect causal link. In the direct case, students who obtain compliance to their requests may learn reading skills as a consequence. In the indirect case, some other intellectual competence(s) promote both the production of requests and responses and reading skills. Further research should be directed to exploring this relationship and the source of individual differences in language use.

The task of developing communicative competence seems formidable, and it is not surprising that the functional aspects are incompletely developed when the child enters school. Children develop knowledge of language forms and functions and the complex rules for their use during the school years. Reading groups provide one context for the learning and practice of this knowledge.

ACKNOWLEDGMENTS

The authors thank Alex Cherry Wilkinson for his help in the statistical analyses and his constructive suggestions on an earlier version of this manuscript. The research reported in this chapter was funded by the National Institute of Education through a grant to the Wisconsin Center for Education Research (OB-NIE-G-81-0009). The opinions expressed in this article do not necessarily reflect the position, policy, or endorsement of the National Institute of Education or the Department of Education. Some of the data reported here are reported in Wilkinson and Spinelli 1983.

NOTES

1. Jackknifing is a method for assessing the degree to which an effect estimated from the data for all subjects persists when a subgroup of subjects is deleted from the analysis. The procedure is recursively applied. In the present analysis, the subgroups are reading groups.

2. For a sample of 40, a Kendall's tau rank order correlation of .20 is the equivalent to a Pearson correlation of about .30, whereas a tau of .30 is equivalent to a Pearson correlation of about .45.

REFERENCES

Bishop, T., Fienberg, S., & Holland, P. (1975). *Discrete multivariate analyses: Theory and practice*. Cambridge, MA: MIT Press.

Cazden, C. (1976). If school is a performance, how do we change the script? *Contemporary Psychology, 21*(2), 125-126.

Eder, D. (1982). The impact of management and turn-allocation activities on student performance, *Discourse Processes, 5*(2), 147-160.

Ervin-Tripp, S. (1976). Is Sybil there? The structure of some American directives. *Language in Society, 5,* 25-66.

Garvey, C. (1975). Requests and responses in children's speech. *Journal of Child Language, 2,* 41-63.

Labov, W., & Fanshel, D. (1977). *Therapeutic discourse*. New York: Academic Press.

Lakoff, R. (1973). Language and woman's place. *Language in Society, 2*(1), 45-79.

Loban, W.D. (1976). *Language development: Kindergarten through grade twelve* (Research Report No. 18). Champaign, IL: National Council of Teachers of English.

McGauvran, M., & Nurss, J. (1976). *Metropolitan Readiness Tests, Level 1*. New York: Harcourt, Brace, Jovanovich.

Mehan, H. (1978). Structuring school structure. *Harvard Educational Review, 48*(1), 32-64.

Miller, J.F., & Yoder, D.E. (1975). *The Miller-Yoder Test of Grammatical Comprehension: Experimental Edition*, Madison, WI.

Montes, R. (1978). Extending a concept: Functioning directly. In R. Shuy and P. Griffin (Eds.), *Children's functional language in the early years*. Washington, D.C.: Center for Applied Linguistics.

Mosteler, F., & Tukey, J. (1977). *Data analysis and regression*. Reading, MA: Addison-Wesley.

Read, B., & Cherry, L. (1978). Preschool children's production of directive forms. *Discourse Processes, 1*(3), 233-245.

Sinclair, J., & Coulthard, R. (1975). *Towards an analysis of discourse: The English used by teachers and pupils*. London: Oxford University Press.

Tukey, J. (1977). *Exploratory data analysis*. Reading, MA: Addison-Wesley.

Webb, N. (1980). Group processes and learning in an interacting group. *Quarterly Newsletter of the Laboratory of Comparative Human Cognition, 2*, 10-15.

Weinstein, R. (1976). Reading group membership in the first grade: Teacher behavior and pupil experience over time. *Journal of Educational Psychology, 68*, 103-116.

Wilkinson, L. Cherry, & Calculator, S. (1982a). Requests and responses in peer-directed reading groups. *American Educational Research Journal, 19*(1), 107-120.

Wilkinson, L. Cherry, & Calculator, S. (1982b). Effective speakers: Student's use of language to request and obtain information and action in the classroom. In Wilkinson, L. Cherry (Ed.), *Communicating in the classroom*. New York: Academic Press, pp. 85-99.

Wilkinson, L. Cherry, & Spinelli, F. (1983). Using requests effectively in peer-directed instructional groups. *American Education Research Journal, 20*(4), 479-501.

QUILL:
READING AND WRITING WITH
A MICROCOMPUTER

Andee Rubin and Bertram Bruce

INTRODUCTION

For a number of years we have been what you might call "friendly skeptics," or maybe "skeptical friends," of the idea of computers in education. On the one hand, we have seen the tremendous value that computers can have in our own work. The modern electronic office has computer systems that assist in organizing information, in revising texts, and in communicating with text and graphics across great distances almost instantaneously. We often find electronic mail more useful than the telephone as a means of communication. We've also been involved in research on artificial intelligence—investigating what could be done if we had computers that were really "intelligent." These experiences suggest that computers can achieve a beneficial role in education. But computers can also make bad situations worse. In the workplace, computers have often dehumanized jobs, compartmentalized work, and separated people from people. In schools, poor uses of computers can

Advances in Reading/Language Research, Volume 3, pages 97-117.
Copyright © 1985 by JAI Press Inc.
All rights of reproduction in any form reserved.
ISBN: 0-89232-389-2

fragment education, putting barriers between subject areas, and separating teachers from students and students from students. This chapter discusses these contrasts in the context of some language arts software our research group has been developing.

USES AND LIMITATIONS OF COMPUTERS IN EDUCATION

We will begin by discussing some problems in the current teaching of writing and then consider how computers might be used to deal with those problems. Consider one popular representation of the problem of teaching writing in a classroom (inspired by a Bil Keane cartoon): A little boy rides the bus to school at the beginning of September with wonderful thoughts running through his head—a trip in the family car, going to the movies, swimming, and so on. When he gets to school, even more thoughts tumble around in his head. He's probably not paying a bit of attention to what's going on in class, thinking instead about a trip to the Capitol and fishing and eating ice cream cones and camping. Then the teacher says, as teachers do, "Okay, you're each to write a composition on 'how I spent the summer.'" And what happens? Poof! All those rich ideas disappear.

This child came to school with a wealth of ideas and experiences, but the activity that he was faced with didn't build on what he knew. There is a large gap between the potential this student has for expressing and communicating and what actually happens in a classroom situation. It is crucial that education find ways to get students to talk and write about topics that are meaningful to them. How do computers deal with this issue? Are they really helping kids to develop and expand on the curiosity and excitement they have when they enter school?

To answer this question, we examined a directory of educational software published by Dresden Associates (1982). In the May 1982 issue there were over 1,600 programs for microcomputers listed, of which 317 were in the language arts area. Figure 1 (top) shows that 60% of the programs were of the drill and practice type. Some were simple games and others were traditional frame-oriented computer instruction. Very few of the programs involved having children use language in an active way. Another way of categorizing the language arts programs is to look at the level of language they were designed to teach. Most of the programs dealt with the letter level (activities like "name the next letter of the alphabet") or the word level ("choose the correct synonym for a word"). Very few of the programs—less than 10%—dealt with language at the level of sentences and whole texts (Figure 1, bottom). Looking at these categorizations together, we found there were only two programs in which kids were actively involved in using whole texts.

When teachers have looked at currently available software, they too have recognized this problem. A recent study (Olds, Schwartz, & Willie, 1980) had

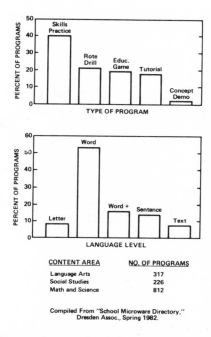

Compiled From "School Microware Directory,"
Dresden Assoc., Spring 1982.

Figure 1.   Types of currently available language arts software.

teachers try out various kinds of software and explore how they might be used. They arrived at a number of conclusions, including the following: "Teachers saw the enormous pedagogic differences between apparent user control and real user control, between answering questions and formulating them, between recognizing someone else's ideas and creating your own" (p. 40). The teachers recognized that the ultimate success of computers in the classroom depends critically on who is in control, the computer or the child.

It is curious that while there is a growing awareness of the need to find ways to get kids to develop higher level thinking and do more writing (Elbow, 1973; Flower, 1981; Murray, 1968), software seems to be focused on the smallest units of language and on drill and practice activities. One explanation for this is that you can think of computer activities in two different ways: You can think of things that are well suited to a computer, or you can think of things that help satisfy educational goals. Unfortunately, software creators have often ended up designing activities that are very well suited to a computer but may not really help in attaining educational goals. Conversely, there are a number of aspects of education in which computers will never be of much use. Having a writing conference with a teacher or a peer (Newkirk & Atwell, 1982) is an important process that will never be replaced by a computer (although computer programs may facilitate it).

USING A MICROCOMPUTER TO DEVELOP READING/WRITING SKILLS

Based on this analysis, our research team has been looking at what can be done effectively with a microcomputer that also addresses pedagogical goals (Rubin & Bruce, in press; Collins, Bruce & Rubin, 1982; Steinberg, Note 4). Beyond that, we have all been studying how to integrate computer activities into a classroom context. The set of microcomputer-based activities for reading and writing that resulted from our work is called QUILL. This section will discuss six aspects of these programs, each in terms of a pedagogical goal in the teaching of writing.[1]

Planning

The first goal is *to help children develop skills of planning and critical thinking*. The centrality of planning processes in writing has recently been recognized and studied by several researchers (e.g., Flower & Hayes, 1981; Scardamalia, 1981). We've developed a program called Planner to encourage students to take notes, write down ideas, and structure the thoughts that will later develop into a piece of writing (Bruce, Collins, Rubin, & Gentner, 1982).

The left side of Figure 2 shows the kinds of questions that might be in a Planner that would lead to a book review: the name of the book, the author, what kind of book it is, who the main character is, and then some less objective kinds of questions—What is the major conflict? What was your principal feeling about the book? A student using this Planner sees these questions and answers them in any order. At the end she gets a piece of paper that has the questions she selected followed by her answers, forming essentially a structured list of notes. The right side of Figure 2 shows one student's answers. The student sees "What is the name of the book?", types in "*A Wrinkle in Time*," and then receives on the piece of paper afterward "Title: *A Wrinkle in Time*." The computer prompts, "Who is the author?"; and the student types in "Madeleine L'Engle"; and it comes out as "Author: Madeleine L'Engle." The output of this Planner can be used as a guide for composing. It can also be used in subsequent class discussions or in a writing conference.

Specific planners are created by a particular teacher and class, representing their ideas of what should be included in a given type of text. For example, students may brainstorm about what might be included in a game review—the name of the game, how to play it, and whether any special equipment is involved.

BOOK REVIEW

- What is the name of the book?
- Who is the author?
- What type of book is it?
  1. Mystery
  2. Science Fiction
  3. Humorous
  4. Non - fiction
- Who is (are) the main character(s)?
- What is the major conflict?
- What was your principal feeling about the book?
- What is the main idea of the review?

(1) Title: A Wrinkle in Time

(2) Author: Madeleine L'Engle

(6) Main Feeling: mystical

(5) Major conflict: a struggle against evil in the fourth dimension

Figure 2.   A Planner for book reviews.

Using the Planner, the teacher can take the topics that the students have suggested and create a set of questions. When she is finished, she has created a Planner that works much as the book review Planner described above: The student answers the questions he chooses, in any order, and skips the rest. After using the program, he gets a printout that he can take back to his seat to use in writing a game review. [Flower (Note 1) and Scardamalia (Note 2) have both emphasized the need to develop Planners that go beyond this genre-based type to facilitate analysis and revision of the text itself as it is generated.]

Integration of Reading and Writing

The second goal is *to integrate reading and writing* (Rubin & Hansen, in press; Tierney & Pearson, 1983). In pursuit of that goal, our group has designed an information exchange, a program we call Library. We arrived at this idea while considering the fact that writers often do research—by reading—before they write; originally, we planned to provide an encyclopedia on the computer containing information that children could access. We then realized that it would be more appropriate for students to write the encyclopedia, with the computer providing the storage facility and a method for accessing different pieces of text once they have been written. We developed this idea into a system that allowed

```
There is information available for these keywords. Type
the NUMBER of the keyword you want. You will be able to
use more than one keyword but you can enter only one at
a time.


1 AMERICAN              8 STEAK

2 MODERATE             9 HUNGARIAN

3 SALAD-BAR           10 MUSIC

4 CROCODILES          11 CANDY

5 SUMMER              12 BOCCE

6 CHEAP               13 WORMS

7 SANDWICHES          14 NONE OF THE ABOVE


Type a NUMBER and press RETURN.
```

Figure 3.   A display from the Library: keyword choices.

students to enter text, assign keywords, and then later read each other's texts, so that reading and writing would be integrated within the same system.

Figure 3 shows a display that a student might see on the screen when using the Library. The entries shown are restaurant reviews. Each review consists of the text itself, two authors, and the title. We have set up the system so that there can be two authors because often the kids work in pairs at the computer. In addition, keywords are attached to each entry for use in accessing what has been written. For restaurants, the authors of these reviews created the keywords in Figure 3: American, moderate, salad bar, and so on.

Suppose you choose the keyword *moderate*, meaning "I want to see all the restaurants that are moderate in price." Figure 4 is a list of the reviews that have been written for which the author had selected the keyword *moderate*. Most of them have other keywords as well. For example, Bertucci's Pizza happens to be a place where you can play bocce, and the person who wrote the review decided that *bocce* would be an interesting keyword. One of these, a review of the "Candy Connection," is by Carolyn Miller, the teacher in one of our pilot classrooms. In addition to *moderate*, she used the keywords *candy* and *sweet* to further define the topic of her review. Her review reads:

```
There are 4 entries with the key
MODERATE.
Type the NUMBER of the entry you would like to see.


        TITLE                        KEYWORDS

1 33 DUNSTER ST.           AMERICAN, MODERATE, SALAD-BAR

2 CLUB CASABLANCA          MODERATE, CROCODILES, SUMMER

3 NEWBURY STEAK HOUSE      AMERICAN, MODERATE, STEAK

4 BERTUCCI'S PIZZA         MODERATE, BOCCE

5 NONE OF THE ABOVE


Type a NUMBER and press RETURN.
```

Figure 4.   A display from the Library: entry choices.

There's a variety of scrumptious candy with a wide selection of yummy chocolates. Fruit dipped in chocolate or chocolate covered nuts and raisins are some of their specialties. Jelly beans in every flavor are available. All candy can be packaged in many unusual containers. Dentists, eat your hearts out.

Keywords: /moderate/candy/sweet/

In May and June of 1982, our research team tried out the Library for the first time in a classroom by having kids write game reviews. Our pilot test was in a fourth-grade classroom in Brookline, Massachusetts. First the teacher conducted a brainstorming session to generate the important points in a game review. The students came up with: what did you try to do, did you like it, how many chances do you get in each turn, what are the rules, how hard is it, what are the secrets for winning, is it fun, where should you buy it, where can you play it, what happens when you reach a certain score, what's the name of the game, etc. Each pair of students used the Planner to begin to specify the contents of their review. Students then composed their reviews (working in pairs) and typed them into the Library. After the first few reviews were typed in, each group that came up to type in their review ended up reading all of the others as well. They wanted to read what others had written and the computer made that easy to do. Here are two examples of their reviews. The first one is called "Jumping Rope."

Jumping rope is not as easy as it looks. You must be well-coordinated and patient. This is how you do it. *Step 1:* Hold the rope in both hands, one on each end of the rope. *Step 2:* Bring the rope over your head. Quickly jump over the rope and start again. When you're first learning how to jump rope, it's best to start with a little help. You play outside. Be careful you don't get tangled up in it. For a good one it is about $1.99. It is great fun and good exercise.

Keywords: /arcade/far-out/home/

(The authors of this review later complained that they couldn't delete *arcade*, which they had mistakenly included as a keyword.)

The second review is on Asteroids (about half of the reviews were about electronic games).

If you like fast-moving space action, then you should try Asteroids by Atari Company. Your ship is a triangle which shoots lasers. You maneuver the ship across the board with a joystick. As you are bombarded by meteorites you try to blast them into space dust. If you succeed, you pile up points. To make the game even more [there should be an "exciting" in here, we were told by the authors], there are randomly shooting UFOs. Asteroids is available for your Atari home computer system. It is also available in most arcades. Asteroids is a very good video game.

Keywords: /electronic/video/space/arcade/home/

For each of these reviews, one of the two authors was a student who spent time in the special-needs resource room. In using QUILL, both of these students got involved in writing with someone else in a way that made them feel successful. They "published" their writing, both by storing it on the computer and by printing out multiple copies on the printer. We watched one of these two pairs typing in their review. The more advanced student typed in the first half of the review, and then there was a moment when he looked at the teacher and said, "Can I go now?" She said, "No, you have to help V type in the other half." V had a lot of trouble, but B stayed and helped him type, showing him which letters to type when he got stuck. B learned more by serving as a tutor and they both shared a sense of pride in creating a publicly available text.

This classroom also offered suggestions for the further development of QUILL. One of us had put up a sign next to the computer saying, "Tell us what you think we should change"; the kids were not bashful. Two of their suggestions were quite interesting. The first was, "If your program is on a disk and you find a mistake, you can fix it." Unfortunately, because we were in the midst of developing the system, we had not been able to provide them with a full text editor. We were surprised, though, by their insistence on being able to change what they had written. They really were committed to the idea of revision and weren't satisfied with their first drafts.

The second suggestion had to do with the printed copy a student can get after writing an entry. We had made the mistake of having the system print out only one copy, but all the reviews had two authors. The students reminded us that each person who contributed to a review should have a copy.

There are myriad classroom activities that might make use of this general information exchange. One disk might contain texts that describe how to accomplish certain tasks: how to build a bird house, how to make ice cream, or how to make chocolate chip cookies, all indexed by relevant categories. A class could create a computerized encyclopedia with expository entries about various topics—animals or ecology or anything that is already being worked on in the curriculum. Finally, because each of these entries has an author attached to it, it is easy for a teacher or a student to look at a portfolio of all of a student's writing at a certain point in the year.

Publishing

Our third goal is *to make writing public*. Writing needs to be read by peers, by people who know its purpose and are expected to be affected by it. Too often students write for their teacher, but for no one else. Making writing public implies "adult" notions of publishing, of presenting texts in formats that are meant to be read by others (see Graves, 1982; Graves & Hansen, 1983).

One of the standard formats that classroom teachers use is a newspaper. Unfortunately, class newspapers are not easy to produce. The first newspaper of the year always sounds like a great idea. Everyone talks about it and thinks it's wonderful; the students write articles; the teacher stays up late at night typing, finally does all the pasting up and formatting and finishes a first issue to everyone's acclaim. Unfortunately, the process is so laborious that the next issue of the newspaper never appears. In a third–fourth-grade class at the Garrison School in Oceanside, California students regularly produce the *Garrison Gazette* using their Apple computer (Levin, Boruta, & Vasconcellos, 1982). Students in the class write their articles on the computer. When they are finished, the computer prints out the articles in the correct column width and prints the date and volume number at the top. After the articles have been written it's a fairly small step to produce the newspaper.

The authorship of several articles in the *Garrison Gazette* is interesting. One "news" article says, "On March 30, Speedy died from a germ. Snoopy started to eat Speedy. A was Snoopy and Speedy's owner. We buried Speedy at 11:00 a.m. Now Snoopy is the only rat in C-2." This was written originally by A, who also put his name on it, but it was edited later by B and L. Thus, it is the product of at least three people's work, and that process is recorded as part of the newspaper.

Another article was written by M and J: "Today is April 2nd, 1981. It was raining this morning. The temperature is 71 degrees Fahrenheit. The sun is coming out now and it is getting warmer. The clouds are big, fat and white." The same kind of collaboration that happened when students used the Library occurred when they wrote this newspaper.

Publisher, the general utility program our group is planning, will publish not only class newspapers but books (with an automatic table of contents so that the page numbers are correct for different chapters of the book). Individual students might write different chapters and put them all together into a class book. The program will also help in formatting memos and personal letters. Any kind of writing with conventional formats can be facilitated by a Publisher.

Addressing Real Audiences

Our fourth goal is *to support meaningful communication with real audiences*. The underlying idea here is that reading and writing have purposes and that being aware of the audience and the intended effect on that audience is an important aspect of writing (Bruce, 1981). The relevance of audience and purpose is most obvious in conversation, where the norm is to know who you are talking to and to expect a response.

In order to create that kind of environment for writing, we've come up with an electronic message system. The students' response to this message system—the Mailbag—has been extraordinarily enthusiastic (Steinberg, 1983). The messages they wrote are not polished compositions, but they are obviously examples of children writing about things they care about. Here's one message from M. to B:

> B., do you think I should get Space Invaders or Quest for the Rings? Can you come over today? I hope you can. Here's a riddle for you. If an athlete gets athlete's foot, what does an astronaut get? I'll give you the answer when you type me a message, but you also have to take a guess. Bye bye, B. Oh, by the way, you won't get the answer from any of my joke books.

Not much later the following message came back:

> Dear M.: I think you should get Quest for the Rings because Space Invaders on Odyssey stinks. Sorry, but I cannot come to your house today. I have to work on my autobiography, get new shoes, and go to a party. Sorry. As for your riddle: Meteor's Foot? Sorry, I can't come over.
>
> [The answer to the riddle, by the way, is "mistletoe."]

These kids sit about three seats apart, but the idea of typing messages to each other on the computer was exciting enough to them that they exchanged several messages over the course of a few days.

In this class the students were writing their autobiographies (using pencil and paper) while they were using Mailbag on the computer and they soon started commenting on each other's autobiographies in their messages. One student would write an autobiography that was read by another student in the class who would then write a message about it that was read by the first student. Here is one example: "Michael, your autobiography was great. I think the pictures are really great too. You should be an artist when you grow up. You'd be very successful. I like the pictures you made in my autobiography too. You're a very, very good artist."

In addition to this relatively free message activity, our group has formulated more structured activities using the Mailbag. The Mailbag allows a student to send a message to all the members of a club at once, just by specifying the club name as an addressee. This facility could encourage the formation of classroom clubs such as dinosaur, video game, and sports clubs. In addition, Mailbag has a bulletin board on which a message to the whole class can be posted. A teacher can put something on the electronic bulletin board like "Today we're going to work on the Civil War." One of the students in our pilot classroom took advantage of the bulletin board option. He wrote the following message: "To Classmates. I don't want to go but I have no choice. I'm going. Going where, you ask? To another school. It is called Solomon Schechter. But do not fear. I am still here, but not for long. I will be gone. Your friend, A." Everyone who logged onto the system got his or her own copy of the message, keeping A from having to write it out many times.

The computer also allows writers to remain anonymous. Some of the messages had signatures like "Guess who?" This facility allows a kind of conversation about personal problems, in which the person who poses the problem and those who respond are all anonymous.

All of the above examples come from a message system within a single classroom. To communicate between classes at the moment teachers have to carry a disk physically or mail it to another class. But we are also working on developing a system that would send messages over longer distances. The scenario for its use is this: Students write the messages they want to send to another school. At the end of the day the teacher leaves the computer plugged in on a local phone line. A program waits until 2:00 A.M., dials the phone number of a large computer, sends its messages to that machine, and "goes back to sleep" until 4:00 A.M. At 4:00 A.M. it wakes up and calls back to pick up any messages that have been left for it on the large computer. In the morning, the teacher comes in and sees on the screen, "Last night you received two messages from Cambridge and three messages from Alaska."

Being able to communicate with distant classrooms introduces new possibilities. Imagine, for example, that in Massachusetts a class is compiling an animal encyclopedia by writing articles about local animals. They could send a message to Alaska or Hawaii and say, "We're doing an animal encyclopedia. Do you have any animals that we might not have that you could write about? Could you send a message that we can include in the encyclopedia we're creating?" Soon their encyclopedia might contain an article on polar bears or tropical birds.

Writing with Peers

A fifth goal is *to encourage writing with and for peers*. In this context, we will describe Story Maker, a program that our BBN team has been working on for the past several years as a reading and writing activity (Rubin, 1980, 1982; Zacchei, 1982). Using Story Maker, students construct stories by choosing already written story parts to put together.

One of the insights that guided Story Maker's development was that when students write, they often *downslide* (Bruce et al., 1982; Collins & Gentner, 1980); they focus on the lowest level of writing—on handwriting, punctuation, and word choice—and spend too little time on idea development and higher level organization. We wanted to reverse the situation and invent an activity in which it was impossible for students to focus on punctuation and word choice because these issues had already been taken care of. Students could then devote all their attention to the connections between ideas in their story.

Here is an example of what happens when a student uses Story Maker. She starts out with the beginning of a story—"Lace opened the front door..." and then she's given several choices of the way that story might proceed. In this case, the options are either "... saw the joker," "... slipped into what looked like a big bowl of spaghetti," or "... stepped on a mouse."

Let's follow the second option. "Lace opened the front door and slipped into what looked like a big bowl of spaghetti." Given this beginning, there are two possibilities for the next story part: either "Frankenstein was cooking it for his dinner" or "It was really the mummy taking a bath." (The mummy taking a bath looked like spaghetti because he was all unwrapped and the wrappings filled the bathtub.) When a student makes a choice, the next choices she sees are determined by her previous choice (unlike Mad Libs, in which the individual choices are independent). The choices are structured as a tree, as in Figure 5. The student goes on making choices until a story has been completed.

Again, the most interesting insights into language use come from watching children use the program. One 10-year-old boy using Story Maker chose a set of stories for his 7-year-old sister. He went through all 25 stories in the Haunted House tree, chose seven that he thought were appropriate, and made them into a book for her. Some of the others he probably thought were too short, too uninteresting, or too scary for his sister. Here is one of the stories that made it into the book.

Lace opened the front door and slipped into what looked like a big bowl of spaghetti. Frankenstein was cooking it for his dinner. Before Frankenstein got too angry, Lace suggested that they go to McDonalds. When Lace and Frankenstein walked up to the counter, Frankenstein ordered twenty five Quarter Pounders with Cheese, six gallons of Coke, and four large fries. The waitress was too scared to ask him for the money. After they carried all the food back to the haunted house, Frank ate every bit of it and then he ate Lace for dessert.

He titled this story "Never Go To McDonalds," illustrated it, paginated it, and bound it with the other six stories. It was interesting that he had chosen as his own task in using Story Maker to compile seven stories for his sister. It was something he could never have done in an hour if he'd sat down with seven pieces of blank paper. In making decisions about how to construct those stories, though, he was paralleling the choices authors make for particular audiences.

THE HAUNTED HOUSE

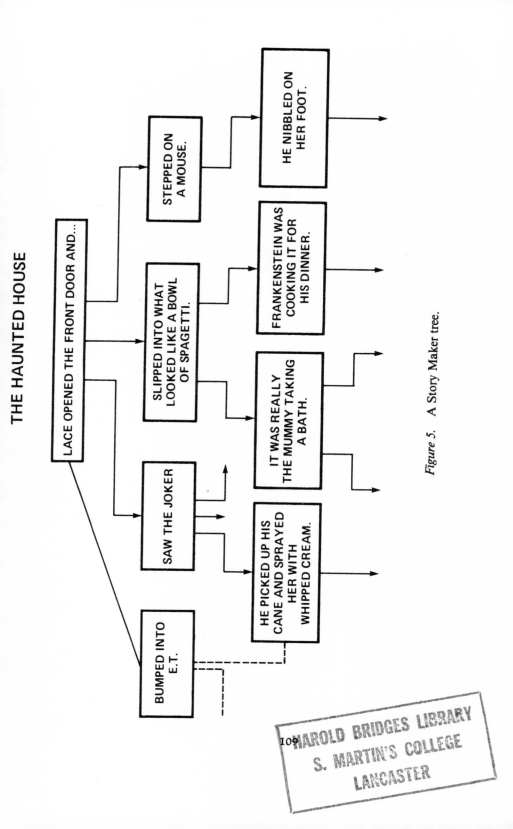

Figure 5. A Story Maker tree.

In order to encourage children to think about the stories as they construct them, we've added goals to some of the Story Maker trees. The computer will present a student with a goal at the beginning and evaluate his story at the end with respect to that goal. Some of the goals for the haunted house story tree are to write a story in which Lace marries the mummy, Lace dies of rat bites, Michelle helps Lace escape from the vampire, and so on. The computer gives a student one of these goals selected randomly, lets him make a series of choices, and then at the end says, "Congratulations, Chip, you've come up with the story that I expected you to come up with" or "I'm sorry, Andee, but you didn't quite come up with the story I expected. For choice number 3, you chose 'Lace walked out of the house' and you should have chosen 'Lace walked into the rat den.'"

A third way to use Story Maker allows students to do their own writing. After reading some of the sets of choices, students often want to add something of their own. Consequently, a program called Story Maker Maker has been added, in which students get to add their own pieces to the story. Given the beginning, "Lace opened the front door and," a student could add, "and bumped into E.T." and then decide whether the new path he or she had initiated should continue on its own or feed back into the existing tree (see dashed lines in Figure 5.)

Using Story Maker Maker, a whole class can get together and construct a story tree one part at a time. The teacher could start it and add the first few choices. Then over a period of weeks students could add their parts, ending up with an entire tree which could even be exchanged with another classroom. The important point here is that the story part each student has written is automatically read by other students. What students write with Story Maker Maker is not only read by other students, but other students actually interact with it. In a sense Story Maker Maker is a tool for collaborative writing because the students who are making the choices among story parts are part of the writing process, as is the person (or people) who made up the original tree. In fact, the haunted house story tree discussed here was written by a fourth grader with the help of one member of our group.

Revision

Our final goal is *to facilitate revision*, and particularly to encourage students to do more kinds of revision—not just to fix the spelling error that the teacher marked on the paper, but to consider putting two texts together to create a longer one, or switching the introduction and conclusion, or other major changes in the text. Even young children can learn to carry out such revisions (Graves, 1982). The text editor included in QUILL (Writer's Assistant, developed by Jim Levin) facilitates such higher level revisions.

Figure 6 is a first draft of a paragraph from a proposal. There are several mechanical and stylistic problems with this text. Using a text editor, all of the changes shown are easy to make. A writer can substitute one word for another

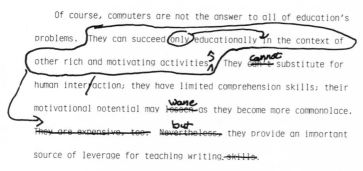

Figure 6.   A text under revision.

("cannot" for "can't," "wane" for "lessen") or change multiple occurrences of the same word. What is even harder to do on a typewriter, and more important in the context of learning about revision, is to move a whole sentence around; to get rid of a complete sentence; or to try out a different order of sentences, decide you don't like it, and return to the original order. With a text editor it is easy to take the entire sentence, "They can succeed educationally only in the context of other rich and motivating activities," move it down, take out "They are expensive too," and connect the moved sentence with the one following it so that it now reads: "They can succeed educationally only in the context of other rich and motivating activities, but they provide an important source of leverage for teaching writing."

The structural changes indicated in Figure 6 definitely improve the paragraph, but with a typewriter or paper and pencil the writer would be forced to recopy the whole piece. On a word processor moving those sentences takes just about as many keystrokes as substituting "cannot" for "can't'." The power of a text editor, especially for kids for whom the thought of editing often has to do with erasing something until there is a hole in the paper, is that now revision is easy to accomplish.

Computers can also help with spelling, punctuation, and subject–verb agreement. Writer's Assistant, for example, includes a command (called "Mix") that displays all the sentences in a student's text starting at the left margin. A student can quickly scan the list of sentences and see if all of the first letters of sentences are capitalized, if end punctuation is missing, if there is a run-on sentence, if the sentence length is varied, and if there are any sentence fragments. The computer doesn't actually identify any of these; it just makes it easier for students to see problems and fix them. The sentences can then instantly be reorganized in paragraph format.

QUILL, then, contains the following components: a set of planning aids (Planner); an information exchange (Library); publication aids (Publisher); a message system (Mailbag), and an activity kit, including Story Maker and Story Maker Maker. A text editor (Writer's Assistant) is also included in QUILL. It was written by Jim Levin at the University of California, San Diego (Levin, 1982; Levin, Boruta, & Vasconcellos, 1982).

TRAINING TEACHERS AND STUDENTS
TO USE THE SYSTEM

Teaching teachers how to introduce students to QUILL is as important as the software itself. QUILL includes a series of lesson plans which guide teachers through the first several weeks in the classroom. As shown in Figure 7, there are computer and noncomputer activities students do as individuals or in pairs, and lessons that the teacher teaches. The teacher starts by teaching a lesson about computers, then goes on to a lesson on the Library system itself—how it's organized and what keywords are—and then a third lesson consisting of brainstorming about the content of reviews. Fourth, students actually go to the

QUILL in the Classroom

Lesson	Writing Time	Computer Time
1. Computer		
2. LIBRARY		
3. Reviews		
		4. See LIBRARY
	5. Pick topic	
6. PLANNER		
		7. Use PLANNER
	8. Conferences; compose draft	
9. Entering & local editing		
		10. Use EDITOR to enter draft into LIBRARY
	11. Conferences; plan revisions	
12. EDITOR		
		13. Use EDITOR to revise review
14. Keywords		
	15. Choose keywords	
		16. Add keywords
		17. See other reviews

Figure 7.   Introducing the class to QUILL.

computer, use the Library program, and read some reviews that have already been entered either by us or by the teacher. The teacher creates a Planner from the brainstorming list so that after a pair of students have chosen the game they are going to review, they can use it. Using the Planner, students generate a structured set of notes which they then use in conferences either with one another or with the teacher. As a result of those conferences they compose a draft on paper. (Eventually, when there are enough computers, students will compose on the computer, but when computers are in limited supply, a classroom runs more smoothly if some composing is done first on paper.) Finally, students use the editor (Writer's Assistant) to enter their drafts and put them in the Library.

Students confer again with the teacher or peers about what they have typed into the Library. The teacher then teaches them more sophisticated revision techniques using the Editor and gives them a chance to use the Editor to revise their reviews. Finally, the whole class discusses which keywords would be useful for their set of reviews, and individual students choose their own keywords and then go to the computer to add those keywords and to read other reviews. In these few weeks they are being introduced to three issues: computer literacy, the QUILL system, and a process approach to writing, including planning, conferencing, and revision.

RESEARCH ON COMPUTERS AND WRITING

The recent growth of computers in education has naturally led to research questions about the effects software can have on classrooms, students, and teachers. One of the first results these investigations have produced is the recognition that the computer alone does not account for the most important changes which take place. Rather, modifications in the social organization of the classroom, such as changing roles of teachers and students and changing attitudes toward learning, are all central mediating factors of the effects of computers.

Unfortunately, most computer software currently available for educational use severely restricts the kinds of interaction that take place between the student and the computer. The implicit model is that of a student working alone on a constrained, predesignated task. Evaluation of responses is done solely by the computer, with little opportunity for either the student or the teacher to alter the model of interaction or adapt it to current classroom needs. These programs may be useful in teaching specific skills, but taken by themselves they exemplify a limited vision of the ways computers can be used in education.

There are related limitations to much of the research on computers in the classroom. First, most evaluation studies have focused on traditional frame-based computer-assisted instruction (Chambers & Sprecher, 1980; Edwards,

Norton, Taylor, Van Dusseldorp, & Weiss, 1974; Moshowitz, 1981), a technology that now appears to be useful primarily for certain tightly defined instructional tasks. Second, studies of specific innovations have typically emphasized the software or hardware (Daiute, Note 1; Malone, 1981) with the general aim of promoting and/or improving it. Although such studies are essential, they need to be followed by investigations of technology's actual impact on the people involved. Third, most studies have been done in a laboratory or model school setting, with enthusiastic, knowledgeable teachers, if not the researchers themselves, introducing the computer to the class. Such a setting is vastly different from the typical classroom with its limited resources and possible indifference or even antagonism on the part of the teacher. Fourth, most studies are product-oriented; they measure learning by means of a standard pretest/posttest design or look at computer-collected data on students' use of the computer. This research by its very design cannot perceive changes in the learning process, classroom structure, students' sense of purpose in learning, or teacher–student roles that may be altered by the computer.

The eventual impact of computers on education will be substantial; in fact, computers have already begun to change the teaching of science (Abelson & diSessa, 1981), math (Bork, 1981; Dugdale & Kibbey, 1975; Papert, 1980), reading (Zacchei, 1982), and writing (Levin et al., 1982; Collins, 1982). The greatest changes will come from programs which not only allow but *require* active involvement and collaboration of students and teachers for their success, e.g., LOGO, QUILL, Interactive Text Interpreter. These more open-ended programs establish new environments for learning or provide tools for carrying out functional tasks. The changes they can bring about are dramatic; at the same time, their use requires substantial support from peers and adults, and much more needs to be learned about their effects on classroom practice.

Unfortunately, the research to date provides only a glimpse of these changes. QUILL, for example, is currently being field-tested in school districts in Connecticut, Massachusetts, and New Jersey. The system will be evaluated by comparing pre- and posttest writing samples from experimental and control classrooms. We have conducted a comparative study of the pattern of use and effectiveness of QUILL's message system in the field test classrooms. Students' messages were analyzed according to the use of purpose, audience, and reciprocity. The rate of message writing was also recorded for each classroom. Several independent variables, such as prior computer experience of students, classroom organization, and teachers' computer knowledge, were examined as potential predictors of classroom success with Mailbag. Findings of this study have been reported by Steinberg (Note 4). Also, limited classroom observation has produced interesting results and hypotheses for future study.

In particular, a major need is for systematic, long-term, ethnographic studies of classroom events and interactions. These must be undertaken if we are to understand such things as how teachers attempt to integrate microcomputers and computer activities into the classroom; the shift of roles for both teachers and students when computers become part of the everyday life of classrooms; and the impact of computer use on students' understanding of themselves and their work.

The most important impact of microcomputers on writing may be changes in the larger classroom writing "system" rather than changes in the technology of writing, e.g., speed, printed output, ease of revision. For example, when milling around the computer waiting for their turn to use it, students may read each others' writing and talk about it. These interactions can affect both the content and form of student writing. Similarly, peer interactions during writing on the computer, student access to other students' work stored in the computer, and programs such as Mailbag in which students send messages to each other can affect students' understanding of purpose in writing and their sense of audience. What is needed is research that looks seriously at the changes brought about in the classrooms, the teachers, and the writing process.

CONCLUSION

All of this writing about writing brings the following to mind. One of us was trying to write a journal article and had really gotten stuck, so as he usually does when in that situation, he tried to procrastinate by reading. He came across the following poem (Roy, 1982) and was struck by its appropriateness:

Author, Author
Susan Davis Roy

By a romance with words
Life-long I've been smitten
I don't want to write
I want to have written.

Computers will never make writing or understanding texts an easy process. But if we try to design and demand computer activities that show a real respect for the learner and for language, it is possible that children will become more actively involved in developing their own reading and writing skills, so that they too will understand the joy of writing and having written.

ACKNOWLEDGMENTS

This research was supported by the U.S. Department of Education under contract Nos. 300-81-00314 and 400-81-0030.

The QUILL system is the result of a joint effort of a group of researchers at Bolt Beranek and Newman, Inc. and the NETWORK, Inc. Those researchers at BBN in addition to ourselves who have played a central role in QUILL's development from initial philosophy and design to implementation and field testing are Cindy Steinberg, Kathleen Starr, and Allan Collins. The team of researchers at the NETWORK who have made major contributions to the project, especially in the areas of teacher training, classroom implementation, and preparation of written materials are Susan Loucks, Denise Blumenthal, David Zacchei, and Joyce Bauchner. Computer programming on QUILL was accomplished by Andy Fox, Maureen Saffi, Adam Malamy, and Rinsland Outland.

We would like to thank Carolyn Miller, a teacher in the Brookline Public Schools who participated in the pilot study and Jim Levin of UCSD for help in some of the work reported here. Thanks also to Cheryl Liebling, a recent member of our research team. Finally, special thanks to Cindy Hunt, Marcia Mobilia, and Abiola Backus for their assistance in preparing this and other QUILL manuscripts.

NOTE

1. Since this paper was originally written, we have changed the design of QUILL to include only Mailbag, Library, Planner, and Writer's Assistant. Publishing utilities are available within QUILL, although there is no explicit Publisher program, and Story Maker is available as a separate program. The pedagogical goals we consider central to the teaching of writing, of course, have not changed. QUILL is available from DCH Educational Software, a division of D.C. Heath and Company.

REFERENCE NOTES

1. Daiute, C. *Child-appropriate text editing*. Paper presented at the Conference on Child-Appropriate Computing, Teachers' College, Columbia University, New York, May 1981.
2. Flower, L. (personal communication, February 1983).
3. Scardamalia, M. (personal communication, February 1983).
4. Steinberg, C. *Can a technological QUILL prove effective in teaching the process of writing?* Talk presented at the American Educational Research Association, Montreal, April 1983.

REFERENCES

Abelson, H., & diSessa, A.A. (1981). *Turtle geometry: The computer as a medium for exploring mathematics*. Cambridge, MA: M.I.T. Press.

Bork, A. (1981). *Learning with computers*. Bedford, MA: Digital Press.

Bruce, B.C. (1981). A social interaction model of reading. *Discourse Processes, 4*, 273-311.

Bruce, B.C., Collins, A., Rubin, A.D., & Gentner, D. (1982). Three perspectives on writing. *Educational Psychologist, 17*, 131-145.

Chambers, J.A., and Sprecher, J.S. (1980). Computer assisted instruction: Current trends and critical issues. *Communications, Association for Computing Machinery, 23*, 332-342.

Collins, A. (in press). Teaching reading and writing with personal computers. In J. Orasanu (Ed.), *A decade of reading research: Implications for practice*. Hillsdale, NJ: Erlbaum.

Collins, A., & Gentner, D. (1980). A framework for a cognitive theory of writing. In L.W. Gregg & E.R. Steinberg (Eds.), *Cognitive processes in writing*. Hillsdale, NJ: Erlbaum, pp. 51-72.

Collins, A., Bruce, B.C., & Rubin, A.D. (1982). Microcomputer-based writing activities for the upper elementary grades. In *Proceedings of the Fourth International Learning Technology Congress and Exposition*. Warrenton, VA: Society for Applied Learning Technology, pp. 134-140.

Dresden Associates (1982). *School Microware*, Spring. (Copies from Dresden Associates, P.O. Box 246, Dresden, Maine 04342.)

Dugdale, S., & Kibbey, D. (1975). *The fractions curriculum, PLATO elementary school mathematics project*. Urbana, IL: Computer-based Education Research Laboratory, University of Illinois, March.

Edwards, J., Norton, S., Taylor, S., VanDusseldrop, R., & Weiss, M. (1974). Is CAI effective? *Association for Educational Data Systems*, Summer 7, 4.

Elbow, P. (1973). *Writing without teachers*. London: Oxford University Press.

Flower, L. (1981). *Problem-solving strategies for writing*. New York: Harcourt Brace Jovanovich.

Flower, L.S., & Hayes, J.R. (1981). Problem solving and the cognitive process of writing. In C.H. Frederiksen, M.F. Whiteman, & J.F. Dominic (Eds.), *Writing: The nature, development and teaching of written communication*. Hillsdale, NJ: Erlbaum, pp. 39-58.

Graves, D.H., & Hansen, J. (1983). The author's chair. *Language Arts, 60*(2), 176-183.

Graves, D.H. (1982). *Writing: Teachers and children at work*. Exeter, NH: Heinemann Educational Books.

Levin, J.A. (1982). Microcomputers as interactive communication media: An interactive text interpreter. *The Quarterly Newsletter of the Laboratory of Comparative Human Cognition, 4*, 34-36.

Levin, J.A., Boruta, M.J., & Vasconcellos, M.T. (1982). Microcomputer-based environments for writing: A writer's assistant. In A.C. Wilkinson (Ed.), *Classroom computers and cognitive science*. New York: Academic Press, pp. 219-232.

Malone, T.W. (1981). Toward a theory of intrinsically motivating instruction. *Cognitive Science, 4*, 333-369.

Moshowitz, A. (1981). On approaches to the study of social issues in computing. *Communications, Association for Computing Machinery, 24*(3), 146-155.

Murray, D.M. (1968). *A writer teaches writing*. Boston: Houghton Mifflin.

Newkirk, T., & Atwell, N. (1982). *Understanding writing*. Chelmsford, MA: The Northeast Regional Exchange, 1982.

Olds, H.F., Schwartz, J.L., & Willie, N.A. (1980). *People and computers: Who teaches Whom?* Newton, MA: Education Development Center, Inc., September.

Papert, S. (1980). *Mindstorms*. New York: Basic Books.

Roy, S.D. (1982). Author! Author! *Journal of Reading, 25*, 381.

Rubin, A.D. (1980). Making stories, making sense. *Language Arts*, 285-298.

Rubin, A.D. (1982). The computer confronts language arts: Cans and shoulds for education. In A.C. Wilkinson (Ed.), *Classroom computers and cognitive science*. New York: Academic Press, pp. 201-217.

Rubin, A.D., & Hansen, J. (in press). Reading and writing: How are the first two "R's" related? In J. Orasanu (Ed.), *A decade of reading research: Implications for practice*. Hillsdale, NJ: Erlbaum.

Rubin, A. & Bruce, B. (in press). Learning With QUILL: Lessons for Software Designers, Teachers and Students. In T. Raphael and R. Reynolds (Eds.), *Contexts of School-Based Literacy*. New York: Random House.

Scardamalia, M. (1981). How children cope with the cognitive demands of writing. In C.H. Frederiksen, M.F. Whiteman, & J.F. Dominic (Eds.), *Writing: The nature, development and teaching of written communication*. Hillsdale, NJ: Erlbaum, pp. 81-104.

Starr, K., & Bruce, B.C. (1983). Reading comprehension: More emphasis needed. *Curriculum Update*, March.

Tierney, R. & Pearson, P.D. (1983). Toward a composing model of reading. Language Arts, 60(5), 568-580.

Zacchei, D. 91982). The adventures and exploits of the dynamic Story Maker and Textman. *Classroom Computer News, 2*, 28-30, 76, 77.

THE NEUROPSYCHOLOGY OF READING ABILITY AND DISABILITY:
PIECES OF THE PUZZLE

Raymond L. Ownby

INTRODUCTION

Although reading is ultimately a process which depends on the same neural substrates as all other human behavior (Schwartz, 1978), its complexity makes it particularly difficult to explain in neurological terms. The underlying neuro-anatomy of simple sensory and motor functions can be specified with a fair degree of certainty, but reading depends on myriad sensory, motor, and high-level cognitive functions which involve many parts of the brain. Reading is widely studied as a psycholinguistic process, but the precise relations between language and reading abilities have not been convincingly demonstrated beyond showing correlations among various types of poor performance on various reading and language measures (Pirrozollo, Campanella, Christensen, & Lawson-Kerr, 1981). Further, anatomical correlates of high-level linguistic processes have not been determined (Blumstein, 1981) except for differentiation of the broad

Advances in Reading/Language Research, Volume 3, pages 119-149.
Copyright © 1985 by JAI Press Inc.
All rights of reproduction in any form reserved.
ISBN: 0-89232-389-2

categories of expressive and receptive language abilities. Even so widely accepted a tenet as dominant hemisphere localization for language processes is challenged, or at least modified, by evidence of the role of the nondominant hemisphere in language (Hecaen & Albert, 1978, pp. 67–74).

Still another problem in discussing the neuropsychological basis of reading is the tentative way in which data from adults, the source of most information about localization of function in the brain, must be generalized to children. This is an especially important consideration in light of evidence that the neurological organization of children's brains may differ from that of adults (Kolb & Wishaw, 1980, pp. 389–409). While it can be cogently argued that adult neuropsychological data can contribute to understanding child neuropsychology (Denckla, 1979), this limitation in the applicability of adult data to children's disorders cannot be lightly dismissed. This discussion has thus been subtitled "Pieces of the Puzzle" because of these problems, which are responsible for the fragmentary nature of our understanding of dyslexia. At this time research evidence is suggestive but certainly not conclusive about the neurological structures involved in normal reading or about what may go awry with neural structures or processes in dyslexia. Neuropsychological discussion of dyslexia must therefore focus primarily on understanding the phenomenon of developmental dyslexia from the point of view of models developed in neuropsychological study of cognitive processes. This approach is certainly not the same as trying to specify one-to-one relations between behavior and brain structures. Rather it is an attempt to understand normal and disordered cognitive processes from the point of view of what can be demonstrated about such processes in known neurological disease.

Given the above-noted problems, the relevant literature points to possible conclusions about what, from the neuropsychological perspective, results in skilled reading and dyslexia. The plan of this chapter will be to set forth basic concepts, discuss several models with which to investigate dyslexia, and review neuropsychological literature pertinent to understanding reading ability and disability. Before turning to research, however, definitions to be used in the discussion and a brief introduction to the anatomy of the brain will be provided so that the reader with determination but little previous training may better understand what follows.

DEFINITIONS

For the purpose of this discussion, reading will be examined as a complex psycholinguistic function differing from most other human language functions in its dependence on the ability to associate patterns of visual symbols with meanings. The general set of skills required in associating visual symbols with meanings includes the ability to segment phonetic strings into their underlying phonemic constituents and to associate phonemes with graphemes. Beyond these elementary abilities, it is likely that reading requires a minimum of competence in general linguistic and cognitive abilities as well as basic levels of attentional, motivational, and control abilities. More recent cognitive models, it should be noted, give increasing emphasis to the effect of higher level cues and top-down effects in understanding reading (cf. Daneman, Carpenter, & Just, 1982; Meyer, 1983).

The problems inherent in defining terms such as "reading disability" or "dyslexia" are extensively discussed elsewhere (Rutter, 1978; Vellutino, 1979). Briefly, they include the fact that dyslexia is primarily a diagnosis by exclusion. Few positive indications of its presence can be relied on; the clinician must infer its presence when a child demonstrates abnormally low reading achievement in the absence of other explanations. In this article the now standard practice of defining reading problems through demonstrating a discrepancy between a child's performances on measures of general intellectual ability and on measures of academic achievement will be followed. Consistent with the neuropsychological literature, the term *dyslexia* will be used rather than the expression "reading disability," which is often used by educators. This usage is not meant to imply that all reading problems result from neuropsychological deficits.

An additional discrimination must also be made between acquired and developmental dyslexia. The first is found most commonly among adults who have suffered brain insult while the second denotes difficulties in reading most commonly found in children and diagnosed through the discrepancy procedure already mentioned. When used without additional qualification, the term dyslexia will be used here to refer to developmental dyslexia.

BRAIN ANATOMY

Brain anatomists use various terms to indicate the directional relationships among parts of the brain. The terms *anterior* and *posterior* will be used here to refer to directions corresponding roughly to toward the front and toward the back of the head, respectively. The terms *superior* and *inferior* will be used to refer to directions corresponding to toward the top of the head and toward the rest of the body, respectively.

The human brain consists of a large number of subunits which are to varying degrees anatomically and functionally discrete (Kolb & Whishaw, 1980. pp. 3–30; Walsh, 1978, pp. 27–58). In addition to the very large cerebral cortex, a number of structures underlie the cortical mantle, many of which should be considered in discussion of cognitive function (see Figure 1). Among these structures are the *limbic system* and in particular, one of its components, the *hippocampus*; the *reticular activating system* (RAS); and the *thalamus*. These structures all play key roles in cognition by mediating learning, attention, and motivation.

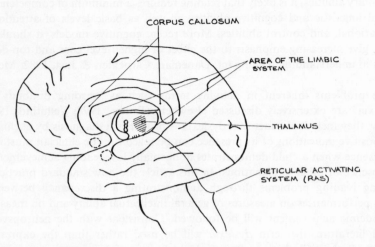

Figure 1.   Medial section of the cerebral hemisphere showing the medial portion of the right hemisphere and brainstem.
(Material drawn from Hecaen & Albert, 1978; Lezak, 1983; Walsh, 1978.)

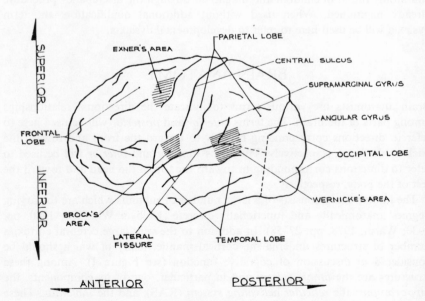

Figure 2.   Lateral view of the left cerebral hemisphere.
(Drawn from Hecaen & Albert, 1978; Lezak, 1983; Walsh, 1978.)

The cerebral cortex is itself divided on the grossest level into two hemispheres which are connected by a large structure consisting of nerve fibers, the *corpus callosum*, through which information from one hemisphere is conveyed to the other. The cerebral cortex is further divided into four major lobes: frontal, temporal, occipital, and parietal. The lobes are still further divided into the *gyri* or convolutions on the cortical surface and the *sulci* or fissures which separate the gyri. Portions of each of the lobes subserve specific sensory and motor abilities in areas of primary and secondary cortex. Adjacent to primary cortexes are secondary association areas which in turn adjoin tertiary association areas (Luria, 1973a), each of which involves higher levels of integration of function.

Temporal Lobe. Primary auditory reception cortex lies on the interior and superior portions of the temporal cortex extending into the large *lateral fissure* (Figure 2). Temporal cortex also mediates some linguistic functions and may play a role in learning and emotional behavior. *Wernicke's area*, receiving input from sensory and association areas, mediates important receptive language functions. Lesions in this area may result in a type of aphasia in which receptive language capacity is severely impaired (Blumstein, 1981).

Frontal Lobe. The frontal lobe is believed to be important in planning and controlling behavior. The large gyrus lying just anterior to the *central sulcus* contains primary motor cortex controlling voluntary muscles. *Broca's area* is involved in motor speech activity; damage to this area results in a type of aphasia in which the person may understand language in an unimpaired fashion but manifests difficulty in expressing himself or herself through speech. *Exner's area*, lying superior to Broca's area and anterior to the primary motor cortex, is believed to regulate complex motor activities required for writing. Damage to this area produces various sorts of writing difficulties (Hecaen & Albert, 1978, pp. 61–67).

Occipital Lobe. The occipital lobe contains primary visual cortex as well as secondary visual association cortex. Lesions in these areas produce visual disturbances which may range from the inability to see in portions of the visual field, to difficulties in seeing particular types of visual stimuli, to total blindness (Walsh, 1978, pp. 233–245).

Parietal Lobe. The parietal lobe contains primary kinesthetic (sense of movement in the body) cortex directly adjacent to primary motor cortex but somewhat posterior to it. Located at the point at which the other lobes meet, it is implicated in the integration of information from the modalities subserved by other areas.

Several other brain structures should be mentioned as possible neural structures involved in reading. The *supramarginal* and *angular gyri*, lying near the junction of the parietal, occipital, and temporal lobes, are believed to be important in the integration of various types of sensory data arriving from primary and secondary areas. Damage to these areas of the dominant hemispheres may produce complex disturbances in finger recognition, right–left orientation, mathematical calculation, and writing skills, a group of difficulties sometimes referred to as *Gerstmann's syndrome* (Walsh, 1978, pp. 220–222). This syndrome of dysfunction in adult brain-damaged patients has received considerable attention, perhaps in part because of its similarity to some of the deficits observed among at least some dyslexics. While controversy exists as to the very existence of the syndrome, it is well established that lesions in these areas in adults produce disturbances in high-level integration of various types of information.

NEUROSCIENCE RESEARCH ON DYSLEXIA: PRELIMINARY CONSIDERATIONS

Doehring (1978) and Applebee (1971) have discussed several of the problems in researching dyslexia, noting that at times the underlying models of the etiology and behavioral effects of dyslexia are not explicitly considered, with resulting confusion. In this context, the distinction between component and process models of dyslexia (Guthrie, 1973) is particularly important. Component models specify that the problem in dyslexia is a defective component, while system or process models specify that the problem is a defect in how the components function.

Much of the neuropsychological research on dyslexia has focused on attempts to isolate a single defective component or process in dyslexia, implicitly accepting the hypothesis that dyslexia is a homogeneous entity stemming from a single cause. While this hypothesis could in fact be correct, the failure to appreciate the implications of this approach has led various researchers each to postulate different defective components or processes in dyslexia, ranging from control of eye movements (Pavlidis, 1981), auditory perception (Johnson, 1977), language difficulties (Wiig & Semel, 1979), and motivational and learning characteristics (Torgeson, 1977), to other equally diverse candidates for the single defective component.

Research guided by single defective component theories of dyslexia is clearly inadequate if the extensive literature on dyslexia is considered since the literature shows the presence of multiple cognitive deficits among dyslexic children. This approach does not demonstrate the relationship of the observed deficit to dyslexia, although many researchers are regrettably apt to neglect the distinction between showing a relationship between two variables and showing that the relation is causal. It is likely that many of the observed deficits among dyslexic children are peripheral, secondary, or simply unrelated to reading. Without a convincing demonstration of the relationship of the deficit to observed reading performance, researchers will continue to explore unsystematically the many ways in which dyslexic children differ from their normally achieving classmates. While this information may be important in its own right, the continuing arguments among proponents of single defective component theories of dyslexia do little to advance understanding of this extremely complex disorder.

Single defective component theories also usually imply a linear stage model of reading in which the defective component interferes with the bottom-up mode of operation of other, presumably correctly functioning, components. An alternative approach is to consider reading as dependent on multiple simultaneously occurring processes. These processes would include at least perceptual, linguistic, attentional, and control processes, aspects of which have been shown to be deficient in some groups of dyslexic children. This model has the important advantage of being consistent with many current views of both information processing and brain function (cf. Daneman et al., 1982; Kinsbourne, 1982; Rumelhart, 1977).

While it would be tempting to organize the literature in terms of studies attempting to assess the presence and relative order of specific processes, research studies in this area don't easily lend themselves to this approach. Most of the studies use one or a cluster of measures that could test for whether at least one of the processes is malfunctioning, but (1) seldom assess whether other processes are also involved; (2) sometimes attribute findings to one kind of process, while, if other measures had been included, the results might as easily have been attributed to a different process; (3) may not have been able to separate out higher level effects of general cognitive or linguistic abilities on estimates of the more specific perceptual processes the studies were intended to examine; and (4) often use a necessarily indirect chain of evidence linking behavioral measures to neural processes. The full linear stage model, while latent in most studies, is never fully operationalized in any one study. This is not so much an indictment of the researchers as a reflection of the complexity of the phenomenon studied.

For these reasons, though, it appears best to organize the literature in broad topical clusters. The reader should recognize that the linear model is often implicitly assumed and should keep in mind the difficulties of using any one study to determine which structure or process is the cause of dyslexia. The notion of simultaneous parallel processing in reading is relatively untested and implies a considerably more complex research strategy than has traditionally been employed. Theoretical parsimony dictates that a simple model be preferred to a complex one if the simple model is consistent with and adequately explains observations. The strategy used in this review will be to survey relevant findings, to assess the degree of support for the linear model, and to discard it in favor of a more complex parallel processing model only if the simpler model is found unsatisfying.

RESEARCH ON CHARACTERISTICS OF DYSLEXIA

Cerebral Dominance

Since Orton's (1928) attribution of dyslexia to poorly developed cerebral dominance, researchers have investigated the ways in which patterns of cerebral dominance may affect the development of reading skills. *Cerebral dominance* refers to the observation that, with development, one of the cerebral hemispheres tends to acquire a greater motor and, in some respects, greater cognitive efficiency than the other. In most people the left hemisphere develops dominance. Cerebral dominance research has progressed from studies based on the simplistic notion that in dyslexia cerebral dominance is delayed or absent to more sophisticated research emphasizing "cognitive strategy preference" (Caplan & Kinsbourne, 1981) or the possibility of "cerebral inattention" in dyslexia (Hynd & Obrzut, 1981a). The central trend in this area of research is to move from reliance on rather broad distinctions in the cognitive abilities presumed to underlie reading to more complex analyses recognizing subtle distinctions in abilities.

Much early lateralization research focused on putative differences between dyslexics and normals in prevalence of mixed dominance for hand, eye, and foot in the two groups. These differences were presumed to reflect incompletely established cerebral dominance. Subsequent research has largely discredited both the ideas that mixed motor dominance bears a significant relation to reading skills and that motor ability testing is an effective means of determining cerebral dominance (Rourke, 1978).

In current research, cerebral dominance is most often assessed through determination of lateral advantages in bilateral simultaneous stimulus presentations. In these procedures, some kind of information is presented to both sides of the body and the extent to which one side shows a performance advantage is assessed. The most frequently used task has been dichotic listening, in which verbal information is simultaneously presented to both ears. Since the pathways which transmit information from the ears to the cerebral cortex cross so that the right ear is primarily involved with the left hemisphere, a right ear advantage is believed to indicate left hemisphere dominance (Kimura, 1967). Researchers have also used visual and tactile stimuli in procedures to determine dominance (see Rourke, 1978, and Satz, 1976, for reviews of this topic).

Researchers have demonstrated some evidence suggesting atypical patterns of lateralization of verbal and visuospatial function in dyslexics (Bakker, Teunissen, & Bosch, 1976; Dalby & Gibson, 1981; Hynd & Obrzut, 1981a, 1981b; Leong, 1976; Witelson, 1976a, 1977; Yeni-Komshian, Isenberg, & Goldberg, 1975). Several of these studies have shown that although some abilities are lateralized in dyslexics as in normals, others may be abnormally (or at least atypically) represented bilaterally. This finding has led to speculation that bilateral representation of some abilities may create interference when the abilities are used (Dalby & Gibson, 1981, Witelson, 1976a). This explanation is in agreement with Kinsbourne's (1982) analysis of the significance of spatial separation of functions in the brain, both within and between the two hemispheres. Kinsbourne suggests that functions which are spatially separated in the brain may be more functionally independent, allowing several cognitive processes to proceed simultaneously until their results are ready to be integrated. This argument is especially cogent if reading is regarded as a process requiring simultaneous utilization of both analytic-verbal and spatial-relational processing (Patterson, 1981). However, the finding of bilateral representation of some abilities in both normal and dyslexic children weakens this argument (Hynd, Obrzut, & Obrzut, 1981).

Another analysis of the lateralization literature suggests that young readers may effectively employ spatial-wholistic strategies in early reading skill acquisition but fail to change to more appropriate analytic strategies in later stages of skill acquisition (Bakker et al., 1976). Sex differences have been demonstrated in the acquisition of lateralization (Witelson, 1976b), with boys becoming more strongly lateralized at earlier ages than girls. Bakker et al. (1976) suggest that because of this earlier lateralization, boys "may run the risk of getting stuck in early reading strategies generated by the right hemisphere" (p. 218).

Still another approach to understanding lateralization of function in dyslexia is presented by Hynd and colleagues (Hynd & Obrzut, 1981a, 1981b; Hynd et al., 1981). One study (Hynd et al., 1981) showed that asymmetric lateralization patterns in normal and learning-disabled (LD) children were unrelated to cognitive abilities measured by the Wechsler Intelligence Scale for Children— Revised (WISC-R) or academic achievement measures. These authors conclude that clinicians should regard asymmetries of this sort as symptomatic of cognitive differences in dyslexics rather than as "pathogenic" (p. 978), the cause of those difficulties. In related articles, Hynd and Obrzut (1981a,b) note that LD and normal children differ in their ability to focus attention on aspects of tasks which are relevant to task solution. These authors conclude that the lateralization issue of greatest importance may be the dominant hemisphere's ability to suppress irrelevant information transmitted from the nondominant hemisphere.

Thus three general hypotheses have been advanced to account for demonstrated atypical lateralization patterns in dyslexics. The first, that bilateral representation of some abilities may produce interference in learning to read, suggests that the pattern of organization of function in the brain may be at fault in failing to learn to read. The second, that varying patterns of development may result in utilization of faulty strategies in reading, is consistent with the point of view that dyslexia represents not a deficit but a maturational lag (Satz, 1976). The third, that observed lateralization differences may be due to a failure to suppress irrelevant information by the dominant hemisphere, is new and without as extensive a research base as the other hypotheses. At this time it would be premature to make judgments about the merits of each of these positions. However, it is unlikely that all reading failure is caused by faulty development of the organization of cerebral dominance, as will be seen from findings reviewed below.

Language Function in Dyslexia

Several authors have discussed language dysfunction in dyslexia, noting the characteristic similarities between children with developmental dyslexia and adults with acquired aphasia. As Denckla, Rudel, and Broman state, "the linguistic errors of the dyslexic group resemble those of residually dysphasic, left-hemisphere-damaged adults" (1981, p. 127).

Others have examined the language abilities of dyxlexics and found that they differ from those of normals in areas as various as rapid naming of common objects or dysnomia, (Denckla & Rudel, 1974; Denckla, Rudel, & Broman, 1981; Rudel, Denckla, & Broman, 1981; Rutherford, 1977; Wiig, Semel, & Nystrom, 1981), ability to segment words into their constituent phonemes (Leonard, 1982; Shankweiler & Liberman, 1976; Tallal, 1976, 1980; Tallal & Piercy, 1973, 1974, 1975), general language abilities, especially verbal encoding (Vellutino, 1978, 1979; Vellutino, Steger, Harding, & Phillips, 1975), use of syntactic structures (Semel & Wiig, 1975; Wiig, Semel, & Crouse, 1973; Vogel, 1974), use of certain pronominal constructions (Fayne, 1981), and the ability to use effectively the pragmatic aspects of language (Olswang, Kriegsmann, & Mastergeorge, 1982; Rees & Shulman, 1978). Pirrozollo et al. (1981) list 11 neurolinguistic variables on which dyslexics have shown performance inferior to normals.

As noted above with respect to demonstrations of ability deficits in dyslexics, these linguistic deficits among dyslexics are once again suggestive but do not usually demonstrate whether, and if so in what way, linguistic deficits affect reading. While the connection is often assumed, some authors (e.g., Shankweiler & Liberman, 1976) have attempted to make it explicit. Shankweiler and Liberman suggest that the deficits in phonemic discrimination observed in dyslexic children may be responsible for their reading problems by making it difficult for them to learn to read phonetically. However, as Pirrozollo and his colleagues note, "the relationship between language and reading is an intimate, complex, and obscure one" (1981, p. 801).

Particularly in the area of difficulties in phonemic perception, authors have suggested mechanisms by which the difficulty is thought to interfere with reading. The difficulty in perception of phonemic segments of words is thought to interfere with recoding printed words into internal speech. This argument's validity is strengthened by demonstrations that dyslexic and LD children can often learn to associate visual symbols directly with words as well as average readers (Nishio, 1981; Rozin, Poritsky, & Sotsky, 1971; Zaidel & Peters, 1981) and arguments that speech recoding is a necessary phase of reading. The argument is less cogent, however, in light of Rudel, Denckla, and Spalten's (1976) demonstration that dyslexics perform worse than average readers in learning Morse code and Braille letter names. On one hand, the fact that some dyslexics can acquire symbol-meaning associations as well as normal readers suggests that the dysfunctional process may be in speech recoding. On the other hand, contradictory evidence such as that provided by Rudel, Denckla, and Spalten (1976) suggests that other dysfunctions may be present. The contradictory nature of these findings is typical of many studies in the area. It is very difficult to isolate from a small group of studies what exactly is wrong with the cognitive abilities of dyslexic children.

Another often demonstrated deficit in the linguistic abilities of dyslexics is their impaired understanding of the phonemic structure of language (the way that the smallest units of meaningfully different sounds are organized into words). These abilities may be assessed by determining whether children can discriminate between various sounds presented to them. It has been shown repeatedly that normal children can make certain discriminations which dyslexics cannot. Numerous researchers have shown this difficulty, and its relation to the development of reading skills is logically compelling. Paula Tallal and colleagues (1976, 1980, Tallal & Piercy, 1973, 1974, 1975; Tallal, Stark, Kallman, & Mellits, 1981) have extensively studied this problem in dyslexic and language-impaired children and conclude that the underlying deficit is in the perception of rapidly changing sequences of sound. Tallal has shown that the ability of dyslexic children to discriminate among phonemes is affected by the length of the stimulus presented, the interstimulus interval, and the phonetic characteristics of the stimulus.

Other authors have suggested that mechanisms other than purely perceptual may operate in this instance. Atchison and Canter (1979) show that word familiarity may influence LD children's phonemic discrimination abilities; for example, Godfrey, Syrdal-Lasky, Millay, and Knox (1981) note that one explanation for their results showing difficulties in phonemic discrimination in dyslexic children might be that the children did not understand the concept of "phoneme," although the researchers explained it in simple terms. Leonard (1982) states that difficulty in discriminating rapidly changing acoustic stimuli is not an adequate explanation of the phonemic skill deficiencies of his sample of dyslexics and suggests that their difficulties should be attributed to a more general perceptual or linguistic deficit.

Savin and Bever (1970) argued that "phonemes are abstract" (p. 301) and that dyslexics' difficulties with phonemic discrimination tasks might be attributed to conceptual rather than perceptual mechanisms. Morais, Cary, Alegria, and Bertelson (1979) demonstrated in a group of illiterate adults that phonemic awareness does not arise spontaneously, a finding which argues against the notion of an innate perceptual mechanism for this skill. It is possible, then, that difficulties in phonemic segmentation skills may be due to deficits in high-level cognitive skills, which are normally developed in part through experience with language, rather than to deficits in low-level perceptual mechanisms.

At least two alternatives are present in explanations of deficits in phonemic discrimination. The first is that phonemic segmentation skill depends on a perceptual mechanism possibly localized in the cerebral cortex near other language areas (Ojemann & Mateer, 1979) and dependent on underlying phonological representations of words. It is unlikely, however, that such a complex cognitive skill is dependent on a small and easily delimited area of cortex. A second hypothesis is that phonemic segmentation skill deficits in dyslexics reflect other, more general linguistic or cognitive problems, possibly in general linguistic awareness, as suggested by Vellutino (1979). At present no definitive experiment has been performed to discriminate among these possibilities, although research in this area would be helpful in elucidating what is responsible for observed phonemic deficits among dyslexics.

Besides poor phonemic segmentation skills, another often demonstrated variable by which dyslexic and normal reader groups may be differentiated is word-finding skill, or when referring to a deficiency in this skill, dysnomia. Groups of average and disabled readers may be distinguished on this variable when the task is naming pictures of common objects, colors, and shapes (Denckla & Rudel, 1974; Wiig et al., 1982). Groups may also be distinguished even when children are trained in order to eliminate the effects of exprience with the words used in naming tasks (Hogaboam & Perfetti, 1978).

The mechanism responsible for dysnomia is not known. As with the deficit in phonemic segmentation skills, it could result from lesions to various sites in the brain (Goodglass, 1980), although Ojemann and Mateer (1979) state that they have discovered sites which may localize this function to areas adjacent to other language areas on the dominant temporal lobe. Goodglass states that lesions to the temporoparietal junction are the most frequent cause of dysnomia, which is one of the most common symptoms of aphasia in adults (Davis, 1983). Luria (1973b) proposes three types of dysnomia, categorized in terms of whether the underlying representations of the sound, meaning, or articulatory expression of the word is disrupted in the disorder.

Goodglass (1980) notes that in aphasic adults, dysnomia may be limited to certain linguistic classes of words or even to specific semantic categories. He suggests a three-stage model to explain the word-finding process, disruptions at any stage of which may cause particular sorts of dysnomic disturbances. The three stages of this model are (1) recognition of the stimulus and arousal of its semantic representation, (2) retrieval of the phonological representation of the word, and (3) activation of the articulatory act patterned on the phonological representation (1980, p. 648).

Dysnomias in adults are not uniform in character but may take the form of failure to respond to queries, response with circumlocution (e.g., "thing that holds the door on" instead of "hinge"), or response with paraphasias. Paraphasias are hallmarks of dysphasic expression and may range from mild disturbances in the phonetic construction of words (e.g., "night" for "might") to insertion or displacement of the phonemes in the words uttered, to production of totally new words. Goodglass suggests that relatively minor alterations of pronunciation may be due to a distortion of the articulatory act (in a person with an intact phonological representation) due to damage to the anterior speech zone; some persons may thus have difficulty only with the last of the three stages of the model. More major speech disturbances suggest disruptions of the phonological or semantic representations of words and occur with lesions in temporoparietal cortex, becoming progressively worse as the lesion site is more posterior.

Naming disturbances have been demonstrated among dyslexic children by several investigators. The most common method of assessment of this characteristic is to observe the child's performance at naming pictures of common objects or colors, to record the length of time required to complete the task, and to note errors. Wiig and Semel's (1979) procedure provides for training the child to name arrays of four simple shapes, four colors, and four colored shapes, and then testing on larger arrays of these forms.

The precise nature of the underlying deficit in dysnomia in dyslexics is not clear. If the type of naming error in dyslexic dysnomia is examined, the frequent minor misarticulations and paraphasias reported (Denckla et al., 1981; Rudel et al., 1981) suggest that the problem may lie in the retrieval of the sensorimotor pattern or its execution, stage 3 of Goodglass's model. The relevance of this type of deficit to learning to read is not easily apprehended, except perhaps in the case of oral reading. Dyslexic children's dysnomia and resulting difficulty in the mechanics of speech present an intriguing possibility: the emphasis on oral reading in early reading instruction may handicap dysnomic children by requiring a difficult performance from them even though they might be able to learn to read efficiently silently if reading aloud were not required of them. Clinical experience suggests that some children may function better in early intermediate than in primary grades (Denckla, 1979); oral reading receives less instructional emphasis in the intermediate grades than reading for meaning.

Related findings from cognitive psychology support to some extent the idea that processes at the phonological level are involved in dysnomia. For example, Hogaboam and Perfetti (1978) showed that even when vocalization latencies were improved in poor readers by providing experience with words to be named, they still performed at lower levels than good readers on naming tasks. This result shows that naming difficulties are probably not due solely to lack of familiarity with words to be named. Further, Perfetti, Finger, and Hogaboam (1978) studied vocalization latencies in less skilled readers under varying circumstances. They conclude that differences between groups were attributable not to word retrieval difficulties but to "processes of verbal coding, including processes operating on subword units" (p. 739).

These results indicate a similarity to previously discussed phonemic segmentation skill deficits in dyslexics. If there were a deficit in the underlying phonological representations of words in dyslexics, it would be expected to produce both of the performance differences observed most reliably between dyslexics and normals. Both poor phonemic segmentation skills and dysnomia could depend on the presence of an internalized phonological representation of the word to be read. Both of these processes might depend on a small area of cerebral cortex in the dominant hemisphere's temporoparietal area, as both Jorm (1979) and Patel (1977) have argued. It is unlikely, however, that such cognitively complex skills depend on a small area of cortex.

Two cautions should be noted before ascribing dyslexia to dysfunction in any single area of the brain. First, linguistic deficits which may depend on non-dominant hemisphere language functions, such as appreciation of context in arriving at meanings, and nonliteral use of language have been described in dyslexic children (Dennis, 1980). Thus the linguistic deficits in dyslexic children have been shown to include abilities which involve both hemispheres—arguing against a single locale for a defective component. This difficulty is not insurmountable, though, since from a theoretical standpoint it could be argued that the dominant hemisphere association area is the "final assembly point" for meanings.

A second caution results from finding language deficits in nondyslexic LD children (Rudel et al., 1981). Therefore even though language deficits are often associated with dyslexia, the relation may not be invariant and it becomes apparent that the coexistence of two deficits may not mean they are directly related. It should be recalled that demonstration of correlation is not demonstration of causation no matter how compelling are the theoretical reasons for making a causal inference. While a linguistic deficit theory of the etiology of dyslexia is appealing, given the rationale that "reading is language written down" and the fact that reading and expressive written language are frequently affected in adult acquired language disorders (Davis, 1983), there has been insufficient attention paid to high-level cognitive and linguistic processes in this research. The exact relations between language and reading remain unclear pending further investigation.

DIFFERENCES BETWEEN
DYSLEXIC AND AVERAGE READERS

This section briefly reviews research on the neuropsychological deficits found in dyslexics and discusses possible relations among ability patterns and dyslexia. A more complete review of the neuropsychological literature on dyslexia, though not organized in terms of the questions examined here, is available in Benton and Pearl (1978).

One problem should be considered when interpreting these findings. In spite of widespread acknowledgments of the presence and significance of attentional difficulties among dyslexics (Bremer & Stern, 1976; Denckla, 1979; Denckla & Heilman, 1979; Ownby, 1983; Rosenthal & Allan, 1978; Schierberl, 1979), few authors have controlled for this problem in research. Thus, skill deficits in the heterogeneous groups of dyslexics usually studied, although attributed to deficits in perceptual or other cognitive processes, may in fact reflect attentional process difficulties. Future researchers should attempt to control for this variable.

Groups of readers described as dyslexic, learning-disabled, or less skilled readers have been shown to differ from average readers on many variables:

a. Control of eye movements (Pavlidis, 1981)
b. Use of syntactic cues in reading (Allington & Fleming, 1978)
c. Use of semantic cues in reading (Allington & Fleming, 1978)
d. Attending to multiple cue systems in reading (Allington & Fleming, 1978; Fay, Trupin, & Townes, 1981)
e. Field articulation (Cotugno, 1981)
f. Developing effective problem solving strategies (Stone, 1981)
g. Associating almost any class of stimulus with another (Rudel & Denckla, 1976; Rudel et al., 1976; Vellutino et al., 1975)
h. Memory and comprehension in tasks requiring spontaneous verbal elaboration and speed (Bauserman & Obrzut, 1981; Doctorow, Wittrock, & Marks, 1978; Kail & Marshall, 1978)
i. Motivational and learning characteristics (Torgeson, 1977)

The significance of these findings is twofold. First, they demonstrate that many high-level cognitive abilities may function at suboptimal levels among dyslexics— evidence that the single defective component approach to research is probably inadequate. Second, their diverse nature can be seen as resulting from still higher level processes which control the operation of perceptual (including eye movements, which may be guided by comprehension processes), linguistic, memorial, and attentional processes. It may be that dyslexic and average readers can be differentiated on almost any task requiring high-level cognitive skills.

Selz and Reitan (1979) have shown that the performances of learning-disabled children on a standard battery of neuropsychological tests are in some ways similar to those of brain-damaged children and that a scoring system assigning weights to various levels and types of performance can discriminate LD children from normals and those with known brain damage at good levels of accuracy. The LD children's performances on the battery of tests shows evidence of lower than average levels of performance, wider than average discrepancies in abilities presumably dependent on right or left hemisphere cortex, and pathognomic signs often indicating the presence of brain dysfunction. Brain-damaged adults and children have been shown to perform worse than non-brain-damaged controls on various sensory, motor, and cognitive tasks (Boll, 1972, 1974; Boll & Reitan, 1972; Boll, Berent, & Richards, 1977; Reitan, 1959, 1974). In addition, Rourke and his associates have demonstrated relations between patterns of scores on several of these measures and academic skills (Rourke, 1975, 1978, 1981; Rourke & Finaylson, 1978; Rourke, Young, & Flewelling, 1971).

These results show (1) that LD children may be discriminated from non-LD children with fair accuracy on tasks known to discriminate between brain-damaged and non-brain-damaged children and adults, and (2) that these performances bear significant relations to academic skills. Beyond quantitative measurement, performances of LD children on many of these measures are qualitatively similar to those of brain-damaged children. Results of this sort suggest the presence of brain dysfunction in LD children generally and by implication among the dyslexics who comprise most of the samples of LD children. It should be remembered here, however, that many cases of reading difficulty are the result of problems other than brain dysfunction, such as poor match of instructional technique to learner.

The significance of these studies lies in the suggestion that the brains of dyslexics, as assessed through neuropsychological tests, are dysfunctional in ways reminiscent of children with known brain damage. These studies also show that the ability deficits associated with dyslexia range across almost every type of high-level cognitive task, especially those which require simultaneous and well-controlled integration of information from several sources, such as the Coding subtest of the WISC-R or the Trail Making Test of the Halstead-Reitan Battery (a task which requires simultaneous memory for letter and number order, knowledge of the alphabet, and a timed visual–motor performance) (Boll, 1974; Reitan, 1974; Selz & Reitan, 1979).

Finally, the multiplicity of deficits shown to be associated with dyslexia strongly suggests that dyslexia should be considered as part of a broader set of cognitive ability dysfunctions, only some of which may be directly associated with reading skill. A task for future investigators will be to determine which ability deficits are of necessity associated in what manner with dyslexia.

SUBGROUPS OF LEARNING DISABILITY

A final area of research bearing on the neuropsychology of dyslexia is that which focuses on defining subgroups of learning disability and on determining what ability patterns are associated with reading skills in these subgroups. This approach to research has gained favor recently, in part because of evidence showing that learning-disabled children are probably not a single, homogeneous group. It has also gained increasing momentum recently, although as long ago as 1963 Kinsbourne and Warrington showed that dyslexics could be grouped according to their patterns of errors on a spelling test. During the last several years, factor analysis (Doehring & Hoshko, 1977; Doehring, Trites, Patel, & Fiedorowicz, 1981) and cluster analysis (Lyon & Watson, 1981; Lyon, Watson, Reitta, & Porch, 1981; Watson, Goldgar, & Fredd, 1982) have been used to find patterns in the cognitive abilities of LD children in order to provide empirical bases for grouping them. These investigators' findings supplement proposed groupings developed by other researchers (Boder, 1971, 1973; Denckla, 1979; Mattis, 1978; Mattis, French, & Rapin, 1975).

Mattis (1978, pp. 46–47) explains the rationale for subgroup analysis of test scores in understanding dyslexia. Reading is a complex process requiring integration of numerous subprocesses, failure in any one of which may impair reading skills. The types of subprocess failures are then expected to be evident in performance on test batteries which include measures of abilities thought to be related to reading, including language, auditory skills, and visual skills. It may be seen that this approach to understanding the deficits present among dyslexics is more nearly consistent with a multiple simultaneous process approach to understanding the disorder than with the single defective component approach. Recognition of patterns of deficits may assist, for example, in identifying which defective processes are related to reading performance and ultimately in determining which instructional strategies may be optimal in particular cases.

Boder (1971, 1973) proposes three subtypes of dyslexia: (1) dysphonetic, (2) dyseidetic, and (3) mixed. Dysphonetic dyslexics display difficulties in auditory comprehension of words and their subunits whereas dyseidetic dyslexics show difficulty in visual recognition of letter patterns composing words. Mixed dyslexics show characteristics of both groups. Boder and Jarrico (1982) published an inventory which helps classify children in these groups.

Another categorization of dyslexia has been proposed by Mattis (1978; Mattis et al., 1975), who suggests that there are three types of dyslexics: (1) a general language disorder group, (2) an articulatory-graphomotor group, and (3) a visual perception group. After completion of a replication study, Mattis added two groups, a mixed type and a group which shows deficits in temporal sequencing. Denckla (1979) suggests categories which are similar to Mattis's. Both Mattis and Denckla include groups of global language difficulties, articulatory-graphomotor difficulties, and sequencing difficulties, although Denckla includes dysphonemic characteristics as a sign among the sequencing group. Denckla states that the most common syndrome is a combination of one form of dyslexia with other forms of dyslexia and hyperactivity.

Doehring and associates (Doehring & Hoshko, 1977; Doehring, Trites, Patel, & Fiedorowicz, 1981), on the basis of results of factor analyses of test scores, have proposed three types of dyslexia, Types O, A, and S. Doehring and co-workers report that their Type O children display close to normal performance on neuropsychological measures and little other evidence of neurological dysfunction. These children's most distinctive feature is their poor oral reading (hence Type O), but difficulties in name retrieval and articulatory and grapho-motor control are also found in this group.

Doehring's Type A (associative) children present difficulty in associating printed and spoken letters, syllables, and words, and scored lowest on the three groups on academic measures. Doehring speculates that this type of disorder might be due to general dysfunction of the dominant hemisphere or a deficit in phonemic perception because these abilities may be dependent on dominant hemisphere cortex. Type S (sequential) children display many signs of neuropsychological deficits as well as difficulty in maintaining information in short-term memory or operating on information of which sequence is a significant part.

Lyon and colleagues (Lyon & Watson, 1981; Lyon et al., 1981) utilized cluster analysis to identify six groups of dyslexics. One group had essentially normal patterns of performance on a battery which included measures of language, memory, sound blending, spatial skills, and fine motor coordination. Two subgroups showed patterns of mixed language and visual perceptual problems varying in degree of severity by group. Two other groups showed patterns of language problems varying in degree of severity by group, and a final group showed primarily visual-motor deficits. Watson et al. (1982) found three subgroups through cluster analysis: (1) a group manifesting general language deficits, (2) a group with visual processing deficits, and (3) a group which showed little deficit on measures included in the test battery.

Several criticisms of subgroup analysis are cogent. First, although the research reviewed above shows that dyslexic children may be differentiated from average readers on many tasks, only a few tasks can be included in any analysis. Those tasks included in multivariate research paradigms logically are believed to bear a relation to reading performance, but the mere demonstration that some dyslexic children perform more poorly than others on subsets of measures leads some to the unjustified conclusion that this performance pattern demonstrates a specific etiology. Such evidence might be adequate to show that some, though not necessarily all, dyslexic children exhibit this deficit, but it cannot show whether other deficits would have been found if other tests had been used, or even whether the deficit caused or was caused by the dyslexia or whether both were caused by some unidentified third factor. Many researchers are careful in their discussions to interpret results cautiously, but the capacity of the credulous or those under the pressure to present a reasoned approach to remediation to jump to inaccurate conclusions should not be ignored. It appears that some investigators have risked interpreting causality in what is, essentially, correlational data. This is a considerable risk in light of the fact that several authors have found subgroups of dyslexics who display little apparent deficit on neuropsychological measures.

Even though particular patterns of ability have been associated with particular patterns of academic skills, the considerable heterogeneity of the groups limits their clinical usefulness. For this reason, Watson et al. (1982) conclude that subgroup models of dyslexia may at least at present be more useful in research efforts in dyslexia than in clinical practice.

Still another difficulty in interpreting these studies is that researchers have varied in test selection and the standards by which they judged the presence or absence of a deficit. For example, Rutherford (1977) argues for the educational significance of a very mild dysnomia whereas several authors reviewed in this section did not even include measures sensitive to this deficit in their analyses, perhaps considering such a mild symptom of linguistic disturbance within the range of normal variation. Finally, because of the difficulty in obtaining subjects, most of these studies have undertandably utilized small numbers of subjects. These samples, often drawn from clinics with a selected population, may not have been truly representative of the population of dyslexics. This possibility restricts the confidence with which these findings may be generalized to other cases.

In spite of these shortcomings, the subgroup studies suggest several hypotheses about ability patterns among dyslexics. Researchers have consistently found evidence of linguistics deficits of many types among groups of dyslexics while at the same time showing that other groups appear linguistically intact but display evidence of deficits in visuospatial abilities. Measures of dysnomia have been used by some to define subgroups. Although temporal sequencing deficit has also been suggested as a defining characteristic of groups, there appears to be little to add to Vellutino's well-reasoned rejection of this concept, which viewed these results as being more parsimoniously explained as basic verbal ability deficits (Vellutino, 1979).

Investigators of subgroups of dyslexics have thus supported others' findings that phonemic segmentation skills, dysnomia, visuospatial skills, and general language skills are important in dyslexia and are useful in defining subgroups. It is apparent when patterns of deficit are examined that one of the major subgroups of deficit, i.e., linguistic, involves skills widely believed to be usually localized in the dominant hemisphere. Another group of deficits, visuospatial, is served by the nondominant hemisphere, especially its posterior portion. Subgroup research interpreted on principles derived from adult lesion research implicates several portions of the cerebral cortex in dyslexia, including language areas in the dominant hemisphere and posterior nondominant hemisphere areas.

THE LINEAR MODEL REVISITED

Having now reviewed some of the neuropsychological literature on dyslexia, it is possible to assess how well the linear stage model fares. First, it is clearly too simple. Linguistic deficits in dyslexia, for example, appear to occur not only in the bottom stages of processing but in higher level stages as well, arguing against a simple explanation which might suggest that a circumscribed deficit in a process such as phonemic discrimination could account for dyslexia. It is possible that higher level linguistic difficulties interact with lower level processes in a complex fashion to affect control processes, once again arguing against a linear, bottom-up model of reading disability. If, as discussed above, the dysnomic problems of dyslexics are in the stage of accessing or executing phonological representations of words subsequent to arriving at their semantic representations, why do these children often show persistent difficulties in silent as well as oral reading? If speech recoding is a disrupted process in dyslexics, why don't they often learn to read (at least initially) primarily by accumulating a large fund of sight words? Answers to these questions will require research aimed at delineating more clearly the relations of observed cognitive and linguistic ability deficits in dyslexics to their reading skills.

Since visual pattern recognition is a skill probably served by nondominant hemisphere structures in adults and, by extension, in children, of what significance is the finding of visuospatial as well as verbal deficits in dyslexics? From a purely localizationist point of view, it might be necessary to postulate dysfunction in both hemispheres to account for dyslexia in children with this pattern of abilities, although lateralization studies suggest that atypical lateralization of functions rather than unilateral dysfunction in an area of cortex may be responsible for the observed patterns of abilities. These arguments would gain force if it were possible to partial out the effects of general pattern recognition or of pattern naming in this study.

The most likely candidate for the single dysfunctional area in dyslexia, if in fact only a single area is involved, is the site of the most elaborate integration of visual and linguistic information at the junction of the temporal, parietal, and occipital cortexes (Jorm, 1979; Patel, 1977). As Masland (1981) indicates, the scant autopsy evidence on dyslexia (two cases) points to abnormal development of language centers in dyslexics; John (1977, p. 203) reports abnormal slow-wave activity in the parietal areas of LD children, a sign of possible dysfunction. This area also mediates other complex integrative activities in which dyslexics are inferior to controls, such as finger localization, the ability to identify shapes by touch, and the ability to recognize numbers written on fingertip.

The strength of the single-location argument is somewhat diminished by related research findings of attentional deficits in dyslexic children because these abilities are probably not mediated by the posterior cortex of either hemisphere but rather by a complex system of frontal cortex and subcortical structures such as the RAS and the limbic system (Ownby, 1983; Schierberl, 1979). Another objection to the single-location hypothesis comes from the observation of similarities between the behavior of animals with lesions of the hippocampus (an element of the limbic system known to play a critical role in learning) and the behavior of LD children (Altman, Brunner, & Bayer, 1973; Rose, 1980). Preliminary results in one study (Ownby, 1984) show that dyslexic children are markedly inferior to normal children on a task which has been shown to be sensitive to hippocampal lesions in adults (Kolb & Whishaw, 1980). This task requires presentation of a series of digits orally and spatial patterns manually on blocks. The pattern contains as many elements as the child's memory span plus one more, and every second time (or third time in older children) the pattern is the same. Normals quickly acquire the repeating pattern even though it is beyond their usual span, whereas dyslexics do not. In fact, some dyslexics show evidence of learned interference on this task, sometimes acquiring incorrect patterns or repeating portions of the nonrepetitive pattern. It is therefore possible that a subcortical system with extensive cortical connections known to be important in learning may be implicated in the search to locate the deficit in dyslexia.

It quickly becomes clear in this sort of speculation that the search for one or even several locations to be made the culprit in dyslexia is likely to be fruitless. Many different sites can plausibly be argued to be important in reading, and it is likely that no single area of cortex subsumes all of the complex processes apparently deficient in dyslexics. Further, in positing locations for the deficits, researchers labor under the continuing burden of generalizing from adult lesion data to child development. As noted at the beginning of this discussion, this generalization can only be tentative. The linear stage model, although useful in the past, probably should now be abandoned in favor of a multiple simultaneous process model. This approach might attempt to describe ability patterns within several domains among dyslexics and ascertain the relations of these abilities to reading skills. The next section briefly reviews research results from this perspective.

MULTIPLE SIMULTANEOUS PROCESS MODEL

Skilled reading requires that the reader simultaneously and interactively integrate visual and linguistic information at multiple levels of complexity within visual, phonological, syntactic, and semantic coding systems. Further, it is likely that the nature of the process varies with the demands of the task, as is shown by Kleiman's (1975) finding that speech recoding is a strategy which may be used even by skilled readers for difficult material, while more direct access to meanings may occur for such readers in speeded or easy reading tasks. Cognitive models such as those proposed by Daneman et al. (1982) or Meyer (1983) are likely to influence the study of reading disability, but the search for sites and processes involved in higher level and top-down processes will require substantially more sophisticated research strategies than those used currently in much neuropsychological investigation of reading. Moreover, neuropsychological research has focused primarily on deficit and dysfunction rather than normal reading and it is in the area of dyslexia rather than skilled reading that its greatest contribution lies.

Having reviewed the research from the perspective of a linear bottom-up model, it is possible now to take another look at these findings within a multiple simultaneous processes framework. Within this model, the findings can be organized according to the cognitive systems involved in dyslexia and the questions which might at this time be addressed by researchers. These systems are chosen because they have a face valid relation to reading and are consistent with the way many neuropsychologists think about cognitive processes (cf. Lezak, 1983).

Perceptual Processes

Speech Perception

Speech perception is often deficient among dyslexics. It is not clear, however, whether this problem results from a basic perceptual mechanism or from more general linguistic skill deficits. Tallal's research (1976, 1980; Tallal & Piercy, 1973, 1974, 1974), showing temporal auditory perception deficits among dyslexics, supports the perceptual hypothesis, but other findings show that dyslexics' linguistic deficits may include a failure to understand the very notion of the phoneme. Since perception of speech sounds is a critical skill in phonics approaches to teaching reading, the differentiation of the source of this observed deficit would be a useful focus of research.

Visual Perception

Dyslexics with apparent visual perceptual deficits have been described. Several subgroup studies have shown that visual perceptual and constructional, e.g., copying geometric designs, difficulties may be a central problem for some dyslexic children. Once again, it is not clear whether the observed deficits are in fact due to perceptual or to constructional processes, since 'visual perception' is typically assessed as the ability to copy geometric designs—a strategy that confounds a number of abilities with visual perception. Difficulties with letter and word confusion may similarly be due to linguistic rather than visuospatial difficulties.

Linguistic Processes

Phonemic Segmentation

Dyslexic children often are unable to segment words into their constituent phonemes, a difficulty which might be due to perceptual difficulties, poor general linguistic development, or lack of specific metalinguistic awarenesses. Spelling difficulties observed among dyslexics suggest difficulty with understanding how various sounds combine in patterns as well. As noted with respect to speech perception, it will be useful to investigate at what level of function these difficulties arise.

Dysnomia

The frequent observation of dysnomia among dyslexics is of interest at least in part because it is a frequent symptom in aphasic disorders (Davis, 1983). However, the significance of this deficit for reading is not clear.

Other Linguistic Deficits

Difficulties with syntactic, semantic, and pragmatic aspects of linguistic function have been observed among dyslexics. These observations may have important implications for understanding dyslexia. Dyslexia might come to be regarded as a symptom of a more general language dysfunction in children, for example.

Attentional Processes

Beyond noting that dyslexic children frequently display attentional difficulties, few researchers have studied these problems. Numerous researchers have investigated the sustaining, alerting, and vigilance aspects of attending among children with learning and behavior problems (for a review, see Rosenthal & Allen, 1978), and Keogh and Margolis (1976a, 1976b) propose a component skills analysis of attention problems among learning-disabled children. Further consideration of the role attentional processes play in dyslexia is warranted because these processes interact with control, linguistic, and perceptual processes in both acquiring and utilizing reading skills.

Control Processes

Some research suggests that the highest level executive functions do not operate optimally among dyslexic children. For example, these children's performances differ most markedly from those of their peers on tasks which require complex organization and direction of memorial, linguistic, and attentional abilities. An exemplar of this sort of task is the Coding subtest of the WISC-R which requires placement of visual symbols in blanks according to a key under timed conditions. This task has been shown to be a fairly sensitive indicator of brain damage among children (Boll, 1974; Reitan, 1974). It has also been shown that control processes may be a significant factor in children's performance on other neuropsychological measures (Ownby & Matthews, 1985). Here again, it might be useful to investigate how perceptual, linguistic, and control processes interact.

Summary

Consideration of these models of the origins of dyslexia suggests first that there is a limited number of possibilities for the nature of the cause of dyslexia and second, that the research favors certain choices over others. For example, the first choicepoint among these options is whether a single cause or multiple causes are responsible for dyslexia. The great variety of processes which have been shown to be deficient among dyslexics argues for a multiple-cause model of the origin of dyslexia.

A second choicepoint within the multiple cause framework is whether the same or different sets of causes are responsible for cases of dyslexia. The varying patterns of abilities among groups of dyslexics suggest that different combinations of deficits may be responsible for dyslexia, so that perhaps someday it may be usual to talk about the "dyslexias" as a group of disorders rather than one "dyslexia."

A third choicepoint within this framework, then, is whether the multiple different causes act independently or interdependently. It is possible, for example, that two deficits such as those in phonemic discrimination ability and in letter shape recognition ability could operate independently to block two major routes to learning to read, resulting in dyslexia. On the other hand, it is possible that two deficits, such as those in phonemic discrimination and in verbal encoding in memorial processes, might operate to impede the acquisition of reading skills by interfering independently at parallel levels with two essential processes while still being interdependent. The deficit in phonemic discrimination, for example, might operate by itself as a necessary but not sufficient cause of dyslexia; the deficit in verbal encoding might operate in a similar way; the two taken together might then interdependently cause dyslexia. It seems likely on logical grounds alone that the effects of the cognitive processes involved in reading depend to a great extent on each other. This hypothesis is further supported by the observation that many cognitive processes involved in reading are interdependent, such as eye movement and comprehension (e.g., see Wanat, 1976). Although it is possible that multiple deficits may function independently of each other in some cases of dyslexia, it seems likely that they are more often interdependent.

Assuming multiple, differing, interdependent causes of dyslexia, a last choice-point is whether the interdependent causes act in a coordinated or interactive fashion. It is possible that interdependent deficits drive each other in a feedback loop—this would be interdependent interactive activity. It is also possible that they do not in fact drive each other in this way, that while distorted input from one system is fed forward to the next, the distorted information is not fed back to the first system. This would be interdependent coordinated activity.

Using the example of phonemic discrimination and verbal encoding deficits, it is possible that they operate interdependently in a coordinated way as suggested above. Alternatively, these two interdependent deficits might drive each other interactively, with the phonemic discrimination system feeding the verbal encoding system inconsistent or inaccurate data about the phonemic characteristics of words to be read while the verbal encoding system might feed back to the phonemic system (dependent on known words for analysis) the same faulty data in a further distorted form. If faulty systems interact in this fashion, the puzzling and frustrating inability of some children to learn to read even at basic levels becomes easier to understand. While it is possible at this choicepoint, as at the previous one, to recognize that some cases of dyslexia may be the result of either pattern of causation, it seems more likely that the multiple causes of dyslexia would operate interactively for the same reasons cited above with respect to whether they act independently or interdependently.

These comments are intended not as a definitive statement but as an initial, admittedly speculative, first approximation of the results of neuropsychological research on reading ability and disability. Some of the choicepoints discussed here have not been directly tested, but the framework may help to stimulate and organize research to examine these issues more definitively.

Consideration of research results within a multiple simultaneous process paradigm highlights the fragmentary nature of current knowledge—truly showing that at this time only pieces of the puzzle are available for consideration. Determining the role and interrelations of high- and low-level processes in dyslexia, for example, is an approach which appears likely to be helpful in understanding dyslexia. Further, this strategy holds the promise of providing neuropsychologists and cognitive psychologists with a common ground for understanding dyslexia.

CONCLUSION

The preceding review suggests the following: First, neuropsychological literature here surveyed provides support for Vellutino's (1979) conclusion that some sort of verbal deficit is frequently present in dyslexics. Several of the studies noted above which did not find linguistic deficits among dyslexic readers may be faulted for not including measures which might have demonstrated the presence of subtle linguistic difficulties such as a mild dysnomia. It remains, however, for researchers to specify the exact relations between language disorders and dyslexia, particularly in light of the finding of linguistic deficits in nondyslexic children who display learning problems in areas such as written language or arithmetic (Rudel et al., 1981). Otherwise, the origin of dyslexia may remain "hopelessly obscure" (Pirrozollo et al., 1981, p. 802).

A second inference to be drawn from this research is that very little has been conclusively demonstrated about dyslexia. It can only be stated with confidence that some ability deficits relative to average readers are often observed in dyslexics. Attempts to explain dyslexia as the result of deficits in only one system—oculomotor, auditory, visual, linguistic, or attentional—are not well founded in research. Until substantiating research is carried out, current theories of dyslexia can only be considered speculation.

An adequate theory of the neuropsychology of reading ability and disability must describe the neurological processes involved in a wide range of levels of processing, including top-down processes (cf. Daneman, Carpenter, & Just, 1982; Meyer, 1983). Recent theory suggests that mathematical models of neural processes may account for some complex cognitive phenomena, but not yet at the very high level of reading processes (Grossberg, 1980). A theory of the neuropsychological bases of reading will also have to allow for the simultaneous existence of several apparently contradictory phenomena: while some dyslexic children may show lower levels of performance on some neuropsychological measures, some normal children and not all dyslexics may show this level of performance. Some who clearly display a specific ability may show difficulty in the reading process to which that ability is believed to be related. When the ability is not specific but a more general linguistic, cognitive, or metacognitive deficit, the likelihood of locating a more direct link to reading problems is increased, but the likelihood of locating a specific neurological substrate for the deficit is decreased. The search may thus increasingly emphasize higher level control and organizational processes.

Another problem which a full neuropsychological model of reading must address is that of developmental change in dyslexics' reading abilities. Since many dyslexics eventually improve in their reading abilities, to what process may this change be attributed? Still another difficult task in model building will be to discriminate between the relative contributions of neural substrate and experience to observed performances. Some neural deficits show little impact on learning processes, and some learning problems occur in the absence of demonstrable neuropsychological deficit.

These sorts of problems inherent in neuropsychological models have moved some researchers on dyslexia to adopt models which infer cognitive processes with little reference to neurological phenomena (e.g., Gerber, this volume). Ultimately the information garnered from these two approaches must be integrated and guide the search for a deeper and more comprehensive understanding of the phenomenon of dyslexia. Research from the multiple simultaneous process perspective suggested above may eventually provide the common ground needed for this integration.

Finally, it is hoped that this discussion has shown that the neuropsychological approach in concert with other paradigms may help to illuminate the work of fitting the dyslexia puzzle together. At present it is evident that some of the pieces are tantalizingly suggestive of their place in the puzzle but cannot yet be confidently put in place. Research of the type discussed above may serve to provide some of the outlining edge pieces of the puzzle, allowing clarity to emerge in the demarcation of where various aspects of neuropsychological research fit in the dyslexia puzzle.

ACKNOWLEDGMENTS

The author wishes to thank James Reed for his comments on a preliminary version of this manuscript. Grateful acknowledgement is also made to Ms. Tessa Lindsay for illustrating the figures in this chapter.

REFERENCES

Allington, R.L., & Fleming, J.T. (1978). The misreading of high-frequency words. *Journal of Special Education, 12*, 417-421.

Altman, J., Brunner, R.L., & Bayer, S.A. (1973). The hippocampus and behavioral maturation. *Behavioral Biology, 8*, 557-596.

Applebee, A.M. (1971). Research in reading retardation: Two critical problems. *Journal of Child Psychology and Psychiatry, 12*, 91-113.

Atchison, M.J., & Canter, G.J. (1979). Variables influencing phonemic discrimination performance in normal and learning-disabled children. *Journal of Speech and Hearing Disorders, 44*, 543-556.

Bakker, D.J., Teunissen, J., & Bosch, J. (1976). Development of laterality-reading patterns. In R.M. Knights & D.J. Bakker (Eds.), *The neuropsychology of learning disorders*. Baltimore, MD: University Park Press, pp. 207-220.

Bauserman, D.N., & Obrzut, J.E. (1981). Free recall and rehearsal strategies in average and severely disabled readers. *Perceptual and Motor Skills, 52*, 539-545.

Benton, A.L., & Pearl, D. (1978). *Dyslexia: An appraisal of current knowledge*. New York: Oxford University Press.

Blumstein, S.E. (1981). Neurolinguistic disorders: Language–brain relationships. In S.B. Filskov & T.J. Boll (Eds.), *Handbook of clinical neuropsychology*. New York: Wiley, pp. 227-256.

Boder, E. (1971). Developmental dyslexia: Prevailing diagnostic concepts and a new diagnostic approach. In H. Myklebust (Ed.), *Progress in learning disabilities* (Vol. 2). New York: Grune & Stratton, pp. 293-321.

Boder, E. (1973). Developmental dyslexia: A diagnostic approach based on three atypical reading patterns. *Developmental Medicine and Child Neurology, 15*, 663-687.

Boder, E., & Jarrico, S. (1982). *The Boder test of reading-spelling patterns*. New York: Grune & Stratton.

Boll, T.J. (1972). Conceptual versus perceptual versus motor deficits in brain-damaged children. *Journal of Clinical Psychology, 28*, 157-159.

Boll, T.J. (1974). Behavioral correlates of cerebral damage in children aged 9-14. In R.M. Reitan & L.A. Davison (Eds.), *Clinical neuropsychology: Current status and applications*. Washington, DC: Winston & Sons, pp. 91-120.

Boll, T.J., & Reitan, R.M. (1972). Motor and tactile-perceptual deficits in brain-damaged children. *Perceptual and Motor Skills, 34*, 343-350.

Boll, T.J., Berent, S., & Richards, H. (1977). Tactile-perceptual functioning as a factor in psychological abilities. *Perceptual and Motor Skills, 44*, 535-549.

Bremer, D.A., & Stern, J.A. (1976). Attention and distractibility during reading in hyperactive boys. *Journal of Abnormal Child Psychology, 4*, 381-387.

Caplan, B., & Kinsbourne, M. (1981). Cerebral lateralization, preferred cognitive mode, and reading ability in normal children. *Brain and Language, 14*, 349-370.

Cotugno, A.J. (1981). Cognitive controls and reading disabilities revisited. *Psychology in the Schools, 18*, 455-459.

Dalby, D.J., & Gibson, D. (1981). Functional cerebral lateralization in subtypes of disabled readers. *Brain and Language, 14,* 34-48.

Daneman, M., Carpenter, P.A., & Just, M.A. (1982). Cognitive processes and reading skills. In B.A. Hutson (Ed.), *Advances in reading/language research* (Vol. 1). Greenwich, CT: JAI Press, pp. 83-125.

Davis, G.A. (1983). *A survey of adult aphasia*. Englewood Cliffs, NJ: Prentice-Hall.

Denckla, M.B. (1979). Childhood learning disabilities. In K.M. Heilman & E. Valenstein (Eds.), *Clinical neuropsychology*. New York: Oxford University Press, pp. 535-573.

Denckla, M.B., & Heilman, K.M. (1979). The syndrome of hyperactivity. In K.M. Heilman & E. Valenstein (Eds.), *Clinical neuropsychology*. New York: Oxford University Press, pp. 574-597.

Denckla, M.B., & Rudel, R. (1974). Rapid "automatized" naming of pictured objects, colors, letters and numbers by normal children. *Cortex, 10*, 186-202.

Denckla, M.B., Rudel, R.G., & Broman, M. (1981). Tests that discriminate between dyslexic and other learning-disabled boys. *Brain and Language, 13*, 118-129.

Dennis, M. (1980). Capacity and strategy for syntactic comprehension after left or right hemicortication. *Brain and Language, 10*, 287-317.

Doctorow, M., Wittrock, M.C., & Marks, C. (1978). Generative processes in reading comprehension. *Journal of Educational Psychology, 70*, 109-118.

Doehring, D.C. (1978). The tangled web of behavioral research on developmental dyslexia. In A.L. Benton & D. Pearl (Eds.), *Dyslexia: An appraisal of current knowledge*. New York: Oxford University Press, pp. 123-135.

Doehring, D.G., & Hoshko, I.M. (1977). Classification of reading problems by the Q-technique of factor analysis. *Cortex, 13*, 281-294.

Doehring, D.G., Trites, R.L., Patel, P.G., & Fiedorowicz, C.A.M. (1981). *Reading disabilities*. New York: Academic Press.

Fay, G., Trupin, E., & Townes, B.D. (1981). The young disabled reader: Acquisition strategies and associated deficits. *Journal of Learning Disabilities, 14*, 32-35.

Fayne, H.R. (1981). A comparison of learning disabled adolescents with normal learners on an anaphoric pronominal reference task. *Journal of Learning Disabilities, 14*, 597-599.

Gerber, M.M. (1985). Spelling as a concept-governed problem-solving: Learning disabled and normally achieving students. In B.A. Hutson (Ed.), *Advances in reading/language research* (Vol. 3). Greenwich, CT: JAI Press, pp. 39-75.

Godfrey, J.J., Syrdal-Lasky, A.K., Millay, K.K., & Knox, M. (1981). Performance of dyslexic children on speech perception tests. *Journal of Experimental Child Psychology, 32*, 401-424.

Goodglass, H. (1980). Disorders of naming following brain injury. *American Scientist, 68*, 647-655.

Grossberg, S. (1980). How does a brain build a cognitive code? *Psychological Review, 87*, 1-51.

Guthrie, J.T. (1973). Models of reading and reading disability. *Journal of Educational Psychology, 65*, 9-18.

Hacaen, H., & Albert, M.L. (1978). *Human neuropsychology.* New York: Wiley.

Hogaboam, T.W., & Perfetti, C.A. (1978). Reading skill and the role of verbal experience in decoding. *Journal of Educational Psychology, 70*, 717-729.

Hynd, G.W., & Obrzut, J.E. (1981a). Development of reciprocal inhibition of normal and learning-disabled children. *Journal of General Psychology, 104*, 203-212.

Hynd, G.W., & Obrzut, J.E. (1981b). Reconceptualizing cerebral dominance: Implications for reading- and learning-disabled children. *Journal of Special Education, 15*, 447-457.

Hynd, G.W., Obrzut, J.E., & Obrzut, A. (1981). Are lateral and perceptual asymmetries related to WISC-R and achievement test performance in normal and learning-disabled children? *Journal of Consulting and Clinical Psychology, 49*, 977-979.

John, E.R. (1977). *Neurometrics: Clinical applications of quantitative electrophysiology.* Hillsdale, NJ: Erlbaum.

Johnson, D.J. (1977). Psychoeducational evaluation of children with learning disabilities: Study of auditory processes. In J.G. Millichap (Ed.), *Learning disabilities and related disorders.* Chicago: Yearbook Medical Publishers, pp. 99-117.

Jorm, A.F. (1979). The cognitive and neurological basis of developmental dyslexia: A theoretical framework and review. *Cognition, 7*, 19-33.

Kail, R.V., & Marshall, C.V. (1978). Reading skill and memory scanning. *Journal of Educational Psychology, 70*, 808-814.

Keogh, B.K., & Margolis, J.S. (1976a). A component analysis of attentional problems of educationally handicapped boys. *Journal of Abnormal Child Psychology, 4*, 349-359.

Keogh, B.K., & Margolis, J.S. (1976b). Learn to labor and wait: Attentional problems of children with learning disorders. *Journal of Learning Disabilities, 9*, 276-286.

Kimura, D. (1967). Functional asymmetry of the brain in dichotic listening. *Cortex, 3*, 163-178.

Kinsbourne, M. (1982). Hemispheric specialization and the growth of human understanding. *American Psychologist, 37*, 411-420.

Kinsbourne, M., & Warrington, E.K. (1963). Developmental factors in reading and writing backwardness. *British Journal of Psychology, 54*, 145-156.

Kleiman, G. (1975). Speech recoding in reading. *Journal of Verbal Learning and Verbal Behavior, 14*, 323-339.

Kolk, B., & Whishaw, I.Q. (1980). *Fundamentals of human neuropsychology.* San Francisco: W.H. Freeman.

Leonard, L.B. (1982). Phonological deficits in children with developmental language impairment. *Brain and Language, 16*, 73-86.

Leong, C.K. (1976). Lateralization in severely disabled readers in relation to functional cerebral development and synthesis of information. In R.M. Knights & D.J. Bakker (Ed.), *The neuropsychology of learning disorders.* Baltimore, MD: University Park Press, pp. 221-231.

Lezak, M.D. (1983). *Neuropsychological assessment* (2nd ed.). New York: Oxford University Press.

Luria, A.R. (1973a). *The working brain.* New York: Basic Books.

Luria, A.R. (1973b). Towards the mechanism of naming disturbance. *Neuropsychologia, 11*, 417-421.

Lyon, R., & Watson, B. (1981). Empirically derived subgroups of learning disabled readers. *Journal of Learning Disabilities, 14*, 256-261.

Lyon, R., Watson, B., Reitta, S., & Porch, B. (1981). Selected linguistic and perceptual abilities of empirically derived subgroups of learning disabled readers. *Journal of School Psychology, 19*, 152-166.

Masland, R.L. (1981). Neurological aspects of dyslexia. In G.T. Pavlidis & T.R. Miles (Eds.), *Dyslexia research and its applications to education.* New York: Wiley, pp. 35-66.

Mattis, S. (1978). Dyslexia syndromes: A working hypothesis that works. In A.L. Benton & D. Pearl (Eds.), *Dyslexia: An appraisal of current knowledge.* New York: Oxford University Press.

Mattis, S., French, J.H., & Rapin, I. (1975). Dyslexia in children and young adults: Three independent neuropsychological syndromes. *Developmental Medicine and Child Neurology, 17*, 150-163.

Meyer, B.J.F. (1983). Text structure and its use in studying comprehension across the adult life span. In B.H. Hutson (Ed.), *Advances in reading/language research* (Vol. 2). Greenwich, CT: JAI Press, pp. 9-54.

Morais, J., Cary, L., & Bertelson, P. (1979). Does awareness of speech as a sequence of phones arise spontaneously? *Cognition, 7*, 323-331.

Nishio, M.R. (1981). Kanji reading by a prekindergarten language-disabled child: A pilot study. *Brain and Language, 13*, 259-289.

Ojemann, G.A., & Mateer, C. (1979). Human language cortex: Localization of memory, syntax, and sequential motor-phoneme identification systems. *Science, 205*, 1401-1403.

Olswang, L.B., Kriegsmann, E., & Mastergeorge, A. (1982). Facilitating functional requesting in pragmatically impaired children. *Language, Speech, and Hearing Services in Schools, 13*, 202-222.

Ownby, R.L. (1983). The neuropsychology of attention deficit disorders in children. *The Journal of Psychiatric Treatment and Evaluation, 5*, 229-236.

Ownby, R.L. (1984). Supraspan learning in learning disabled children. Unpublished manuscript.

Ownby, R.L., & Matthews, C.G. (1985). On the meaning of the WISC-R third factor: Relations to selected neuropsychological measures. *Journal of Consulting and Clinical Psychology, 53*, 531-534.

Patel, P.G. (1977). The left parieto-occipital junction, semantic aphasia and language development around age seven. *Linguistics, 196*, 35-48.

Patterson, K.E. (1981). Neuropsychological approaches to the study of reading. *British Journal of Psychology, 72*, 151-174.

Pavlidis, G.T. (1981). Sequencing, eye movements, and the early objective diagnosis of dyslexia. In G.T. Pavlidis & T.R. Miles (Eds.), *Dyslexia research and its application to education.* New York: Wiley, pp. 99-163.

Perfetti, C.A., Finger, E., & Hogaboam, T. (1978). Sources of vocalization latency differences between skilled and less skilled young readers. *Journal of Educational Psychology, 70*, 730-739.

Pirrozollo, F.J., Campanella, D.J., Christensen, K., & Lawson-Kerr, K. (1981). Effects of cerebral dysfunction on neurolinguistic performance in children. *Journal of Consulting and Clinical Psychology, 49*, 791-806.

Rees, N.S., & Shulman, M. (1978). I don't understand what you mean by comprehension. *Journal of Speech and Hearing Disorders, 43*, 208-219.

Reitan, R.M. (1959). Impairment of abstraction ability in brain damage: Quantitative versus qualitative change. *Journal of Psychology, 48*, 97-102.

Reitan, R.M. (1974). Psychological effects of cerebral lesions in children of early school age. In R.M. Reitan & L.A. Davison, (Eds.), *Clinical neuropsychology: Current status and applications.* Washington, DC: Winston & Sons, pp. 53-89.

Rose, D. (1980). Some functional correlates of the maturation of neural systems. In D. Caplan (Ed.), *Biological studies of mental processes.* Cambridge, MA: MIT Press, pp. 27-43.

Rosenthal, R.H., & Allen, T.W. (1978). An examination of attention, arousal, and learning dysfunctions of hyperkinetic children. *Psychological Bulletin, 85*, 689-715.

Rourke, B.P. (1975). Brain-behavior relationships in children with learning disabilities. *American Psychologist*, *30*, 911-920.

Rourke, B.P. (1978). Neuropsychological research in reading retardation: A review. In A.L. Benton & D. Pearl (Eds.), *Dyslexia: An appraisal of current knowledge*. New York: Oxford University Press, pp. 139-171.

Rourke, B.P. (1981). Neuropsychological assessment of children with learning disabilities. In S.B. Filskov & T.J. Boll (Eds.), *Handbook of clinical neuropsychology*. New York: Wiley, pp. 453-478.

Rourke, B.P. & Finlayson, M.A.J. (1978). Neuropsychological significance of variations in patterns of academic performance: Verbal and visual-spatial abilities. *Journal of Abnormal Child Psychology*, *6*, 121-133.

Rourke, B.P., Young, G.C., & Flewelling, R.W. (1971). The relationships between WISC verbal-performance discrepancies and selected verbal, auditory-perceptual, and problem-solving abilities in children with learning disabilities. *Journal of Clinical Psychology*, *27*, 475-479.

Rozin, P., Poritsky, S., & Sotsky, R. (1971). American children with reading problems can easily learn to read English represented by Chinese characters. *Science*, *171*, 1264-1267.

Rudel, R.G., Denckla, M.B., & Broman, M. (1981). The effect of varying stimulus context on word finding ability: Dyslexia further differentiated from other learning disabilities. *Brain and Language*, *13*, 130-144.

Rudel, R.G., Denckla, M.B., & Spalten, E. (1976). Paired associate learning of morse code and Braille letter names by dyslexic and normal children. *Cortex*, *12*, 61-70.

Rumelhart, D.E. (1977). Toward an interactive model of reading. In S. Dornic (Ed.), *Attention and performance VI*. Hillsdale, NJ: Erlbaum, pp. 573-603.

Rutherford, D. (1977). Speech and language disorders and MBD. In J.G. Millichap (Ed.), *Learning disabilities and related disorders*. Chicago, Yearbook Medical Publishers, pp. 45-50.

Rutter, M. (1978). Prevalence and types of dyslexia. In A.L. Benton & D. Pearl (Eds.), *Dyslexia: An appraisal of current knowledge*. New York: Oxford University Press.

Satz, P. (1976). Cerebral dominance and reading disability: An old problem revisited. In R.M. Knights & D.J. Bakker (Eds.), *The neuropsychology of learning disorders*. Baltimore, MD: University Park Press, pp. 273-294.

Savin, H.B., & Bever, T.G. (1970). The nonperceptual reality of the phoneme. *Journal of Verbal Learning and Verbal Behavior*, *9*, 296-302.

Schierberl, J.P. (1979). Physiological models of hyperactivity: An integrative review of the literature. *Journal of Clinical Child Psychology*, *8*, 163-172.

Schwartz, G.E. (1978). Psychobiological foundations of psychotherapy and behavior change. In S.L. Garfield & A.E. Bergin (Eds.), *Handbook of psychotherapy and behavior change: An empirical analysis* (2nd ed.). New York: Wiley, pp. 63-99.

Selz, M., & Reitan, R.M. (1979). Rules for neuropsychological diagnosis: Classification of brain function in older children. *Journal of Consulting and Clinical Psychology*, *47*, 258-264.

Semel, E. & Wiig, E. (1975). Comprehension of syntactic structures and critical verbal elements by children with learning disabilities. *Journal of Learning Disabilities*, *8*, 46-51.

Shankweiler, D., & Liberman, I.Y. (1976). Exploring the relations between reading and speech. In R.M. Knights & D.J. Bakker (Eds.), *The neuropsychology of learning disorders*. Baltimore, MD: University Park Press, pp. 297-313.

Stone, C.A. (1981). Reasoning disorders in learning-disabled adolescents. *Exceptional Child*, *28*, 43-53.

Tallal, P. (1976). Auditory perceptual factors in language and learning disabilities. In R.M. Knights & D.J. Bakker (Eds.), *The neuropsychology of learning disorders*. Baltimore, MD: University Park Press, pp. 315-323.

Tallal, P. (1980). Auditory temporal perception, phonics, and reading disability in children. *Brain and Language*, *9*, 182-198.

Tallal, P., & Piercy, M. (1973). Developmental aphasia: Impaired rate of non-verbal processing as a function of sensory modality. *Neuropsychologia*, *11*, 398-398.

Tallal, P., & Piercy, M. (1974). Developmental aphasia: Rate of auditory processing and selective impairment of consonant perception. *Neuropsychologia, 12*, 83-93.

Tallal, P., & Piercy, M. (1975). Developmental aphasia: The perception of brief vowels and extended stop consonants. *Neuropsychologia, 13*, 69-74.

Tallal, P., Stark, R., Kallman, C., & Mellits, D. (1981). A reexamination of some nonverbal perceptual abilities of language-impaired and normal children as a function of age and sensory modality. *Journal of Speech and Hearing Research, 24*, 351-357.

Torgeson, j.K. (1977). The role of nonspecific factors in the task performance of learning disabled children: A theoretical assessment. *Journal of Learning Disabilities, 10*, 27-34.

Vellutino, F.R. (1978). Toward an understanding of dyslexia: Psychological factors in specific reading disability. In A.L. Benton & D. Pearl (Eds.), *Dyslexia: An appraisal of current knowledge*. New York: Oxford University Press, pp. 61-111.

Vellutino, F.R. (1979). *Dyslexia: Theory and research*. Cambridge, MA: MIT Press.

Vellutino, F.R., Steger, J.A., Harding, C.J., & Phillips, F. (1975). Verbal vs. non-verbal paired-associates learning in poor and normal readers. *Neuropsychologia, 13*, 75-82.

Vogel, S.A. (1974). Syntactic abilities in normal and dyslexic children. *Journal of Learning disabilities, 7*, 103-109.

Walsh, K.W. (1978). *Neuropsychology, a clinical approach*. New York: Churchill Livingstone.

Wanat, S.F. (1976). Relations between language and visual procesing. In H. Singer & R.B. Ruddell (Eds.), *Theoretical models and processes of reading* (2nd ed.). Newark, DE: International Reading Association, pp. 108-136.

Watson, B.U., Goldgar, D.E., & Fredd, R.D. (1982). *Subtypes of specific reading disability*. Paper presented at the meeting of the American Psychological Association, Washington, August.

Wiig, E., & Semel, E. (1979). *Clinical evaluation of language function*. Columbus, OH: Charles E. Merrill.

Wiig, E., Semel, E., & Crouse, M. (1973). The use of English morphology by high-risk and learning disabled children. *Journal of Learning Disabilities, 6*, 457-465.

Wiig, E., Semel, E., & Nystrom, L.A. (1982). Comparison of rapid naming abilities in language-learning-disabled and academically achieving eight-year-olds. *Language, Speech, and Hearing Services in Schools, 13*, 11-23.

Witelson, S.F. (1976a). Abnormal right hemisphere specialization in developmental dyslexia. In R.M. Knights & D.J. Bakker (Eds.), *The neuropsychology of learning disorders*. Baltimore, MD: University Park Press, pp. 233-255.

Witelson, S. (1976b). Sex and the single hemisphere: Right hemisphere specialization for spatial processing. *Science, 193*, 425-427.

Witelson, S.F. (1977). Early hemisphere specialization and interhemisphere plasticity: An empirical and theoretical review. In S.J. Segalowitz & F.A. Gruber (Eds.), *Language development and neurological theory*. New York: Academic Press, pp. 213-287.

Yeni-Komshian, G.H., Isenberg, D., & Goldberg, H. (1975). Cerebral dominance and reading disability: Left visual field deficit in poor readers. *Neuropsychologia, 13*, 83-94.

Zaidel, E., & Peters, A.M. (1981). Phonological encoding and idiographic reading by the disconnected hemisphere: Two case studies. *Brain and Language, 14*, 205-234.

STYLES IN EDUCATIONAL RESEARCH ON TWO SIDES OF THE ATLANTIC

W. B. Dockrell

INTRODUCTION

Most introductory psychology textbooks include the classic figure–ground experiment. The line drawing can be seen either as a vase or as two profiles. The author of an article on educational research in different countries is faced by the same dilemma. He can either see the similarities as the figure and the differences as the ground or the differences as the figure and the similarities as the ground. There is much that is common in educational research on the two sides of the Atlantic. Many themes recur and the techniques seem to be universal.

It is hardly surprising that there is an international flavor to educational research, for there has been collaboration at least since the International Examinations Enquiry of the 1920s and 1930s. The giants of those days, Thorndike and Munroe, Spearman and Thomson, Arseneau and Hanniger, met

Advances in Reading/Language Research, Volume 3, pages 151-166.
Copyright © 1985 by JAI Press Inc.
All rights of reproduction in any form reserved.
ISBN: 0-89232-389-2

under the auspices of the Carnegie Corporation to plan and carry out a cooperative program of research. From the 1950s onward the pace of mutual involvement has grown. There has been the exchange of scholars made possible by travel grants like those provided under the Fulbright Act. The improvement in travel makes it possible for researchers to attend conferences on one side of the Atlantic or the other as easily as in their own countries. We can therefore not only read each other's books, monographs, and articles, we can listen to each other's papers, join in discussion, and get to understand each other's perspectives. That, however, is still for a minority.

For the majority a much more important factor is that the lingua franca of educational research is English. By far the largest number of research journals and those with the greatest circulation are produced in the United States. Second in this particular international league comes Britain with a substantial number of journals which are widely read. The international journals are also for the most part written in English. Journals like *Studies in Educational Evaluation* may be edited in Israel with associate editors in Germany and the United States or, like the *International Journal of Behavioural Development*, edited in Holland with associate editors in France, England, and the United States, but they are written in English.

Even national publications are written in English. Such journals as *Didakometry and Sociometry* and *Educational and Psychological Directions* from Sweden are written in English. The German journal *Mitteilungen und Nachrichten* has some articles in English and *Kasvatus*, the Finnish journal of education, is helpfully subtitled in English and has summaries of articles and a list of contents in English.

Even articles which are not written in English carry many references to American authors and even occasionally references to publications by foreign authors in English translation rather than the original. Some of the articles in *Kasvatus* and some in *Mitteilungen und Nachrichten* have only Finnish/German references but those articles which have foreign references always include U.S. publications. Paradoxically, even an article in the *European Journal of Education* on "Higher Education in Scotland" had two American references tucked in among the Scots. There is, therefore, a strong American flavor to educational research carried out in Europe.

Although the American influence is large everywhere, there are national differences. Protected perhaps by language barriers, German-speaking and French-speaking countries appear to be less influenced by American sources. Three years ago the French journal *Enfance* produced a special issue for the centenary of Henri Wallon. How many American readers have heard of Wallon? Even fewer would have heard of the authors who contributed to that special issue. Their concerns were with a French thinker and his influence on educational practice in French-speaking countries. Similarly, the German journals often carry articles which are dependent exclusively on German or other European sources and which are concerned with German issues.

There is a great deal in common but there are considerable differences in emphasis. There are certain features of educational research which are much more marked in Europe than they are in the United States, each, of course, has American parallels but they are less dominant. There are also those characteristics which seem to be particularly American though they too have their European parallels but again to a lesser extent.

MAJOR DIFFERENCES IN AMERICAN AND EUROPEAN RESEARCH

There are three major differences of emphasis between American and European research. One is that American work is predominantly empirical and positivist whereas European work is much more likely to be speculative and phenomenological. American work is often more pragmatic and with less concern for general theory, or perhaps implicitly behavioristic, whereas European work is much more likely to be related to a general theory. Finally, educational research in Europe is much more likely to be sociological in its orientation than American research.

EMPIRICAL VS. ANALYTIC/SPECULATIVE EMPHASIS

An analysis of the four numbers of the *American Educational Research Journal* published in 1982 shows that the articles contained in it are overwhelmingly reports of experimental or quasi-experimental studies. The standard article consists of an introduction, a review of previous evidence, or a statement of the model or theory to be tested, a second on methods, one on results and, finally, one containing conclusions or discussion. The pattern is so standard that it is hard to find one that deviates from it. There are, however, a few articles of two other types. One type consists of meta-analyses which are themselves empirical in that they consist of a structured analysis of previously published materials and the other consists of methodological articles which analyze the merits of particular experimental or analytic techniques.

A comparison with the *British Educational Research Journal* for 1982 is revealing. The British journal has only two issues per year but that is far from being the most striking difference between them. Most of the articles in the British journal are empirical in the sense which I have used above and could as easily have appeared in the American journal. There are two articles concerned with technique, the Rasch model, for example. They, too, could have appeared in the American journal.

There are however, also speculative or analytic articles which would not have appeared in the American journal. In part that is because American journals are more specialized so that an article like Hewitt's "A Critique of Research Methods in the Study of Reading Comprehension" might, in principle, have appeared in the *Review of Educational Research* but is unlikely to have done so because it is not a meta-analysis in the sense of analyzing quantitatively the European and American research. Rather it is analytic, arguing for "naturalistic research using observational techniques" (p. 19). "We need to describe what readers do while reading and after they have read and to theorise about and discover what influences their comprehension and their conception of comprehension. We need to discover what kinds of meanings reading has for different individuals and what the socio-political determinants are of these meanings" (p. 20).

An article like Watson's "Idealism and Education: T.H. Green and the Education of the Middle-class," which analyzes the educational theory of a nineteenth-century philosopher, its relation to the social and economic circumstances of the time, and its ultimate impact on educational practice, would no doubt have found an outlet in the United States but would it have been seen as part of the mainstream of educational research, something that educational researchers would want to read? An article like Chambers's "School-based Curriculum Research" might well have found an American audience, though its emphasis on providing "an ideological basis for justifying school-based curriculum research" (p. 133), might well have seemed alien.

By contrast the American articles seem to a European to be marked by a positivist emphasis on facts that is reminiscent of Mr. Gradgrind. There is no lifting of the eyes from the evidence or questioning of what is evidence. The facts appear to be sufficient. This emphasis on the facts seems to be deeply embedded not only in American educational research but in American education generally. Is it part of the influence of Thordndike or are there other sources?

It is not that there is no American concern with the issues raised in the British journal. Some of the articles in *Philosophical Re-Directions of Educational Research* (Thomas, 1972), especially those by Dunkel and Gowan and some of the contributions to *Philosophy of Educational Research* (Broudy, Ennis, & Krimerman, 1973), do recognize the issue. There is also some talk of the value of hermeneutics. These concerns, however, have not permeated the practice of educational research in the United States as they have in Europe. It is not merely that there is the tradition of "Geisteswissenschaft" (and not only in Germany) but that this tradition has deeply influenced what educational researchers do, at least in the course of the last decade or so, as Kallos (1980) points out in *Rethinking Educational Research*.

These European studies are distinguished from the positivist studies, partly by method and partly by purpose. Cronbach (1975), in his well-known paper "Beyond the Two Disciplines of Scientific Psychology," describes the procedure as well.

> An observer collecting data in one particular situation is in a position to appraise a practice or proposition in that setting, observing effects in context. In trying to describe and account for what happened he will give attention to whatever variables were controlled but he will

give equally careful attention to uncontrolled conditions, to personal characteristics, and to events that occur during treatment and measurement. As he goes from situation to situation his first task is to describe and interpret the effect anew in each locale, perhaps taking into account factors which were unique to that locale or series of events. As results accumulate a person who seeks understanding will do his best to trace how the uncontrolled factors could have caused local departures from the modal effect, that is, generalisations come late and the exception is taken as seriously as the rule (pp. 124–125).

That describes the method; it is open, exploratory, wide-eyed or, as Cronbach says, "intensive local observation goes beyond discipline to an open-eyed, open-minded appreciation of the surprises nature deposits in the investigative net" (p. 125).

HYPOTHESIS TESTING VS. ILLUMINATIVE EMPHASIS

There is a difference in purpose as well as method, a different idea of what research is for most articles appearing in the American journal are what Kuhn (1970) calls normal science, i.e., they are attempting in the style of Popper (1963) to test hypotheses derived from established theories. That is not the purpose of illuminative research. As Cronbach says, "though enduring systematic theories about man in society are not likely to be achieved, systematic enquiry can realistically hope to make two contributions. One reasonable aspiration is to assess local events accurately to improve short-run control. The other reasonable aspiration is to develop explanatory concepts, concepts that will help people use their heads" (p. 126). The illuminative approach questions the value of existing theory in the social sciences. The purpose of research—systematic enquiry—is therefore not to test theory but either "to assess local events to improve short-run control" or "to develop explanatory concepts that will help people use their heads." This style of research is often referred to in Britain as illuminative research because of the use of the word illumination in an influential monograph (Parlett & Hamilton, 1972).

Cronbach is of course an American and his article was addressed to an American audience. Two features are striking. The first is the minimal impact of his paper on those to whom it was addressed: educational psychologists. The 1982 volume of the *Journal of Educational Psychology*, for example, had nearly 100 articles, of which only one can be said to take the position advocated by him. The second is the extent to which the approach that he advocates permeates European research. It is not the only and in some countries not the dominant form of research but it takes its place in research practice with other traditions.

Studies of this kind are typical of a widespread approach to educational research in Britain. They are supported financially by the major funders of research. These are the central government departments, the Department of Education and Science in England, the Scottish Education Department, the local educational authorities, and the Social Science Research Council. This council is the major public agency in Britain funding research in the social sciences, including education. Such studies are accepted by the major funders as part of that mainstream of educational research.

It is worth emphasizing that this is an approach not only to evaluation but to research. It involves a definition of what knowledge is in the social sciences (including education) and how it is likely to be increased.

European research has both of Cronbach's purposes. There is great emphasis placed on "school-based research" or "collaborative research." This is when those in schools attempt to assess their own local events as accurately and as systematically as possible so that they might understand them better and therefore improve their own short-run control. Manifestly research of this kind is not intended to be of general value. Rather its purpose is to be relevant to a specific situation. It may well use theory as a guide to possible understanding of what is taking place, but it is not attempting to test theory. Theory may be contributing implicitly to understanding, lying behind the questions asked and the explanations offered, but it is not a case of experiments being specifically designed to test theory. The research is not generally published for it is intended to "assess local events" and therefore not likely to be of interest to others.

Chambers and Powney (1982), for example, argue that

> unless educational research becomes part of every teacher's professional repertoire and is specified conceptually and practically in ways that demonstrate its centrality, its development is likely to remain embryonic. The importance of research must be established in initial teacher education so that it is got over to teachers in training that research is a part of teaching. As they take up their roles as teachers they should also take up a commitment to evaluating their teaching performance and researching into effectiveness of what they do (p. 138).

They go on to suggest that "three values that should shape school-based research policy [are]:

a. a recognition of a value of applied research and development;
b. an acknowledgement of the importance of both small scale and co-operative research;
c. an understanding that a major outcome of educational research will be its sensitising influence on teachers, helping them make sense of educational processes rather than necessarily expecting fundamental evidence to shape educational policy" (pp. 138-139).

The group which has practiced this approach and been most active in analyzing it has been associated with the University of East Anglia and particularly with Stenhouse and his colleagues. The most comprehensive statement of the approach is still Stenhouse's *Introduction to Curriculum Research and Development* (1975), in which he states his philosophy of educational research and of the role of the teacher.

Stenhouse makes the case for assessing "local events accurately to improve short-run control" in the schools as follows:

> I believe that long-term improvement of education through the utilization of research and development hinges on the creation of different expectations in the system and the design of new styles of project in harmony with those expectations.
>
> The different expectations will be generated only as schools come to see themselves as research and development institutions rather than clients of research and development agencies. Against that background assumption a project will see itself as helping schools to undertake research and development in a problem area and to report this work in a way that supports similar work in other schools" (pp. 222–223).

This approach is not an alternative to Cronbach's second purpose. It is rather a different emphasis and, as Stenhouse points out in the quotation given above, one outcome of assessing local events is a report "that supports similar work in other schools."

Other members of the "East Anglia" school are MacDonald and Walker. They begin their analysis of curriculum change (1976) with a warning: "In some fields of education, theory is fully developed, sophisticated, complex and demanding. Such theory can trap the beginner, offering him elegant substitutes for his own analysis of and reflections upon the phenomena they address. Or it may undermine the student who seeks his own understanding of the field, interposing a set of baffling obstacles between him and his data" (p. 4). For student read scholar.

The same suspicion about theory and emphasis on the understanding of the practitioners is found in a Scottish study reported at about the same time. The Scottish Council published a case study of the transition to open plan in a single primary school (Hamilton, 1977). In his preface to that book Hamilton harks back to an even earlier publication by the Scottish Council (Corrie, 1974). He comments that the book "did not set out to test a range of pre-specified hypotheses or even to survey every aspect of open-plan schooling, instead it tried to respond in an accessible manner to some of the questions posed at that time by teachers and administrator" (p. v). He goes on to say that his current study "utilises a similar research perspective. It identifies the general phenomena of open-plan schooling and locates them in the day-to-day work in one school . . . its principal concern is to contribute—in a concise but sensitising manner—to wider discussions about the problems and possibilities of open-plan schooling" (p. v).

The study was based on a conscious approach to educational research. Hamilton goes on to assert that educational research has in the past failed to provide the help to practitioners that it might because there has been a separation between theory and practice:

> Until recently efforts to overcome this separation of theory and practice have been hindered by the absence of suitable two-way communicational channels. Questions posed by practitioners have been obscured or trivialised by the specialised processes and languages of

educational research. Not surprisingly the answers offered by researchers frequently turned out to be inadequate, incomprehensible or irrelevant.

The essays in this volume are an attempt to re-consider such deficiencies in educational research. They arose from a belief that educational research can gain a great deal from the insights and experiences of educational practitioners—especially those who work in areas of development and innovation (p. 2).

Hamilton continues:

In a more general sense this places researchers and teachers on opposite sides of the theory/practice divide. Researchers tend to be articulate about practice but incompetent in practice whereas teachers tend to be competent in practice but inarticulate about practice. Fortunately, these perspectives are complementary. Thus, this report attempts to merge the skills of researchers and practitioners by making explicit and accessible some of the ideas and practices which have developed alongside the growth of open-plan schooling (p. 3).

This project was funded by the Social Science Research Council.

Perhaps the most significant contribution of this school of thought is the emphasis on collaboration between teacher and researcher, not always as clearly differentiated as in the quotation from Hamilton above. A recent example of the approach is the report on the school accountability project (Elliot, Bridges, Ebbut, Gibson, and Nias, 1981). This too was funded by the Social Science Research Council. In his introduction Elliot gives the reasons for adopting the case study approach in this project:

First, we wanted our research to contribute to the development of self-accounting practices in participating schools.... [I]f the project was to help schools in developing their responsiveness to local audiences then it needed to understand the problems and effects of self-accounting in the light of the particular circumstances they faced.

Second, since the self-accounting procedure adopted by schools, and the problems and effects which arise as a result, will depend on their own situation, we were skeptical [sic] about the possibility of producing a definitive set of "research findings" in the form of generalisations which could be applied to all schools irrespective of the settings in which they operated.

However, we felt that by comparing and contrasting the "problems and effects" of self-accounting across a small number of cases and explaining them in terms of similarities and differences between settings we could generate some ideas and hypotheses which staff in schools outside the project could usefully explore and examine in relation to their circumstances (p. xiv).

There are many examples of case study work which have a basis different from that of Stenhouse, Walker, MacDonald, Hamilton, and others from East Anglia. Parsons (1981) takes issue with Walker's position on the use of fiction in educational research:

Whatever process of testing a fictional account may go through, however it may capture the flavour of the reality experienced by the researcher, it defies authentication. It is a duty of researchers to reveal to an audience the way the data were collected and demonstrate stringency in analysis. Walker . . . holds an extreme position even within new wave evaluation. By journalistic and literary standards it outshines much educational research. It sacrifices so much for these advantages that its reliability and hence utility for decision makers must be questioned (pp. 60–61).

He goes on to say that

further, the debate, even schism, between traiditional and nontraditional evaluators has been unhelpful, since the more recently advocated modes of enquiry are not substitutes for measurement programmes of pupil's outcomes. However important we might regard studies of process—how schools are organized, how teachers teach, the nature of pupil activity—we are still interested in the result in terms of pupils' development (p. 61).

He asserts further "that evaluation can most profitably be relocated in discipline-based, policy-oriented research. He does, however, concede that what he calls the new wave is still in the ascendant. The East Anglia group do indeed hold an extreme position, as Parsons asserts, but their approach has deeply penetrated the practice of educational research" (p. 62) in the United Kingdom to a greater extent than similar thinking in the United States has affected research there. Eggleston's collection of case studies (1980) is more clearly a part of normal practice in Britain than would be a parallel book in the United States.

The second of Cronbach's purposes is for the "person who seeks understanding." The case studies not only try "to describe" but also "account for" what happened by paying attention to "local departures" as well as "modal effect." In this circumstance the researcher describes in order to "interpret the effect." The critical word is understanding. It is the purpose of this research to illuminate. The reader will first be led to understand phenomena which were previously puzzling and then to ask about the relevance of these new understandings to his specific situation. There is dual emphasis on the uniqueness of the individual situation and on explanatory concepts which arise from a shared understanding.

Among the more recent publications of the Scottish Council for Research in Education are three reports of research in this qualitative or illuminative style. First, *Routes and Results* (Ryrie, 1981) is a study of the later years of schooling. It looks at the courses of programs available in eight high schools up to the point of graduation. There are a considerable number of tables reporting, for example, the percentage of students in each program by father's occupation; the grades obtained at graduation; the student's intention on leaving school, university, polytechnic, further education college (junior college) or work; and results of multiple regression and other analyses. In many respects it is like the educational research I have called positivistic, but it includes and uses to interpret the findings what the students, their parents, or their teachers said in interviews. The question asked is, how do the people concerned see the process of progression through the secondary system? Is there a common perception or set of perceptions which runs across schools or do students see schooling differently according to the policy and practice of the schools which they attend? This study was funded by the Scottish Education Department.

The second publication, *Making the Change* (Cumming, Lowe, Tulips, & Wakeling, 1981) is a study of guidance, discipline, and sanctions in a number of schools which eliminated corporal punishment. It was funded jointly by the Scottish Education Department and the local authorities. Corporal punishment has in the past been a much more common feature of Scottish than American schools, although now, partly as a result of the research, it has been banned by the two largest authorities in Scotland, covering between them well over half of the schools and pupils. This book is descriptive. It is based on carefully accumulated data including systematic classroom observation, questionnaires, and structured interviews. These data were the bases for a series of case studies which described the practice in the five schools that were making the change from corporal punishment. The studies place particular emphasis on the guidance systems and the use of alternative sanctions. The main body of the book, however, is an analysis, an integration, and indeed an application of the procedures that were used in those schools. It was not merely that the individual schools were described in detail but that an attempt was also made to understand them, to relate them to particular sets of circumstances, and to show how the behavior of children was influenced by them. It was not an attempt to test theory in the classical sense; rather it was an attempt to provide a structured understanding of school management, particularly the management of change as it applied to a particular issue. The analytic, the conceptual, the attempt to understand the meaning of actions is not divorced from the gathering of facts but is derived from the facts and related back to them. In Cronbach's words, "generalisation comes late and the exception is taken as seriously as the rule."

The third book, *Classroom Management Strategies* (Corrie, Haystead, & Zaklukiewicz, 1981), places its emphasis on the interpretations and actions of the individuals concerned. The attempt is made "to identify and describe the factors influencing the strategies typically used by teachers to cope with their interactions with pupils in the classrooms as they see them and undertand them" (p. 1). The aim was "to develop a description of the nature of teachers' classroom management strategies which would be as consonant as possible with the experience of individuals" (p. 2). In this case too it is not merely that the researchers carried out a series of observations of what teachers actually did. They attempted to make sense of them in light of the teachers' interpretations of their own actions.

There are, of course, American examples of work of this kind. It is not that they exist in Europe and not in the United States but that in Europe they are a common approach to educational research. Of the 10 studies reported by the Scottish Council for Research in Education in the last two years, five were of this kind.

SPECIFIC THEORY VS. MACRO THEORY EMPHASIS

My next distinction in emphasis between European and American research is paradoxically the importance of theory to European research. Perhaps it should be referred to as "grand theory" (grand in the French sense of big) or macro theory, attempting to explain on a general rather than a narrow psychological or sociological basis. American research is theoretical in the sense that many studies are attempts to test in a precise and explicit way hypotheses which are drawn from theory, but the theory is narrow and specific. Theory in the European context is rather different.

The work of Jean Piaget is familiar to American educators and there is much American research derived from his work, but much of it misses what Europeans see as the essential philosophical basis of his work. The American research has been concerned with the specifics of Piagetian theory, questioning whether the stages mark discrete points in the growth of intelligence, trying to accelerate development, or attempting more specific measurement of different kinds of operations. Much European research has been different. It accepts the Piagetian technique of close and careful observation of children's actual performance in different sets of circumstances as a means of questioning some of Piaget's own interpretations (Dockrell, 1983; Donaldson, 1979) or it takes Piaget's theory as a structure or framework within which to operate (Lovell, 1971; Shayer, 1972). Theory in this sense is providing a framework, a structure for thinking about thinking.

The important point is not only that the European researchers and the Americans have tended to use Piaget's theory in different ways but that there is no American parallel to Piaget's general theory which provides a structure for viewing the growth of intelligence. Nor is there any American equivalent to Bourdieu, no general way of thinking about the relationships between teaching and the social system which provides a perspective for viewing education as a whole. The relationship between theory and research is well illustrated in the way that Bernstein (1980) relates his work to Bourdieu's (1977) thinking. It is not that a series of hypotheses has been formulated and tested, rather that a particular theory provides a way of understanding particular observations or empirical findings. Bernstein is perhaps the most influential British researcher not primarily because of his empirical studies but because of the dialogue in his writing between general theory and specific instance. His concern is to understand and to relate his understanding of what is happening to a theory, a world view.

Bourdieu himself makes the point. He distinguishes between the development of his conceptual framework, "a system amenable to logical verification" (p. ix), and "the application, to a particular historical case, of principles whose generality would support other applications" (p. ix). The logical analysis on which Bourdieu places so much emphasis is a more significant part of the whole educational research activity in Europe than it is in the United States.

The same approach to theory can be found in Nathan (1973). He makes the distinction between a Lamarckian and a Darwinian view of language. "The burden of the arguments that follow—or at least the basis for which the other arguments may be inferred—is that there are two views of communication. One that we might call Lamarckian, the other Darwinian" (p. ix). The theory is the basis from which other arguments may be inferred.

There have, of course, been Marxist or neo-Marxist analyses of American education (Bowles, 1976) in recent years, but Marxism and neo-Marxism as a framework for thinking about education is not ingrained in American educational research as it is in European. The concern about the relationship between society, state, and schooling and its dependence on a Marxist framework for the analysis of this relationship is a common theme of much European research (Althusser, 1971; Bourdieu & Passeron, 1977; Entwistle, 1978). Marxism is seen as a structure for defining what the issues are and for directing the attention of researchers to particular questions, not as providing a series of hypotheses for empirical testing. The role of theory is to clarify the issues in order to direct the attention of researchers to particular questions and to provide a framework for understanding the processes involved.

Who would be the American parallels to Pierre Bourdieu, to Jean Piaget, to Claude Lévi-Strauss, or, in an earlier generation, to Sigmund Freud? There are, of course, seminal American thinkers like Noam Chomsky but they do not seem to play the role in American research that their European parallels play. European sociologists have shown a considerable interest in education for many years. Durkheim's (1977) writings were influential in France and Mannheim's (1936, 1952) in Britain.

THE IMPORTANCE OF SOCIOLOGY

Sociological research has been prominent too for many years. The work of Halsey and Floud (1961) is known to American sociologists of education. What is perhaps not recognized is that their research of the 1940s and 1950s played an important role in Britain in educational thinking and ultimately in policymaking. Their book *Social Class and Educational Opportunity* (Floud, Halsey, & Martin, 1956) made a significant contribution to the decisions about the form of secondary education. A major educational reform was based in part, at least, on research evidence like theirs. Not only did they contribute to the general climate of opinion but they provided specific evidence on a crucial issue of public concern. It is significant too that the authors were all sociologists interested in education and not educators who had turned to sociology. The same is true of Bourdieu (1976) and Althusser (1972), whose thinking has been taken up because of its relevance to educational issues.

When the most substantial program of educational research carried out in Britain was commissioned by the Social Science Research Council in the early

1970s, it was coordinated by Halsey (1972). The issues were thought to be sociological issues which could be investigated most appropriately by sociologists using their conceptual framework and techniques. The most recent major work from this perspective is a study of family class and education (Halsey, Heath, & Ridge, 1980). For many years, perhaps since the writings of Durkheim, sociological thought has been a prominent if not a dominant strain in educational research in Europe. Perhaps the best known of British educational researchers over the course of the last 20 years has been Bernstein, and Bourdieu has been the most prominent among the French. They are both sociologists.

It is not that this influence is limited to one or two atypical figures. The work of Jackson and Marsden (1962), Hargreaves (1976), Lacey (1970), Davies (1976), and particularly Young (1971) has been important to Britain. In France, in addition to Bourdieu there are Boltanski (1969), Chamboredon and Prevot (1973). Among German writers (in addition to Althusser) are Heinrich (1973) and Masuch (1973). These writers have been influential in a way that sociology has not been in the United States. That is not to say that there are not prominent sociologists or sociological research in the United States, but rather that in the *American Educational Research Journal* there is no evidence of a comparable stream of sociological educational research and certainly no sociological thinkers who have the same significance for education as the European sociologists.

CONCLUSION

The three differences which I referred to above are obviously related, but not necessarily. Many of the British sociologists are in the empiricist and positivist traditions. The users of qualitative techniques are not necessarily sociologists nor devotees of an all-embracing theory, but they do in total provide a difference of flavor to the research on the two sides of the Atlantic. Britain and Sweden are closer to America. The differences between Germany and France and the United States are greater, though there is now in Germany (Ingenkamp, 1977) and indeed in French-speaking Europe (de Landsheere, 1976) a growing empiricist approach.

As we noted at the beginning, there are few European researchers who are not aware of American writing. The reverse does not seem to be true. In the articles published in the Volume 19 of the *American Educational Research Journal* there were few references to British studies, fewer still to writing from elsewhere in Europe, and none at all to the writers I have referred to in this chapter, with the exception of reference by one writer to the work of Piaget. In his invited address to Division B of the American Educational Research Association in 1979 Philip Jackson drew attention to fresh winds that were blowing across the Atlantic from Norwich and from London. He did not assume that his audience would be familiar with the works of Stenhouse, MacDonald, and Walker in Norwich or with the more recent writings of Bernstein and Young in London. There is more to European research than the occasional significant book like Rutter and colleagues' *Fifteen Thousand Hours* (1978).

The differences between European and American research have been emphasized for the sake of contrast. There are parallel forces at work on both sides of the Atlantic. In the United States one can name theorists, like Chomsky, qualitative researchers, like Stake, sociologists of education, like Havighurst, but they do not play the same prominent part in the mainstream of educational thinking as do their European counterparts. There are in Europe prominent researchers who are empiricists, do not subscribe to one of the major theories, and are not sociologists. In a recent study of the citations of British writers (Rushton, Littlefield, Russell, & Meltzen, 1983), Bernstein's name is prominent, with approximately 200 citations in each of 1980 and 1981, but by far the most cited of British educational writers was Rutter, with 600 citations in 1980 and 800 in 1981. Though he is British conducting his research into British education, he is "American" in the sense that I have used it here.

Different styles are to be found on both sides of the Atlantic. It is a question of emphasis. On the whole, however, educational research in Great Britain is more marked than its American and Canadian counterparts by greater interest in illumination than in testing formal hypotheses, by the influence of broad theory, and by sociological orientation.

NOTE

1. There are no formal tracks in the American sense in these schools; rather individual student programs were made up of a different balance of academic (college preparation) courses and general or vocational courses.

REFERENCES

Althusser, L. (1971). *Lenin and philosophy and other essays*. London: New Left Books.
Bernstein, B. (1980). Class and pedagogies: Visible and invisible. In W.B. Dockrell & D. Hamilton (Eds.), *Rethinking educational research*. London: Hodder & Stoughton, pp. 115-139.
Bernstein, B. (1971, 1972, 1973). *Class codes and control* (3 vols.). Boston, MA: Routledge & Kegan Paul.
Boltanski, (1969). *Prime Educationet Moraledo Classe*. Paris-La Haye: Mouton.
Bourdieu, P., & Passeron, J. (1977). *Reproduction in education, society and Culture*. Beverly Hills, CA: Sage Publications.
Bowles, S., & Gintis, H. (1976). *Schooling in capitalist America*. New York: Basic Books.
Broudy, H.S., Ennis, R.H., & Krimerman, L.I. (Eds.) (1973). *Philosophy of educational research*. New York: Wiley.
Chambers, P., & Powney, J. (1982). School based curriculum research. *British Educational Research Journal, 8*, 133-141.
Chamboredon, J.C., & Prevot, J.Y. (1973). Le Metie d'enfant definition sociale de la prime enfance et fonctions differentielles de l'ecole maternelle. *Studies in the Learning Sciences*, 3 (CERI/OECD).
Corrie, M. (1974). *Space for Learning*. Edinburgh: Scottish Council for Research in Education.

Corrie, M., Haystead, J., & Zaklukiewicz, S. (182). *Classroom management strategies*. London: Hodder & Stoughton for Scottish Council for Research in Education.

Cronbach, L. (1975). Beyond the two disciplines of scientific psychology. *American Psychologist*, *30*, 116-127.

Cumming, C., Lowe, T., Tulips, J. & Wakeling, C. (1981). *Making the change*. London: Hodder & Stoughton for Scottish Council for Research in Education.

Davies, B. (1976). *Social control of education*. New York: Methuen.

Dockrell, J.E., Neilson, U., & McKechnie, J. (1983). Does repetition of the question influence children's performance in coversation tasks? *British Journal of Developmental Psychology*, *1*, 163-174.

Dockrell, W.B., & Hamilton, D. (1980). *Rethinking educational research*. London: Hodder & Stoughton.

Donaldson, M. (1979). *Children's minds*. London: Fontana/Collins.

Dunkell, H.B., Gowan, D.B., & Thomas, L.G. (1972). Introduction. In L.G. Thomas (Ed.), *Philsosophical redirection of educational research*. Chicago: University of Chicago Press, for National Society for the Study of Education, pp. 1-8.

Durkheim, E. (1977). *The evolution of educational thought*. Boston: Routledge & Kegan Paul. Originally published as L'Evolution pédagogique en France. Presses Universitaire de France, 1938.

Eggleston, J. (1980). *School-based curriculum development in Britain*. Boston, MA: Routledge & Kegan Paul.

Elliot, J., Bridges, D., Ebbut, D., Gibson, R., & Nias, J. (1981). *School accountability*. London: Grant McIntyre.

Entwistle, H. (1978). *Class, culture and education*. New York: Methuen.

Floud, J.E., Halsey, A.H., & Martin, F.M. (1956). *Social class and educational opportunity*. New York: Heinemann Educational Books.

Halsey, A.H., Floud, J., & Anderson, C.A. (Eds.) (1961). *Education, economy and society*. New York: The Free Press.

Halsey, A.H. (1972).*Educational priority: E.P.A. problems and policies*. London: Her Majesty's Stationery Office.

Halsey, A.H., Heath, A.F., & Ridge, J.M. (1980). *Origins and destinations*. London: Clarendon Press.

Hamilton, D. (1977). *In search of structure*. London: Hodder & Stoughton, for Scottish Council for Research in Education.

Hargreaves, D.H. (1976). *Interpersonal relations and education*. Boston, MA: Routledge & Kegan Paul.

Heinrich, R. (1973). *Zur polilischen okonomie der schulreform*. Frankfort am Main: Europaische Verlagsanstalt.

Hewitt, G. (1982). A critique of research methods in the study of reading composition. *British Educational Research Journal*, *8*, 9-23.

Ingenkamp, K.H. (1977). *Educational Assessment*. Windsor: NFER.

Jackson, B., & Marsden, D. (1962). *Education and the working class*. Boston, MA: Routledge & Kegan Paul.

Kallos, D. (1980). On educational phenomena and educational research. In W.B. Dockrell & D. Hamilton (Eds.), *Rethinking educational research*. London: Hodder & Stoughton, pp. 140-152.

Kuhn, T.S. (1970). *The structure of scientific revolutions*. Chicago: University of Chicago Press.

Lacey, C. (1970). *Hightown grammar*. Manchester: Manchester University Press.

de Landsheere, G. (1979). *Dictionnaire de l'evaluation et de la recherce en education*. Paris: Presses Universitaires de France.

Lovell, K. (1971). *The growth of understanding in mathematics*. New York: Holt, Rinehart & Winston.

MacDonald, B., & Walker, R. (1976). *Changing the curriculum*. Berkeley, CA: Open Books.

Mannheim, K. (1936). *Ideology and Utopia*. New York: Harcourt Brace.

Mannheim, K. (1952). *Essays on the sociology of knowledge*. Boston, MA: Routledge & Kegan Paul.

Masuch, M. (1973). *Politische okonomie der ausbildung, lernabeit and lehrabeit im Kapitalismus*. Hamburg: Rowohlt.

Nathan, H. (1973). *Stable rules: Science and social transmission*. London: Her Majesty's Stationery Office for Organization for Economic Cooperation and Development.

Parlett, M., & Hamilton, D. (1972). Evaluation as illumination. Edinburgh: University of Edinburg, Center for Research in Educational Sciences.

Parsons, C. (1981). A policy for educational evaluation. In C. Lacy & D. Lawton (Eds.), Issues in evaluations and accountability. New York: Methuen, pp. 39-68.

Popper, K. (1963). Logic of scientific discovery. Brooklyn, N.Y.: Hutchinson.

Rutter, M., Maughan, B., Mortimore, P., & Ousten, J. (1979). *Fifteen thousand hours*. Berkeley, CA: Open Books.

Rushton, J.P., Littlefield, C.H., Russell, R.J., & Meltzen, S.J. (1983). Research production and scholarly impact in British universities and departments of psychology: An update. *Bulletin of the British Psychological Society, 36*, 41-45.

Ryrie, A.C. (1981). *Routes and results*. London: Hodder & Stoughton, for Scottish Council for Research in Education.

Shayer, M. (1972). Conceptual Demands in the Nuffield "O" level physicals course. *School Science Review, 186*, 26-34.

Steinhouse, L. (1975). *Introduction to curriculum research and development*. New York: Heinemann.

Thomas, I.G. (Ed.) (1972). *Philosophical re-directions of educational research*. Chicago: University of Chicago Press for National Society for the Study of Education.

Watson, D. (1982). Idealism and education: T.H. Green and the education of the middle class. *British Educational Research Journal, 8*, 73-83.

Young, M.F.D. (Ed.) (1971). *Knowledge and control: New directions for the sociology of education*. New York: Collier-Macmillan.

LET'S BE TECHNICALLY RIGHT
ABOUT TECHNICAL WRITING

Paul Sorrentino

Various scholars, such as Anderson (1980), Walter (1980), and Winkler (1983) have emphasized the need for a theory of technical writing.[1] As Winkler notes, "The challenge facing teachers of technical and scientific writing in the eighties is to develop an interdisciplinary problem-solving rhetorical theory to improve the teaching of technical, scientific, and professional writing while also guiding research in communication theory" (p. 111). Without a coherent framework of principles to explain and verify experience, technical writing will remain—to paraphrase Sommers (1979) on composition research—a technology in search of a science. An appropriate theory should evolve from both theoretical and empirical research. Mere collection of data without interpretation leads to a morass of details; mere theory is simply speculative until it is tested and verified. To develop a theory one needs to know what questions to ask and where to find answers. I, therefore, review some of the significant scholarship, offer a heuristic

Advances in Reading/Language Research, Volume 3, pages 167-182.
Copyright © 1985 by JAI Press Inc.
All rights of reproduction in any form reserved.
ISBN: 0-89232-389-2

for generating questions about areas of research, and give examples of its application.

Until recently only a few scholars such as Mills and Walter (1953) seriously considered developing a theory of technical writing, for two reasons. Traditionally, technical writers have been primarily trained as engineers and scientists. Faced with a writing task and limited time, their approach has been pragmatic. If something worked, fine. There seemed little need to ask why it worked. Some professionals have even been hostile toward theoretical questions. When *Technical Communication* (Corey, 1978) devoted a special issue to the relationship between rhetoric and technical writing, it received a rash of letters, of which the following was typical: "Never before has an entire issue of *Technical Communication* gone completely over my head, but the Fourth Quarter 1978 features a series of articles that left me wondering which of the following might be the case: (1) I am so far out in the bayous that current thinking about technical literature has passed me by; (2) I am working on a level at which philosophical and policy considerations are irrelevant; (3) The authors are suffering from acute epidemic ivory-tower disease" (Boynton, 1979, p. 1). The writer, an employee of Computer Sciences Corporation, concluded that item 3 was the answer.

The primary place for developing a theory is academia, but the status of technical writing in departments of English has stymied research. For years most teachers of the course were junior faculty with graduate degrees in literature. With no training in technical writing and no one with experience to turn to for advice, they quickly assembled a course that too often could have been labeled advanced freshman English. If they turned to their colleagues for intellectual companionship, they found themselves isolated. In 1973, John Harris wrote:

> The teacher of technical writing often feels like an orphan. His colleagues in English departments are likely to view his subject matter as an industrial craft inferior to Renaissance drama or Victorian poetry, and the faculty of the colleges of science and engineering may look at him as an ivory tower humanist.
>
> Nor do the professional organizations have a real place for him. The NCTE [National Council of Teachers of English] and especially the CCCC [Conference on College Composition and Communication] have provided space for him on convention programs, but their journals carry few articles on teaching technical writing (p. 1).

Today, however, the attitude on campus has changed. The Association of Teachers of Technical Writing has helped to schedule heavily attended sessions on technical writing at CCCC, NCTE, and MLA (Modern Language Association). *College English* and *College Composition and Communication* now regularly publish articles on technical writing. Schools are hiring specialists to staff undergraduate and graduate degree programs in professional writing and are offering workshops to train teachers interested in the field.

Currently the discipline most frequently examined for a taxonomy of technical writing is discourse theory (e.g., Harris, 1981). Discourse is defined as the complete text of an oral or written situation; researchers examine how a writer or speaker uses language purposefully to convey information to an audience. Modern discourse theory criticizes Bain's (1890) influential classification of modes of discourse according to five forms: description, narration, exposition, argumentation, and poetry (which is not germane to this discussion). Each form has its own function, subject matter, methods of organization, and style. Though many teachers have structured a course in technical writing around the first four modes, the approach is unrealistic because writers do not simply describe a device, narrate an event, explain a procedure, or argue a point. These are merely means of achieving an end; instead, they describe a machine so that a customer will know whether to buy it, narrate a company's activities so that stockholders reading an annual report will be informed, explain procedures so that employees will know a company's policy regarding sick leave, and argue for or against building a new plant so that corporate executives will know whether the project is feasible. Consequently, a theory of technical writing centered on techniques of writing is inadequate; instead, it should be organized around the purpose of writing. The first question to ask is not how to write a document, but why.

Recognizing the inadequacy of a course based on technique rather than purpose, Eckhardt and Stewart (1979) argue for a functional taxonomy of writing. They point out that the traditional division of modes of discourse is confusing because whereas description, narration, and exposition are only means of organizing material, argumentation is a means that implies purpose. One writes to clarify what the subject is, to substantiate a thesis about it, to evaluate it, or to recommend a course of action regarding it. Hence, the four purposes in writing are definition, substantiation, evaluation, and recommendation. The categories are incremental; each incorporates the preceding one(s). To recommend that a company begin manufacturing a new product, for example, requires that management know what the product is, whether the claims about it are valid, and whether it is worth doing, given the company's resources and interests. Eckhardt, Stewart, Holahan, and Sorrentino (1976) have edited an anthology organized around this taxonomy of purpose.

Of the various recent approaches to discourse, Kinneavy's (1971/80) has had the most influence on technical writing. Like Bain, Kinneavy believes that each mode of discourse has its own logic, organization, and style; but like Eckhardt and Stewart, he is more interested in a theory based on purpose, which he calls "aim." Though he draws on such cognate fields as linguistics, philosophy, and information theory, he relies heavily on communication theory. As Figure 1 shows, all communication, whether oral or written, involves components that can be graphically depicted as a triangle.

Because all communicative acts involve the four components—encoder, decoder, reality, and signal—the difference among acts is in aim. In expressive discourse—such as private journals, diaries, and prayer—the primary aim is to express the thoughts, emotions, and beliefs of the encoder. In persuasive

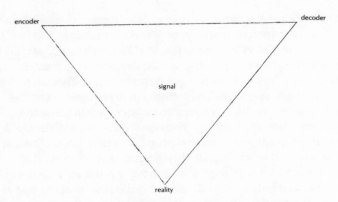

Figure 1. Components of the Communication Triangle.
(From Kinneavy, 1971/1980.)

discourse—as in advertising, religious sermons, and editorials—the primary aim
is to persuade the decoder. In literary discourse—short stories, poems, and
songs—the primary aim is to draw attention to the text as literary artifact. And in
referential discourse—such as lab reports, news articles, and textbooks—the
primary aim is to refer to some reality preexisting the encoder and decoder. Each
aim can involve narration, description, evaluation, and classification, but not
argumentation (persuasion) because it is an aim, not a mode. Referential
discourse can be "informative" if it simply presents facts about known reality,
"exploratory" if it investigates unknown reality, or "scientific" if it systematically
tests the validity of a proposition about reality. (Scientific discourse is not limited
to writing or speaking about the sciences.)

Scholars have begun to test and modify Kinneavy's theory. Freisinger (1981) is
exploring an unexamined assumption in the theory, i.e., that the aim of and
audience for a text influence a writer's "voice" and style, by examining
documents from academia and industry. To date, he has concluded that
industrial texts involve a wider range of aims and audiences than do academic
texts. Harris (1979) has shown the practical applications of the theory by
describing how she divides her technical writing course into informative,
exploratory, scientific, and what she calls persuasive-referential writing. The last
category combines two aims of discourse to account for forms (e.g., recommendation reports) that do not easily fit into one of Kinneavy's categories.

Despite the popularity of Kinneavy's theory, other scholars have criticized its
emphasis on static form. The analysis of the process of discourse, as Odell (1979,
p. 54) notes, "is troublesome for two reasons. First, his statement about process is
based primarily on an analysis of written products, rather than an analysis of the
choices writers have made as their texts evolve through a succession of drafts.
Second, in analyzing a written product, Kinneavy does not usually refer to the

reasoning of the writer who actually produced the discourse." No basis exists "for assuming that analysis of products will let us find out everything we need to know about the writing process. Nor can we assume that writers' own insights will not be useful to us as we try to understand this process." Knoblauch (1980, p. 154) has criticized Kinneavy (as well as other discourse theorists) for not distinguishing between "generic purposes" and "operational purposes." Generic purposes, such as Kinneavy's four aims of discourse, "merely define categories in which completed discourses may be located." Writers "do not set out to 'be referential' except in an unhelpfully general way." Operational purposes, however, "actually initiate discourse"; they "are specific to real situations and often quite complex." The generic purposes of, say, a proposal are referential and persuasive; but because the document is treated as a completed text, the classification does not explain the rhetorical choices a writer makes while composing the document. A classification according to operational purposes is more helpful. In a consulting agency, for example, a proposal writer might want to explain a highly sophisticated service like systems planning to a prospective client, define a contractual obligation between the client and agency, and convince superiors that as a writer he or she is efficient and promotable.

Miller (1980)[2] responds to this criticism of Kinneavy by adapting Bitzer's 1968 analysis of the rhetorical situation. Every rhetorical situation, according to Bitzer, consists of an exigence, which is the specific need or problem that a writer or speaker addresses, an audience, and constraints such as persons or events that affect how the exigence is treated. In composing an article on advances in the research of technical writing, for example, a writer must respond to the need of a disparate audience to know about the current state of the field and areas for future research. Among the constraints are the audience's knowledge of and experience with the subject, deadline for submission of the manuscript, and editorial policies concerning its length and style. Miller argues that if the theory "is based on a classification of exigences, rather than a classification of functions or purposes, it becomes a dynamic, social force rather than a static, formulaic pattern" (pp. 8–9). More recently, O'Banion (1982) objects to Kinneavy's "inconsistent methodology: he does not consistently apply his own insights into any one particular aim to his theory as a whole. His chapter 'Expressive Discourse,' for instance, contains some of his best material, but its phenomenological and existential values fail to inform the rest of the book" (p. 198).

As scholars examine Kinneavy's work, they might find useful an heuristic for generating questions about areas of research. Harper's adaptation (1979) of the Greco–Roman model of human communication theory is appropriate. Though she is mainly concerned with oral communication, her discussion is applicable to technical writing as a daily activity and as a scholarly discipline. Because the model treats communication as a process rather than a product, it can account for objections raised by Odell, Knoblauch, and Miller against Kinneavy. The

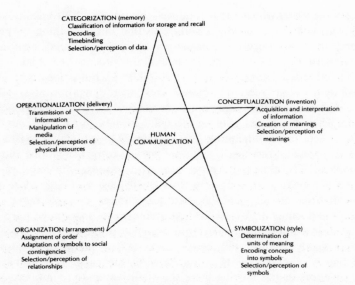

Figure 2.   A model of the processes involved in human communication.
(From Harper, 1979.)

prevailing view in composition research is that writing must be regarded as a "process."

As Figure 2 shows, Harper's model (p. 2) depicts human communication graphically as a star, with each of its points representing one of the five processes involved in 'message making.' The connecting lines of the star suggest the interdependence of categorization, conceptualization, symbolization, organization, and operationalization. Though the five "points" are discussed separately, something said about one often overlaps with another. Throughout message making, for example, rhetorical choices about what to write and how to write it are a function of audience and purpose. Categorization and conceptualization discover ideas; symbolization, organization, and operationalization transmit them. The order in which the five processes are considered depends on whether one is sending or receiving a message.

Categorization is the process by which we perceive, store, and recall information. From our reading and experience, we gather data relevant to our job, classify it in our memory, and recall it when we encounter new data that are more easily understood in the light of what we already know. Because we do not all use the same methods of classification, what we select and perceive as relevant depends on our needs and preconceptions. In Korzybski's words (1958, passim), we become "timebinders": our ability to see relationships between data selected in the past and those selected in the present and to categorize both groups accordingly allows us to bind and order our world. The time-binding process shapes our expectations of what to see and look for in the future. Just as what we have perceived shapes what we will perceive, the language available structures our view of reality.

To further understand categorization, scholars should explore information-processing theory, a subfield of cognitive psychology. The theory assumes that categorization is the main function of the human brain: the mind perceives, selects, stores and retrieves information. The pace, or speed, at which the mind stores and recalls data is important. Technical writers have always believed that the more complex the subject, the slower the pace should be in describing it because the reader must assimilate new with existing information. Writers know that pace depends on audience and subject matter, but they need more precise guidelines. Smith's discussion (1975, pp. 51–58) of the limitations and rate of information processing offers a provocative introduction applicable to ways in which technical readers categorize information. He describes an experiment in which participants looked at a clear white screen. Twenty-five randomly arranged letters appeared on the screen for a split second. Asked to recall as many letters as possible, they could remember only four or five. When the experiment was repeated, but this time the letters were arranged into words, they could remember more than a handful of letters. Since the amount of visual information and the length of time to view it were the same in both experiments, why was more information recorded the second time? Smith answers that the participants used nonvisual information, which was not on the screen. By recalling prior knowledge about the structure of the English language, they processed the letters more quickly the second time; therefore, the way readers process (decode) language should govern the way writers construct (encode) documents.

Knowing how readers categorize information is especially vital for teaching students with English as a second language (ESL). Currently about 70% of the foreign students studying in the United States are in technical fields, and many of them take a course in technical writing. They are bright but have trouble with linguistic structures in English. Teachers should thus consider the kinds of problems foreign students encounter in processing English. I suspect that most people involved with technical writing know little, if anything, about two orientations within ESL, English for Specific Purposes (ESP) and English for Science and Technology (EST). A good, though brief, introduction is Olsen (1981).

With the increasing use of computer data banks to store and retrieve information, computer science is another discipline valuable for understanding categorization. Many current programs can flag misspelled words, calculate readability, evaluate word choices, and assess writing style. To date, however, a computer's capability to generate new text is in its infancy. Algorithms necessary for the task will require additional research in such fields as artificial intelligence and psycholinguistics. Yet a program like TALE-SPIN can already produce new

Aesop-like fables, and the Navy is developing a program that lets a computer write a set of instructions by recalling from its memory information that is then rearranged according to a specified format (Coke, 1982). In Japan, the government and several of the country's major electronics firms have formed the Institute for New Generation Computer Technology, which is involved in a 10-year, $800 million research program to develop computers that can actually think as humans do. Less dramatic but perhaps as significant are research and development on children's computer-assisted composition, as exemplified in Rubin and Bruce's (1984) chapter in this volume. Much research is still needed to show how artificially stored and retrieved information will affect technical writing. Indeed, computer technology will influence not only our understanding of categorization but Harper's other four processes involved in human communication.

After categorization, the next process is conceptualization, which is the making of meaning from data. Linguistics, sociology of knowledge, and history and philosophy of science are especially helpful in explaining how scientists and technologists interpret data. One aspect of the interpretation is the relationship between the observer and what is observed. Is it possible for the observer to be objective in dealing with and writing about facts? Despite criticism of the belief in objectivity, some writers still contend they can free themselves from any bias toward facts. Kelley and Masse's definition of technical writing (1977, p. 95) is typical:

> *Technical Writing* is writing about a subject in the pure sciences or the applied sciences in which the writer informs the reader through an objective presentation of facts.... *Objective* refers to a state of mind. If a writer is objective, he is free from any bias toward his subject. If he writes objectively, he presents the facts as they are, unaffected by his thoughts and feelings about them. These *facts* are pieces of information that can be verified objectively. In other words, they are pieces of information that can be proved accurate by simple experience or by scientific observation and experimentation.

Their definition reflects the positivist legacy in science, which asserts that only facts verifiable empirically and known without reference to a scientific theory can assure the objectivity of science. As a result, positivists claim there must be a strict duality between subject and object for legitimate research.

Kelley and Masse's definition reiterates the popular view in technical writing that language should not "interfere with" the presentation of facts; consequently, many readers treat scientific and technological documents, or discourses, as if the language were like a window through which they can see. Research in linguistics and the history and philosophy of science, however, has challenged this view. If language precedes and shapes thought and is the product of a particular scientific or technological discipline at a particular time, language does not simply duplicate the phenomenal reality to which it refers. Meaning does not simply lie in data; instead, the making of meaning is complicated. Because it is humanly impossible to perceive and record all data, the process of conceptualization is highly selective.

What one conceptualizes and makes meaning out of depends on what the scientific and technological community deems worth pursuing and examining. This attitude is part of what Kuhn (1970) calls a "paradigm." A paradigm, or a theoretical world view, shapes the way scientists perceive, what kind of research they do, and how they do it. As the group of beliefs shared by the scientific community changes, so does the paradigm. The paradigm dictates what kind of empirical evidence to select and how to interpret it. The processes of categorization and conceptualization are thus theory laden; and as the theory changes, so do the processes. Consider, for example, the shift from the Ptolemaic to the Copernican world view: one's view of reality reflects the paradigm currently maintained by the scientific community. Essentially, then, the process of making meaning is what Berger and Luckmann (1966; reprinted 1980) call "the social construction of reality"; an interpretation of data is valid if it is accepted communally. As Harper says, "Human beings not only *sense* their world, they also *make sense* of it" (p. 6).

Whereas categorization and conceptualization are concerned with discovery of ideas, the remaining three processes in Harper's model deal with transmission of ideas. Symbolization is the process of encoding meaning into symbols. The symbols can be regarded as either denotative or connotative and discussed syntactically, semantically, or pragmatically. Syntactics involves the structure of symbols; semantics, the relationship between meaning and symbols; and pragmatics, the use of symbols. A better understanding of how connotation affects usage might have prevented the costly error General Motors once made. No one realized why an expensive advertising campaign in Spanish-speaking countries failed to sell the Nova car until someone noticed that "Nova" looks like "no va," which in Spanish means "no go."

Because in technical writing the symbols are verbal and nonverbal (visual aids), we need to understand better how words and pictures interrelate. How does one know, for example, when to use visual aids? How much of a presentation of a subject should be done visually and how much verbally? Are certain kinds of information better conveyed visually? Where should visual aids appear in a text? We need, in other words, a rhetoric for visual aids because, as Burke (1969, p. 43) argues, rhetoric should include all of the "symbolic means of inducing cooperation in beings that by nature respond to symbols."

As with language, we should be able to discuss the syntactics, semantics, and pragmatics of a nonverbal symbol. To date, because little research exists, technical writers must rely more on their own judgment than on empirically tested principles when they answer questions about visual aids. Currently, however, researchers are developing a rhetoric for visual aids or, more broadly, for graphic design. The Document Design Center in Washington, D.C. has been studying how to make documents easier to understand and use. With the help of Carnegie-Mellon University and Siegle & Gale, a design firm in New York specializing in the effective use of language, the Center has been testing what appear to be effective principles in graphic design. Among its extremely useful publications are the newsletter *Simply Stated* (November 1979-present); Felker, Pickering, Charrow, Holland, and Redish's *Guidelines for Document Designers* (1981); and Felker, Atlas, Charrow, Holland, Olkes, Redish, and Rose's *Document Design: A Review of the Relevant Research* (1980), which surveys not only typography/graphics but also psycholinguistics, cognitive psychology, instructional research, readability, and human factors.

Jonassen (1982) also reports recent research and suggests areas for more. He is interested not just in graphic design, but in the design of the whole document, i.e., *"the technology of sequencing, structuring, designing, and laying-out of the printed page, whether that text is reproduced on paper or in electronic signals on a cathode ray tube"* (p. ix). Recognizing that traditionally the approach to document design has been unsystematic, he wants to develop *"a scientific approach to text design"* (p. x) based on theories and research that will provide better instructional material. His edition contains essays based on research in cognitive psychology, reading, and information processing that offer heuristics for document design.

Several of the essays examine the process of nonverbal symbolization. The authors correctly assume that because there is no categorically best way to communicate visually a specific body of information, there should be a rhetoric for graphic design that supplies operative principles. Winn and Holliday (1982) discuss "the logical or syntactical relationships" as well as the 'semantic distance' existing among concepts that diagrams and charts describe (pp. 277, 278), and they develop from their research nine principles regarding the use of diagrams and charts in instruction. Principle 9 typifies the sort of advice they offer: "Do not use complex and redundant diagrams and charts with low-ability students. Remember, understanding diagrams requires certain mental skills. Diagrams are *not* necessarily 'easier' forms of instruction" (p. 297). As with diagrams and charts, little empirical evidence exists to explain when and why to use pictures in instructions. Brody (1982) describes how pictures affect text and offers six principles for their use, e.g., "placement of pictures should be based on the function the picture is to serve" (p. 315). Brody's article is especially helpful in the light of recent research concluding that pictures can affect cognitive processes:

> While the precise relationship between picture elements and cognitive processes has not been clearly delineated, the implications are clear. Through careful analysis, it may be possible to design pictures that will not only help the student gain content competence, but also develop a specific cognitive skill or strategy. For example, not only can graphic techniques be used to help isolate pictorial elements so that the viewer can better acquire the information, but also to better develop the skills related to isolating relevant information (p. 303).

Wright (1982) evaluates choices in, and offers principles for, the design of tables and flowcharts. "Eliminating redundancy," for example, "can be a false economy"

(p. 337). She and the other authors in Jonassen's edition realize the need to make a document user friendly.

Professonal writers have always recognized the importance of visual aids. As Gombrich (1972) notes, "The real value of the image . . . is its capacity to convey information that cannot be coded in any other way. In his important book *Prints and Visual Communication*, William M. Ivins, Jr., argues that the Greeks and Romans failed to make progress in science because they lacked the idea of multiplying images by some form of printing (1953; reprinted 1969, p. 87). Visual aids are vital in a world once described by Marshall McLuhan as a global village. If a company wishes to sell its products worldwide, it can write instructions only in English, in selected languages, or in every language from Abnaki to Zuñian, or it can use one set of instructions using only visual aids in order to overcome language barriers. IBM, for example, is experimenting with instructions without words, just 17 pictures that portray how to remove an electric typewriter from its packing crate, set up the machine, and position the ball. Admittedly, a more complicated procedure would probably require verbal instructions as well, but the set of instructions emphasizes the value of pictorial representation.

Organization, the fourth part of Harper's model, is the process of adapting and arranging verbal and nonverbal symbols in time and space. Generally speaking, the organization may be natural (i.e., spatial or chronological), as in an annual report, or logical, as with a feasibility study. Both sequences may appear in the same document. A lab report describes the sequence in which an experiment was conducted and argues for certain conclusions inferred from the results. In a survey of 1,000 engineers asking them to identify the biggest problem they face in writing, the most frequent answer was "organization and outlining" (Smith, 1976). The same holds true, I am sure, for other professionals. Yet, as Kinneavy mentions about the organization of reference discourse, the category for technical writing, "the systematizing techniques of science, as such, have not been subjected to analysis with anything remotely resembling the care accorded to the logical techniques of science. . . . [T]here is not a corresponding analytical tradition for the organization of scientific and informative discourse paralleling the 'arrangement' . . . tradition in rhetoric. This is undoubtedly regrettable" (1971, p. 151). There is, however, a deep reservoir of research in discourse processing by such researchers as Daneman, Just, and Carpenter (1982) and Meyer (1983) on text processing and by Stone and Crandell (1982) on integration of text and technical illustrations. While the focus in their work is on the text and its interpretation, there are clear implications for guiding and assessing the processes of composing text.

Most likely the difficulty with organization that the engineers faced resulted from their inability to distinguish between what Mathes and Stevenson (1976, chap. 3) call the technical task and the rhetorical task. Solving a technical problem and taking notes on it compose the technical task. We write information down in writer-based prose, which is for our eyes only. We know what the crossouts, question marks, and arrows moving one section to another place mean. But writing something *down* for our use differs from writing something *up* for the reader. In reader-based prose, our rhetorical task is to organize information in a way best suited to our audience and purpose. I tell students how I organized papers in high school. Page 2 appeared where it did simply because I wrote it after page 1. Because I had no idea how to organize a paper, I made the opening sentence so general that it could subsume anything following it: "One of the most interesting things about... is...." I did not realize that writers at first frequently do not know what to say and how to organize it; but as they revise a first draft, they discover how to turn writer-based prose into reader-based prose. As Middleman (1981, p. 17) says, they move "from 'Oh, Oh!' to 'Aha!'"

Although the current emphasis in composition research on writing as a process is yielding significant findings for dealing with organization and writing in general, we still need to know more about the cognitive process involved in revising writer-based into reader-based prose and how best to teach the process. A useful textbook that approaches writing as a process is Flower's *Problem-Solving Strategies for Writing* (1981). Based on her research with John Hayes, a cognitive psychologist, the book treats writing as a problem-solving activity. The steps supplied for developing strategies that transform a vague idea into a final draft are useful for technical writing. In discussing argumentation, for example, Flower describes Rogerian argument, based partly on the work of psychologist Carl Rogers, to clarify the difference between winning an argument and persuading a reader. She then demonstrates how a specific letter reorganized and revised could make the difference between the acceptance or rejection of its argument. An argument is successful, Flower concludes, only if it is organized into reader-based prose. As with her book, Felker et al. (1981) supply principles for organizing text. Each principle is followed by a review of the appropriate research.

Just as research is needed to derive principles regarding organization of text, so too is it necessary for visual aids. The organization of an aid is typically discussed spatially. Because the cliché "A picture is worth a thousand words" is true, the arrangement in space of a pie chart tells the reader more quickly than words can the distribution of, say, the gross national product. Yet there is also a temporal sequence inherent within a visual aid. Unlike a camera, the brain does not record instantaneously what the eye sees. The brain first records the dominant features of the chart, then its details. The order in which the brain perceives the components of an aid depends on such visual rhetorical devices as color, kind and style of typography, and white space. A rhetoric for graphic design will explain how to control the temporal sequence.

The last part of Harper's model of human communication is operationalization, the process of embodying content in a physical form such as a letter, memo, or progress report. Because an audience first notices the document itself before starting to read it, technical writing has emphasized the physical construction of the document. Readers will perceive a document in the light of experience with similar documents. If they are reading the fourth progress report of a project, their knowledge of the first three reports will shape their expectations. The operationalization of a document, as well as its symbolization and organization, is a form of persuasion; the packaging of verbal and nonverbal symbols influences an audience's acceptance or rejection of them. Felker et al. (1981), for example, suggest using unjustified right margins: "Some readers find that ragged right margins make the text easier to read. When each line looks different, the eye is less likely to stray to another line because it can quickly separate and identify each line. Also, the eye does not have to adjust to the different spacing between letters in each word which is necessary to justify the type. In contrast, justified type may be harder to read because the lines do look the same, and the spaces between letters are different in each word" (p. 85). The authors' suggestion is based in part on research showing that poor readers find it easier to understand material with an unjustified right margin. Traditionally, writers have thought justified margins look "more professional." Deciding how to type a document, though, involves more than aesthetics.

Another instance of the significance of operationalization is the ethos that a document projects. Ethos, the audience's perception of the writer's character, influences the way an audience processes information. A young man writing a letter of application for a sales job with a company wanting someone to start at the bottom reversed the layout of his letter. The address, date, and salutation were at the bottom of the page, and the complimentary close was at the top. The body was also reversed. Part of the letter read, "You state that you have a position open for a young man, who isn't afraid to start at the bottom, to become a sales representative for your firm. Well, as you can see, I am not afraid to start at the bottom" (Leonard, 1979, p. 228). The unorthodox format might discourage many employers, but the applicant projected an ethos appropriate for sales—that he was creative, assertive and imaginative.

The layout of the signature block can also determine ethos. In the Army, the close can be written in two ways:

FTC	Paul Sorrentino		James A. Boyle, Jr.
	First Lieutenant	or	Lieutenant Colonel
	Adjutant		Commander

In the first case, "FTC" (for the commander) means that although the adjutant has written the letter, the commander has approved its contents. The letter might deal with a change in policy or with standard operating procedure. If the second block appears, the same letter takes on added authority simply because of the commander's position. Similarly, a letter in business and industry that ends

Sincerely yours,

Doug Henning
Sales Manager

is written by Henning in his role as sales manager; but if the letter ends

> Sincerely yours,
> The Merlin Corporation
>
> *Doug Henning*
> Doug Henning
> Sales Manager

the tone is more formal and implies that he is writing officially for the company. In both examples, the physical layout of the complimentary close creates an ethos to which the audience responds. Such labels as "Commander" and "The Merlin Corporation" influence whether the audience finds the writer credible. Before readers can be persuaded to accept the contents of any document and be moved to act on it, they must first accept the writer's character. Job titles and company names, in other words, generate an ethos. To quote a popular commercial, "Like a good neighbor, State Farm is there."

As with any framework, there is always the danger of treating its components as discrete. It is worth remembering that because Harper's model consists of five processes, it is itself a process. Also, the process is not linear, but recursive. Decisions made at any time may force us to revise previous ones. The model is thus dynamic rather than static. As such, it generates the kinds of questions to ask in developing a theory of technical writing and points out where answers will come from. Using research from various disciplines, scholars will be able, I am sure, to be technically right about technical writing.

NOTES

1. Other scholars have more recently written about a theory of technical writing. See, for example, P.V. Anderson, R.J. Brockmann, & C.R. Miller (Eds.) (1983), *New Essays in Technical and Scientific Communication: Research, Theory, Practice*, Baywood's Technical Communication Series, Vol. 2 (Farmingdale, N.Y.: Baywood); M.G. Moran & D. Journet (Eds.) (1985), *Research in Technical Communication: A Bibliographic Sourcebook* (Westport, Ct.: Greenwood); and the *Journal of Technical Writing and Communication*, 15 (1985).

2. C.R. Miller has since published "Genre as Social Action," *Quarterly Journal of Speech*, 70 (1984), 151-67.

REFERENCES

Anderson, P.V. (1980). The need for better research in technical communication. *Journal of Technical Writing and Communication, 10*, 271-282.
Bain, A. (1890). *English composition and rhetoric* (rev. ed.). New York: Appleton.
Berger, P.L., & Luckmann, T. (1980). *The social construction of reality: A treatise in the sociology of knowledge*. New York: Irvington. (Originally published by Doubleday, 1966.)
Bitzer, L.F. (1968). The rhetorical situation. *Philosophy and Rhetoric, 1*, 1-14.
Boynton, B.F. (1979). Correspondence. *Technical Communication, 26*(2), 1.

Brody, P.J. (1982). Affecting instructional textbooks through pictures. In D.H. Jonassen (Ed.), *The technology of text: Principles for structuring, designing, and displaying text*. Englewood Cliffs, NJ: Educational Technology Publications, pp. 301-316.

Burke, K. (1969). *A rhetoric of motives*. Berkeley, CA: University of California Press.

Coke, E.U. (1982). Computer aids for writing text. In D.H. Jonassen (Ed.), *The technology of text: Principles for structuring, designing, and displaying text*. Englewood Cliffs, NJ: Educational Technology Publications, pp. 383-399.

Corey, R.L. (Ed.) (1978). Rhetoric and technical writing [Special issue]. *Technical Communication, 25*(4) , 2-18.

Daneman, M., Carpenter, P.A., & Just, M.A. (1982). Cognitive processes and reading skills. In B.A. Hutson (Ed.), *Advances in reading/language research* (Vol. 1). Greenwich, CT: JAI Press, pp. 83-124.

Eckhardt, C.D., & Stewart, D.H. (1981). Towards a functional taxonomy of composition. In G. Tate & E.P.J. Corbett (Eds.), *The writing teacher's sourcebook*. New York: Oxford University Press. (Reprinted from *College Composition and Communication*, 1979, *30*, 338-342.)

Eckhardt, C.D., Stewart, D.H., Holahan, J., & Sorrentino, P. (Eds.) (1976). *The Wiley reader*. New York: Wiley.

Felker, D.B., Atlas, M., Charrow, V.R., Holland, V.M., Olkes, C., Redish, J.C., & Rose, A.M. (1980). *Document design: A review of the relevant research*. Washington, DC: American Institutes for Research.

Felker, D.B., Pickering, F., Charrow, V.R., Holland, V.M., & Redish, J.C. (1981). *Guidelines for document designers*. Washington, DC: American Institutes for Research.

Flower, L. (1981). *Problem-solving strategies for writing*. New York: Harcourt.

Freisinger, R. (1981). *Style in the universe of industrial and academic discourse*. Paper presented at the meeting of the Modern Language Association, New York, December.

Gombrich, E.H. (1972). The visual image. *Scientific American*, September, *227*, 82-97.

Harper, N. (1979). *Human communication theory: The history of a paradigm*. Rochelle Park, NJ: Hayden.

Harris, E. (1979). Application of Kinneavy's *theory of discourse* to technical writing. *College English, 40*, 625-632.

Harris, E. (1981). Discourse theory for technical writing. In M. Marcuse & S. Kleinmann (Eds.), *Proceedings of the Inaugural Conference of the Maryland Junior Writing Program, 17 March 1980*. College Park: University of Maryland, March, 125-131.

Harris, J.S. (1973). From the president. *The Technical Writing Teacher, 1*, 1-2.

Ivins, W.M., Jr. (1969). *Prints and visual communication*. New York: Da Capo Press. (Originally published by Harvard University Press, 1953.)

Jonassen, D.H. (Ed.) (1982). *The technology of text: Principles for structuring, designing, and displaying text*. Englewood Cliffs, NJ: Educational Technology Publications.

Kelley, P.M., & Masse, R.E. (1977). A definition of technical writing. *The Technical Writing Teacher, 4*, 94-97.

Kinneavy, J.L. (1980). *A theory of discourse*. New York: Norton. (Originally published by Prentice-Hall, 1971.)

Knoblauch, C.H. (1980). Intentionality in the writing process: A case study. *College Composition and Communication, 31*, 153-159.

Korzybski, A. (1958). *Science and sanity: An introduction to non-Aristotelian systems and general semantics* (4th. ed.). Lakeville, CT: The International Non-Aristotelian Literary Publishing Co.

Kuhn, T.S. (1970). *The structure of scientific revolutions* (2nd. ed.). Chicago: University of Chicago Press.

Leonard, D.J. (1979). *Shurter's written communication in business* (4th. ed.). New York: McGraw-Hill.

Mathes, J.C., & Stevenson, D.W. (1976). *Designing technical reports: Writing for audiences in organizations*. Indianapolis, IN: Bobbs-Merrill.

Meyer, B.J.F. (1983). Text structure and its use in studying comprehension across the adult life span. In B.A. Hutson (Ed.), *Advances in reading/language research* (Vol. 2). Greenwich, CT: JAI Press, pp. 9-54.

Middleman, L.I. (1981). *In short: A concise guide to good writing*. New York: St. Martin's Press.

Miller, C.R. (1979). A humanistic rationale for technical writing. *College English, 40*, 610-617.

Miller, C.R. (1980). *The rhetorical genre: An explanatory concept for technical communication*. Paper presented at the meeting of the Modern Language Association, Houston, December.

Mills, G.H., & Walter, J.A. (1953). *The theory of technical writing* (circular no. 22). Austin, TX: Bureau of Engineering Research at the University of Texas.

O'Banion, J.D. (1982). *A theory of discourse*: A retrospective. *College Composition and Communication, 33*, 196-201.

Odell, L. (1981). Teachers of composition and needed research in discourse theory. In G. Tate & E.P.J. Corbett, (Eds.), *The writing teacher's sourcebook*. New York: Oxford University Press. (Reprinted from *College Composition and Communication*, 1979, *30*, 39-45.)

Olsen, L.A. (1981). Issues in ESL and their relevance for technical writing teachers. *Proceedings: 28th International Technical Communication Conference, 28*, E74-E77.

Rubin, A., & Bruce, B. (1985). Quill: Reading and writing with a microcomputer. In B.A. Hutson, (Ed.), *Advances in reading/language research* (Vol. 3). Greenwich, CT: JAI Press, pp. 97-117.

Simply Stated. (Monthly newsletter of the Document Design Center, American Institutes for Research, 1055 Thomas Jefferson Street, N.W., Washington, DC 20007, November 1979-present.)

Smith, F. (1975). *Comprehension and learning: A conceptual framework for teachers*. New York: Holt.

Smith, T.C. (1976). What bugs people most about report writing. *Technical Communication, 26*(4), 2-6.

Sommers, N.I. (1979). The need for theory in composition research. *College Composition and Communication, 30*, 46-49.

Stone, D.E., & Crandell, T.L. (1982). Relationships of illustrations and text in reading technical material. In B.A. Hutson (Ed.), *Advances in reading/language research* (Vol. 1). Greenwich, CT: JAI Press, pp. 283-307.

Tate, G., & Corbett, E.P.J. (Eds.) (1981). *The writing teacher's sourcebook*. New York: Oxford University Press.

Walter, J.A. (1980). ATTW: In retrospect and in prospect. *The Technical Writing Teacher, 7*, 91-93.

Winkler, V.M. (1983). The role of models in technical and scientific writing. In P.V. Anderson, R.J. Brockmann, & C.R. Miller (Eds.), *New essays in technical and scientific communication: Research, theory, practice*. Farmingdale, NY: Baywood, pp. 111-122.

Winn, W., & Holliday, W. (1982). Design principles for diagrams and charts. In D.H. Jonassen (Ed.), *The technology of text: Principles for structuring, designing, and displaying text*. Englewood Cliffs, NJ: Educational Technology Publications, pp. 277-299.

Wright, P. (1982). A user-oriented approach to the design of tables and flowcharts. In D.H. Jonassen (Ed.), *The technology of text: Principles for structuring, designing, and displaying text*. Englewood Cliffs, NJ: Educational Technology Publications, pp. 317-340.

PERSONAL COMPUTERS IN LANGUAGE AND READING RESEARCH:
THREE VIGNETTES

Daniel W. Kee and Patricia E. Worden

INTRODUCTION

Advances in microelectronic technology have fostered the development and widespread availability of personal computers. Personal computers can perform many of the same functions as "big" computers and they consist of many of the same components. For example, a typewriter keyboard is used to input information to the computer system, while a television or printer serves as an output device. In contrast to 'big' computers, however, the "brains" or central processing unit of personal computers can be located on a single silicon-based microprocessor "chip" less than one centimeter square. The central processing unit is responsible for interpreting instructions and controlling the flow of information through the computer system. Because of the small size of this

Advances in Reading/Language Research, Volume 3, pages 183-205.
Copyright © 1985 by JAI Press Inc.
All rights of reproduction in any form reserved.
ISBN: 0-89232-389-2

microprocessor chip, most personal computers are small enough to fit on a desktop and some are briefcase size. Another important component of computers is memory, which is used in the storage of data and programs. The larger the memory, measured in kilobytes, the larger and more complex the computing activity that can be performed. The cost of memory 'chips' has declined dramatically over the last few years whereas their sophistication has increased. Thus, very powerful personal computers are available at reasonable prices.

The widespread availability of personal computers will have a substantial impact on many facets of language and reading research. Historically, computers were used primarily to facilitate the data analysis phases of research. For example, after a study was completed a data base would be established on computer cards or computer tape for subsequent statistical analysis on a mainframe computer housed at a computer center. Some investigators may have had "mini computers" in their laboratories for the control of experiments, including on-line data collection and analysis. Such computers, however, were expensive and often required a trained technician for the support of the project. In contrast, personal computers will change the role computers can play in the research activities of many investigators. Because of the low cost and small size of personal computers, applications will emerge in all phases of research, from data collection to word processing of manuscripts. Furthermore, the kinds of research questions asked about the development of reading and language skills will undoubtedly be affected.

This chapter provides vignettes illustrating the impact personal computers and microelectronic learning devices can have on research in child language and reading. The examples are drawn from programmatic research concerning diverse issues: (1) brain specialization and language functions; (2) joint parent–child reading with books vs. computers; and (3) learning and motivational aspects of a hand-held microelectronic language game. These are obviously diverse topics, but each provides an example of the use of personal computers to facilitate reading/language research. Each vignette describes the results from an initial study in the area. These studies will illustrate how research tactics were influenced by the availability of personal computers and/or how new research questions were suggested by the presence of the new computer technology. The research examples described explore both basic and applied research issues; the computers employed were relatively inexpensive and simple to use. Illustration of both observational and experimental methodology is provided.

VIGNETTE 1:   USING A PERSONAL COMPUTER FOR DUAL-TASK STUDIES OF LANGUAGE ASYMMETRY

One role for personal computers in language and reading research will be to provide inexpensive and flexible instrumentation for data collection activities.

Because the function of the computer is controlled by the nature of the program executed, personal computers can be used for a variety of data collection activities. Our first vignette illustrates how a personal computer was used in a dual-task study of left-hemisphere language specialization.

The dual-task method is a relatively new procedure, in contrast to other experimental measures of brain organization for language function such as visual half-field and dichotic listening (see Kinsbourne & Hiscock, 1983). The application of dual-task procedures in language laterality research assumes that two independent tasks will interfere with each other more when they are programmed or controlled by the same cerebral hemisphere than when they involve different cerebral hemispheres. In a typical dual-task study, a subject's performance on a simple manual task such as finger tapping is evaluated. The finger tapping of the index finger of each hand is compared under conditions with and without a concurrent verbal/language task such as reciting a rhyme or solving anagrams. Because the motor activity of each hand is programmed primarily by the contralateral cerebral hemisphere—the left hemisphere controls right-hand tapping, while the right hemisphere controls left-hand tapping—differential tapping interference produced in the left vs. right hands by the verbal concurrent task indicates which cerebral hemisphere is primarily involved in the processing of the verbal/language activity. For example, for right-handed persons, right-hand tapping is disrupted to a greater extent than left-hand tapping with a verbal concurrent task, presumably because both verbal tasks and right-hand motor tasks are controlled by the same hemisphere (left). This pattern of lateralized interference in manual performance implicates the left hemisphere as the primary processing hemisphere in the verbal concurrent task. This procedure has been used successfully to estimate hemispheric language laterality in both adults and children (see Kinsbourne & Hiscock, 1983; Kee, 1984).

Personal computers are ideal for dual-task instrumentation. For example, a computer program can be written which directs the computer to (1) time tapping trials; (2) record finger-tapping responses; (3) record and tabulate different measures of manual performance such as rate and variability; and (4) present detailed statistics concerning manual performance at the conclusion of tapping trials. It could at the same time present stimuli and record performance on a concurrent verbal task. In the past, manual devices such as typewriters have been used in dual-task studies. For example, a record of the number of times a specific key is struck provides a measure of manual performance. The dual-task literature indicates, however, that simple rate measures of performance are not always sensitive to language laterality effects. Measures of tapping variability based on the intervals between taps, measured in fractions of a second, can provide a more sensitive index of left-hemisphere language specialization under certain conditions (see Kee, Morris, Bathurst, & Hellige, in press; Kinsbourne & Hiscock, 1983). Thus an appropriately programmed personal computer can provide the necessary precision for the recording of tapping variability data and thereby increase the probability that a decisive estimate of left-hemisphere language laterality will be provided.

The flexibility and utility of personal computers for this kind of dual-task research is underscored in the following description of a recently completed study of language laterality in preschool-age children. The study was prompted by a *Science* article by Gottfried and Bathurst (1983). They reported that intellectual precociousness was related to handedness differences in preschool-age females but not males. Their findings were based on a longitudinal study of early development conducted at the Infant Study Center at California State University, Fullerton. The middle-class normal children in their study had been evaluated every 6 months since the age of 1 year with standardized intelligence scales including the Bayley Mental Scale and McCarthy Scales of Children's Abilities. Children's handedness information was based on evaluation of the hand used for drawing picture illustrations across five assessments conducted between the ages of 18 and 42 months. The data analysis was based on a contributing sample of 89 children (48 males and 41 females). Within each gender group, about equal numbers of children were found to be consistent (24 boys and 23 girls) or inconsistent (24 boys and 16 girls) in their across-time use of their right hands for drawing pictures. Gottfried and Bathurst conducted their data analysis within gender group and observed that at every assessment period between 18 and 42 months of age, the females who were consistent in their use of the same hand for drawing outperformed the inconsistent females on the intelligence scales. For the boys, however, the two handedness groups did not differ on the intelligence scales at any time between 18 and 42 months of age.

Gottfried and Bathurst's findings are unique and indicate for the first time that consistency in hand preference across time is related to advanced intellectual development for females, but not males. They note that "the relationship between these variables is apparently sex-specific. Why this relation between consistency in hand preference and intellectual skills holds for females and not males is not known. Whether this relation is based on differences in neural anatomy, neural proximity, maturational factors, or degree of hemispheric lateralization remains to be determined" (p. 1075).

The literature on brain organization and language indicates that handedness differences are related to variation in degree of left-hemisphere specialization for language functions (see Bryden, 1982; Ownby, 1985). For example, evidence indicates that right-handed persons from right-handed familial backgrounds are most consistently associated with the "typical" pattern of left-hemisphere language specialization (Bathurst & Kee, 1983; Kee, Bathurst, & Hellige, 1983). Lesser degrees of right-handedness and/or familial left-handedness can be associated with more bilaterality of language representation. Thus, it is quite plausible, as Gottfried and Bathurst suggest, that the female handedness groups differ in their hemispheric lateralization for language function. Furthermore, the intriguing possibility exists that differential language laterality may serve to mediate the relationship between handedness and intellectual precociousness observed for females. Such a finding would be unique and add significant new evidence concerning the relationships between handedness and the development of mental abilities (see Porac & Coren, 1981).

Because access to Gottfried and Bathurst's subjects was possible, we had a unique opportunity to evaluate the hypothesis that the handedness groups differ in cerebral hemispheric lateralization for language. Prompt testing of the children from the Gottfried and Bathurst study with a measure of language laterality was necessary. Prompt testing was required because the possibility exists that the handedness differences might represent a maturational or developmental lag. For example, adults are typically more consistent in their hand use than children. Thus, hand consistency differences found in Gottfried and Bathurst's children might represent corresponding differences in developmental maturity. Thus, if testing were delayed too long, the "gap" between the two handedness groups might close sufficiently to mask testable differences in the cerebral lateralization of the groups for language function.

Selection of a language laterality task that could be easily transported to the homes of each child for testing was required. The dual-task procedures, implemented on a portable personal computer, appeared ideal for our assessment needs. We were familiar with the computer instrumentation for this task from previous work (e.g., Kee, Hellige, & Bathurst, 1982; Kee, Bathurst, & Hellige, 1983; 1984). However, the Apple II personal computer used in our laboratory was not available for the in-home testing of the Gottfried and Bathurst children. Luckily, Kathy Brown, a graduate assistant, volunteered her children's Atari 400 personal computer for the project. The Atari 400, a computer typically thought of as a game machine, is light in weight and is about the size of a small portable typewriter. Thus, it was a perfect size for transportation to the homes of the children for testing. A computer program was written which allowed the Atari to control the dual-task experiment and collect various measures of tapping performance.

Forty-one of the females (22 consistent and 15 inconsistent) from the Gottfried and Bathurst study were tested with the dual-task procedure described. The mean age of the children at testing was 4.61 years (S.D. = .06). Thus, at testing the children were about 12 months' older than the last assessment reported by Gottfried and Bathurst (1983). Each child was given a series of 10-second tapping trials programmed by the computer. The concurrent verbal task required children to recite lists of three or five words. Subjects tapped equally often with the two hands, and counterbalancing of the tapping trials (tapping alone vs. tapping while reciting words) was included. Recall that the dual task was used to determine if the two handedness groups differed in cerebral lateralization for language. Analysis of the children's performance was based on a score reflecting the percentage of reduction in tapping rate when a verbal concurrent task is added. This score was calculated by the following formula:

Table 1. Language Laterality Study:
Mean Percentage Reduction in Finger Tapping Rates

| Handedness | Tapping Hand | |
Group	Left	Right
Consistent	36.87	45.14
Inconsistent	51.07	52.63

percentage reduction in tapping rate $= (TA - TC)/TA \times 100$

where TA equals the taps per second while the subject is tapping alone and TC equals the taps per second while the subject is tapping and reciting words (the concurrent task). This score, an indicator of interference, is tabulated separately for each hand. Interference should be largest in the hand which is programmed by the cerebral hemisphere which also serves as the primary processor of the verbal concurrent task (right hand/left hemisphere). These percentage reduction scores were analyzed using analysis of variance procedures. Table 1 displays the results on the percentage reduction measure for the two female handedness groups by tapping hand. Both groups showed generalized interference in tapping performance under dual-task conditions, i.e., tapping performance was disrupted in both the left and right hands when subjects performed a concurrent verbal task. Only the females belonging to the consistent handedness group, however, showed significant lateralized interference in tapping performance ($p < .05$), i.e., their right hand was disrupted to a greater extent than their left hand with concurrent verbal activity. This outcome indicates that the females consistent in their across-time hand consistency are also more left-hemisphere-specialized for language function. In contrast, the equivalent disruption in the tapping performance of the left and right hands observed for the females inconsistent in handedness suggests that their language functions are more bilaterally represented. This initial analysis of the female dual-task results is based on a *rate* measure of performance. It may be that the variability measures of tapping performance based on the time intervals between taps may prove more sensitive to language laterality effects. Thus, subsequent analysis of the variability data—the collection of which was made possible by the use of the personal computer—will indicate whether any evidence of cerebral hemispheric language specialization can be found for the inconsistent female group.

Our finding of differential cerebral laterality for language function in Gottfried and Bathurst's female handedness groups provides some unique evidence about correlates of language lateralization in young children. Whether or not language laterality *mediates* the relationship between handedness and intellectual precociousness in the females will become clearer when the results from our evaluation of the two male handedness groups is complete. The personal computer's flexibility and portability extend the possibilities of basic research on hemispheric specialization/integration which can be explored in environments familiar to young children or to adults who would not normally participate in psychological laboratory testing. The capacity for fine-grained data gathering and analysis, sometimes on-line, may allow us to capture patterns that might be overlooked without such methods.

Personal computers can be used in many phases of research activities. In this first example, the computer was programmed to control an experiment and to record/tabulate information on the subject's performance. Because the computer's activity is controlled by the nature of the program written, the computer can be readily reprogrammed to perform different functions in other experiments. In this regard, the computer becomes a true "utility" for the investigator. In our next vignette, the increasing use of computers by children for early learning activity prompted the research question. Also, the same computer that provided the medium for the experiment was programmed to facilitate the data gathering and data analysis associated with the study of parent–child reading activity.

VIGNETTE 2:   JOINT PARENT–CHILD READING WITH BOOKS VS. COMPUTERS

One of the most important accomplishments of the preschool years is learning the alphabet. Recently a potentially significant new medium for learning the alphabet has been introduced: the personal computer. "My First Alphabet," marketed by Atari, is an example of educational software available for personal computers. The program allows the child to select a letter on the keyboard, draws a colorful graphic picture of an appropriate object or animal, draws the letter selected, and also presents several additional words beginning with that letter, all accompanied by music. We wondered how parent–child interaction with such a computer program would compare with the more traditional and familiar activity of reading an alphabet book.

Traditionally, preschoolers gain experience with the letters of the alphabet via interactions with family members, from children's television, in nursery school, from playing with certain toys (e.g., alphabet blocks), and from alphabet books (reading alone or jointly with others). Parenthetically, since it has been reported that such early picture book reading is done primarily by mothers (Laosa, 1982), and the existing studies of picture book reading with preschoolers (Guinagh & Jester, 1972; Mendoza, 1983; Ninio, 1980; 1983; Ninio & Bruner, 1978) have primarily examined mothers' actions, the focus of our study was on mother–child interactions.

Alphabet book reading was selected as the best activity with which to compare the computer activity for several reasons. First, the content presented in such books and by the computer is fairly similar, consisting of a target letter and an object or animal, and often a few words that begin with the letter. Second, both elicit a high degree of parent–child interaction. Third, while virtually no previous research exists on computer interaction in preschoolers, there are several previous studies of parent–child picture book reading (Guinagh & Jester, 1972; Mendoza, 1978; Ninio, 1980, 1983; Ninio & Bruner, 1978). From these studies we know that joint picture book reading seems to involve a great deal of direct teaching by the mother. For instance, mothers are much more likely to label objects pictured in books than real objects (Ninio & Bruner, 1978). Interactions involving picture books seem tailormade for instruction in naming things (Mendoza, 1983). We wondered whether computer interactions would be as instructive.

There are a number of differences in the two situations. In the computer alphabet game examined in this study, the child (or mother) pushes a key on the keyboard. A color graphic design is drawn showing an object or animal, the letter selected, and three other words; a little man is shown running back and forth across the bottom of the screen. When the design is complete (this takes 15–30 seconds), a short musical passage is played. Thus, the computer is "active" in the sense that it develops the visual input and determines the timing of letter episodes. In contrast, the book requires that participants direct their own attention to particular pictures, via pointing or a verbal narration, and the timing of letter episodes is self-determined. Would the computer game hold the child's attention as well as (or perhaps even better than) the book? Looked at another way, would the parent direct the child's attention more actively in one setting vs. the other? How would the pace of the interaction differ? Would the language behavior of the parents and children differ in the two settings?

In order to address such questions, 10 preschoolers and their mothers were videotaped in 12-minute sessions. Three-year-olds were selected because we wished to test the youngest children who could interact appropriately and easily with the computer. Subjects participated in both book reading and computer sessions in order to ensure that any differences found were due to the media rather than subject characteristics (order was counterbalanced). Although it was not possible to find a commercially available alphabet book with pictures that exactly resembled the graphic displays of the computer game, three alphabet books appropriate for this age range (Allen, 1980; Eastman, 1974; Williams, 1957) were selected on the basis of the simplicity of their pictures and their inherent interest to preschoolers (tested informally with pilot subjects).

Subjects were five girls and five boys between the ages of 3 and 4 years, recruited from local Orange County preschools, and their mothers. The average age of the girls was 3;6, and the average age of the boys was 3;7. Children and mothers came to the observation room at the Child Study Center at California State University, Fullerton. During an introductory period the number of letters the child could correctly identify was assessed with a recognition test and by asking the child to sing the Alphabet Song. Then (for the computer-first subjects) the mother and child were seated on the couch in front of the computer. The parent was given basic instructions in how to operate the computer. The alphabet program is so simple that all the child has to do is push a key and watch what happens. After the mother and child were video- and audiotaped for 12 minutes, a break allowed the child some physical activity. The experimenter removed the computer apparatus during this time. The mother and child then returned to the couch for a 12-minute book-reading session. Instructions in this condition were brief and unstructured, e.g., "Please read this alphabet book to your child as you would at home."

Our data analyses were designed to provide information concerning the patterns of parent–child reading activity under the two media. A substantial amount of information is provided by the observational techniques used in this study, not all of which will be presented in this brief vignette. Presented below are three categories of result: (1) preliminary descriptive data, (2) verbal events, and (3) behavioral analyses. For the different categories of results, a high degree of interrater reliability was observed for the initial coding of verbal and behavioral events (mean rating reliabilities ranged between .90 and .98). All tests of statistical significance were conducted at an alpha of .05.

Preliminary Descriptive Analyses

Audio recordings were transcribed and the transcriptions were corrected by a second observer. Utterance boundaries were determined on the basis of syntax and intonation contours following Masur (1982). Table 2 presents preliminary data gathered while preparing the transcripts. The mean length of utterance of the children (MLU), an indication of language complexity, was not affected significantly by the different media (book reading vs. computer game playing). The number of turns (defined as a change of speaker) per 12-minute sample was a rough measure of the amount of overall verbal interaction. Mothers and children took significantly more turns speaking in book reading than in the computer game. The total number of letters discussed in the book-reading task was more than double the number of letters discussed during the computer game. (It should be noted that we have at present no way of knowing whether

Table 2.   Parent–Child Study:
Preliminary Descriptive Results

Task	Dependent Measure			
	MLU	*Turns*	*Letters*	*Repeats*
Book	2.67	127.60	43.40	20.90
Computer	2.80	92.60	18.40	3.30

presenting fewer letters is good or bad—in terms of retention it might be better to present only a few at one time.) In addition, the number of letters repeated (either by reviewing previously read sections of a given book, reading another book, or selecting the same letter more than once during the computer game) was more than five times as great in the book task as the computer task.

This was undoubtedly a result of the self-paced nature of book reading. Whereas the computer game took an average of 25.15 seconds to present each letter, the book readers preferred to explore letters at a much faster rate. A rough indicator of pacing is provided by dividing the total number of letters by the 12 minutes in the sample. In this way we can estimate that children in the computer game viewed approximately one and a half letters per minute ($M = 1.53$) whereas in the book task they explored an average of over three and a half letters per minute ($M = 3.62$).

Verbal Events

Analysis of speech content directed from the mother to the child (and vice versa) in the two settings investigated whether the computer game elicits quantitative or qualitative differences in the kinds of verbal messages children and mothers exchange with each other in comparison with book reading. Specifically, a preliminary review of the transcripts showed that all of the verbal events could be categorized into 10 classes. These were identifications, requests for identification, comments, directives, questions (other than requests for identification), positive utterances (e.g., yes, OK, good, etc.), negative utterances (e.g., no, nope), laughter, use of a name or other personal reference, and extraneous references (reference to something not shown in the book or on the computer). Mothers' and children's utterances were analyzed separately because the categories were not independent (verbal events produced by one person can influence the responses given by the other).

Informal comparison showed that different patterns of verbal events were found for the mothers than for the children. Overall, mothers talked more, averaging 227.45 verbal events, compared with 139.30 for the children. As Table 3 shows, children predominantly gave identifications and (to a lesser degree) made comments, whereas mothers distributed their verbalizations more evenly across the 10 categories. Comparison between the book and computer tasks for the mothers showed that their verbal events differed significantly in five categories. In the book-reading situation mothers made significantly more requests for identification, identified items significantly more often, and made significantly more extraneous references than in the computer game. On the other hand, there were significantly more directives and mothers were also more prone to make negative utterances in the computer game than in the book task. The categories of positive remarks, comments, use of name or other personal references, questions, and laughter did not differ significantly as a function of task.

Table 3. Parent–Child Reading Study:
Frequency of Occurrence of Verbal Events by Category[a]

Category	Mothers			Children		
	Book	Computer	Mean	Book	Computer	Mean
Requests for identification	65.40*	36.60	51.00$_a$	7.80*	3.60	5.70$_c$
Identifications	65.50*	35.70	50.60$_a$	95.80*	50.30	73.05$_a$
Positive remarks	31.00	32.30	31.65$_b$	9.50	8.80	9.15$_c$
Comments	27.90	28.80	28.35$_{bc}$	25.30	30.20	27.75$_b$
Directives	20.80*	33.50	27.15$_{bc}$	3.30	4.90	4.10$_c$
Questions	19.60	18.40	19.00$_{bc}$	6.30	10.60	8.45$_c$
Negative remarks	6.30*	9.70	8.00$_{bc}$	5.40	4.60	5.00$_c$
Name, personal references	4.80	4.70	4.75$_c$	2.80	1.70	2.25$_c$
Laughter	4.10	3.90	4.00$_c$	4.00	2.10	1.55$_c$
Extraneous references	4.00*	1.90	2.95$_c$	1.00	.60	.80$_c$

[a]Significant differences in rows for particular book vs. computer comparisons are indicated by an asterisk. For category effects, column means that do not share subscripts differ from one another significantly at the $p < .05$ level (Newman–Keuls test).

The children's verbal events were associated with only two significant differences between the book and computer tasks. Children made nearly twice as many identifications in the book-reading task, and requests by children for identification were also significantly higher in the book than in the computer condition. No significant differences were found for the other verbal categories.

A more qualitative way of looking at verbal behavior is to examine the percentage of the total number of verbal events for each task found in each category, as shown for mothers and children separately in the two panels of Figure 1. This analysis allows a more direct comparison of the distribution of verbal events into the various categories by controlling for overall differences in frequency. Figure 1 shows the mean percentages for the seven categories in which mothers, children, or both showed significant differences as a function of task. The categories of laughter, name or other personal reference, and extraneous references were not included in Figure 1 because they were not affected by task and because they each represented less than 5% of the overall sample.

On the left of Figure 1 are the mothers' verbal behaviors. Although their verbal events were distributed differently into the various categories, these differences across categories were gradual rather than sharp. Mothers gave significantly greater proportions of identifications and requests for identification in the book-reading situation. In the computer game, on the other hand, mothers made a greater proportion of comments, directives, and negative remarks. Negative remarks in this context are not necessarily unpleasant—they may be a useful form of corrective feedback.

For children, the proportion of identifications significantly exceeded those in all other categories. The next highest proportion, comments, also was significantly

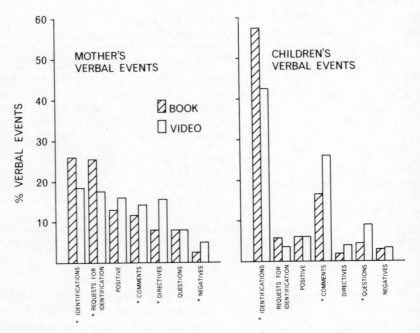

Figure 1. Parent–child reading study. Mean percentages of verbal events in seven categories for mothers and children. An asterisk indicates a significant book vs. video difference ($p < .05$).

different from all other categories. Analysis showed that children made a significantly greater proportion of identifications in the book-reading task. During the computer task, on the other hand, they produced a significantly greater proportion of comments and questions.

In summary, alphabet book reading was associated with more overall verbalization than was the computer game. In particular, both mothers and children made more identifications and requests for identification when reading, a finding that extends the previous report by Ninio and Bruner (1978) that mothers label objects and pictures in books more frequently than they name real objects. Apparently the book-reading situation is particularly conducive to instruction in naming things, as confirmed in the present study in which books prompted even more labeling than a computer display specifically designed to showcase letters and objects for learning purposes.

Mothers' verbalizations were more strongly affected by the task differences than were those of the children. This may be because mothers spoke a great deal more and produced a greater variety of messages than did children, who mostly identified letters and objects and (to a lesser extent) made comments. When percentages rather than frequencies were examined, mothers and children still differed in their distribution of verbalizations into various categories of verbal events. Different distributions as well were produced by the two tasks, and because these results were equated for overall differences in production they could not be a spurious result of the relatively slow pace of the computer game, which provided less to talk about than the book-reading task. Mothers shifted from a predominance of identifications and requests for identifications in the book task to a more even distribution where identifications and requests for identifications were balanced by an increased proportion of comments, directives, and negatives in the computer task. Thus reading was more exclusively tutorial in the naming of pictures, whereas the computer game elicited controlling and directing statements as well as labeling and requests for labeling; an increased proportion of comments about the pictures and the computer game was also found on the part of mothers. For children, identifications were the chief verbal behavior in both tasks, with comments at a relatively high level as well. Nevertheless the computer task, as presented here, caused children to lower their proportion of identifications and to increase their proportion of comments and, to a lesser extent, questions.

Thus, the computer task did not serve so exclusively as a medium to teach naming of objects and pictures as did the alphabet books. The computer game prompted mothers (and to a lesser degree, children) to vary their messages, probably to some extent because of the necessity to talk about how to operate the keyboard, which letter to select next, the need to wait until the computer was done drawing the picture, and so forth. In contrast, mothers and children were well acquainted with the "rules" of how to "operate" a book (don't tear the paper, turn one page at a time, read the book in a forward direction, etc.) and thus concentrated more directly on naming the pictures. Whether these differences would attenuate as participants gain more experience in computer operation is an empirical question that needs to be investigated.

Behavioral Analyses

The frequency and duration of various behavioral events were tallied using a timing and counting computer program run on the Atari personal computer used in the study. In this case the data collection was not on-line, but coded later from video- and audiotapes. The measured behaviors included pointing (at the book, computer, or monitor), looking (at the book, computer, screen, parent–child, or away), and page turning. These analyses were designed to assess the degree of interest and involvement on the part of parents and children in the book vs. computer setting. Three general classes of behavior were analyzed: manipulation, pointing, and looking.

Manipulation. The first analyses concerned the amount of physical manipulation, as defined by frequency of page turning in the book task, and frequency of pointing at the computer keyboard. (Frequency of key pressing was not tallied separately from that of pointing, but most points to the keyboard involved keypresses and thus gave a rough indication of this activity.) There were no significant effects for page turning, indicating that mothers and children turned pages an equal number of times. In the computer task, children's activity significantly exceeded that of mothers. Children pointed at the keyboard more than three times as frequently ($M = 31.54$) as mothers ($M = 8.94$). Thus while mothers and children were equally active in turning pages while reading, the children were predominantly responsible for operating the computer.

Pointing. The second set of analyses concerned the duration of pointing as a function of actor and task. Pointing at the book was first compared with overall pointing at the computer, defined as pointing at the keyboard plus pointing at the screen. This analysis indicated that across both groups there was more pointing at the book ($M = 142.11$ seconds) than at the computer ($M = 70.50$ seconds). Furthermore, mothers pointed at the book for more time ($M = 203.19$ seconds) than children did ($M = 81.03$ seconds), whereas children pointed at the computer ($M = 114.27$ seconds) more than mothers did ($M = 26.43$ seconds).

We next repeated these analyses using the pointing data for the computer screen and the keyboard separately because pointing at the screen is analogous to pointing at pictures in the book, whereas pointing at the keyboard indicated operation of the computer. The mean for a given category of pointing to screen is thus less than the mean for the same category of pointing to computer. Results showed that mothers pointed longer ($M = 36.04$ seconds) than children ($M = 14.73$ seconds). However, although mothers pointed at the book more than did children, mothers and children did not differ in the amount of pointing at the screen. This finding suggests that the initial finding that children pointed more at the computer was due primarily to the children's manipulating the keyboard, and this was confirmed when the extent of pointing at the book vs. keyboard was analyzed. This analysis showed that mothers pointed more at the book and children pointed more at the keyboard.

In summary, even though pointing at the screen is analogous to pointing at pictures in the book, the participants pointed at the book over 10 times longer ($M = 142.11$ seconds) than at the computer screen ($M = 13.59$ seconds). Evidently, book reading elicits more physical involvement with the medium than does computer watching, and this was even true when the analysis included both pointing at the screen and pointing at the keyboard (which included key pressing, the physical activity necessary to operate the computer). The increase in pointing may have been due in part to the fact that most pages of the alphabet books showed more than one letter. Mothers typically pointed to a particular letter or figure, perhaps to direct attention to that specific object, while they queried their child about its name or other characteristics. However, the book pages never contained as many as 10 letters, so that the 10-fold increase in pointing was not due to the addition of a simple constant amount of pointing for that letter. In other words, it is likely that there would be more pointing associated with book reading than with computer watching, even if there were only one letter per page or more than one letter depicted on the computer screen.

Looking. The third set of analyses involved looking duration. The direction of looking could be at the other person (mother looks at child or vice versa), at the book/computer, or away. The overall analysis defined looking at the computer as the duration of looking at the screen plus looking at the keyboard. Results showed that looking at the book or the computer ($M = 668.46$ seconds) significantly exceeded looking at the other person ($M = 69.96$ seconds) and looking away ($M = 33.39$ seconds), which did not differ from one another. When looking at the computer was defined as looking at the screen, analyses showed that participants looked longer at the book ($M = 690.12$ seconds) than at the screen ($M = 536.80$ seconds).

The looking results showed that participants spent the vast majority of time looking at either the book or the computer, with only occasional looks at each other, and with only a minimum amount of looking way. Thus, the computer task and book reading were similar in that they both were highly engaging and there was no differential tendency for children's attention to wander in one of the activities. The tasks were different in that book reading elicited more looking at the content of the book whereas there was less looking at the pictures on the computer screen, partly because participants spent some time examining the keyboard in order to select the next picture. Whereas looking at the next picture can be accomplished directly during reading, it must be accomplished by looking away from the screen, i.e., at the keyboard, when interacting with a computer. Children looked away significantly more than mothers did, and mothers looked at their children more than vice versa, but this did not differ as a function of task. Mothers and children did not differ in looking at the screen or in looking at the keyboard.

In summary, some of our initial findings concerning joint parent–child reading with books in comparison with computers have been presented. Because our study was preliminary there are a number of limitations to our findings which will require attention in future work. For example, one obvious difference between our computer and book conditions was novelty. None of the subjects had had much experience with a personal computer before (and none had seen the "My First Alphabet" game) whereas all had previously read alphabet books. Since personal computers are just beginning to gain wide consumer acceptance, it was not possible to recruit a subject pool of "computer-literate" 3-year-olds for this study. Another remedy for the novelty problem would be to test subjects repeatedly, a costly and time-consuming procedure. In the future, however, it will be important to discover whether differences between interactions around a computer and interactions around a book persist after subjects have had repeated experience with the computer program.

Even more basic, perhaps, is the need for studies exploring the *impact* of program variations and of mothers' teaching behaviors with and without computers. An emerging undercurrent in many current studies is the role of classroom organization and social interaction around the computer. While it will be useful to explore presentation variables such as speed, frequency, and salience of display of stimuli, it will also be important to explore the social context of computer usage in preschool, school-age, and adult users. Background for such exploration can be found in sources such as the older tradition of studying interaction during mother–child teaching situations (e.g., studies by Hess and Shipman and by the Infant Stimulation Projects at the University of Florida) and in more recent ethnographic studies (cf. Cochrane-Smith, 1983; Green & Smith, 1983) as well as in projects more explicitly studying children's responses to computers (e.g., Rubin & Bruce, 1983). The use of personal computers in reading/language research can generate both new questions and new approaches to old questions. For example, the study presented here described in some detail the process of learning and particularly the child's interaction with mother, book, and computer, but it did not seek to assess how well the children learned the alphabet. Although it is easy to assume that elicitation of more identifications is desirable, it is possible that the young child's learning could be diminished by an information overload.

The results from this study provide a foundation for future work in this area. For example, investigation across a broader range would show how preschool children's interactions with computers change as a function of cognitive and linguistic development. Furthermore, studies using different prereading and reading primer software would show whether interactions around some computer learning situations have important features that remain more or less constant across tasks or whether the type of interaction varies widely depending on aspects of the program or even the technology. Finally, an assessment of the learning and cognitive consequences associated with book vs. computer learning experience will provide important evidence concerning the relative effectiveness of the two media. Other researchers could use tasks like those studied here to examine very different issues. For example, the very effort required to search out the letter key might help to secure the links between letter form, letter name, and associated key words. The effects of program dimensions such as speed of presentation might interact with age; if so, future software should be designed to permit changes in pace. Similarly, task variables, such as requirement to predict the letter as soon as its emerging form permits, changing the task into active hypothesis testing and confirmation, might enhance learning as well.

Thus availability of personal computers for reading and language learning activities will prompt a variety of new research questions. The study described above provides one example of the kinds of questions that can be asked. Other kinds of questions may concern the educational implications of this new technology. Our last vignette describes a study concerned specifically with the educational uses of a variant of microelectronic technology, the hand-held learning aid.

VIGNETTE 3: LEARNING AND MOTIVATIONAL ASPECTS OF A HAND-HELD MICROELECTRONIC LANGUAGE GAME

The microprocessor technology used in personal computers is also found in a myriad of hand-held electronic learning aids. Many of these learning aids have been designed to support the development of children's basic reading skills. For example, Speak & Spell is a very popular book-size learning aid produced by Texas Instruments. It includes a one-line display screen and an A-to-Z touch-sensitive keyboard. Different spelling activities can be selected by the child. For many of these activities, the Speak & Spell presents a to-be-spelled word in a synthesized voice and the child responds by entering the correct spelling of the word on the keyboard. As each letter is entered, it is pronounced in the synthesized voice and appears on the screen. Synthesized voice and visual print feedback is provided concerning the correctness of entries. The interactive nature of Speak & Spell in the three senses of touch, vision, and hearing creates an attractive and sustaining learning activity for both children and adults (Kee, 1981).

Our last vignette concerns a study which examined some applied questions prompted by children's interest in Speak & Spell. We wondered if children's use of Speak & Spell would enhance their interest in spelling and/or related academic activities. If reliable enhancement effects were found, Speak & Spell could be used by parents and teachers to help sustain high interest in spelling activities or encourage children to develop interest in spelling activities when interest is initially low (see A. E. Gottfried, 1983). Presumably, children will spend more time with tasks that are interesting, thereby increasing opportunities for learning and skill development.

A second issue examined in this study concerned whether or not the instructional method associated with initial Speak & Spell use would influence the children's self-reported interest in using the learning aid and/or their learning performance with the device. In this regard, research indicates that children's activities that are high in intrinsic motivation can be undermined by external constraints such as rewards, directions, and surveillance of the activity (see Lepper & Greene, 1979). Activities high in intrinsic motivation are those performed for their own sake, tasks for which pleasure is derived from the task itself, and tasks performed in the absence of obvious external rewards. For such tasks, external rewards may serve to diminish interest in the task and/or negatively affect task performance. Thus provisions were made in the study to vary the presence vs. absence of a reward for Speak & Spell participation. Evidence provided by this manipulation will identify optimal conditions for introduction of devices like Speak & Spell to foster interest and efficient learning.

Participants in our study were 30 male and 30 female third-grade children (modal age = 8 years) from a middle-class community serving Orange County, California. Third-grade children were selected for the study after consideration of the difficulty level of the word set found on Speak & Spell and consultation with elementary school teachers. With a third-grade sample, the spelling activity on Speak & Spell was expected to be not too easy or too difficult. These children were pretested in intact classrooms to evaluate their initial attitudes toward various educational activities and their potential interest in playing with Speak & Spell. Specifically, they were asked to rate on a 6-point scale how much they "liked" (1 = do not like it very much; 6 = like it a whole lot) the following activities: spelling, reading, arithmetic, playing games, playing word games, and playing arithmetic games. In addition, after a brief introduction to Speak & Spell, they were also asked to rate how much they would enjoy playing with this learning aid. These same rating questions were administered to the children at the conclusion of their individual sessions described below.

About 2 weeks after this pretest, the children participated in individual 30-minute sessions with a female experimenter. These children had no prior experience with Speak & Spell, with the exception of the brief in-class demonstration described. During this session children were introduced to two of the activities on Speak & Spell: "Say it" and "Spell it." In both activities, children use the keyboard to spell a word presented in a synthesized voice by the Speak & Spell. "Say it" provides a preliminary trial on which the child is asked to repeat the word orally prior to entering the spelling on the keyboard. "Spell it" does not include this pronunciation trial. After this introduction, each child was asked to rate on a 6-point scale how much fun Speak & Spell was to play and which activity they would prefer to play with again ("Say it" or "Spell it"). These two rating questions were also asked at the conclusion of their individual sessions. After this rating, children were assigned to a no-reward or reward condition. In the no-reward condition children were asked to explore a spelling activity on Speak and Spell. The children were left on their own while the experimenter sat some distance from the subject, apparently engaged in an unrelated activity. In a reward condition, subjects were promised a certificate of merit for their participation. An example certificate was mounted on a poster board displaying the child's name under a heading which read: "Speak & Spell Project." Subjects were told that they would receive the certificate at the end of the session. The experimenter also indicated that she would directly monitor the child's progress. Equal numbers of children were assigned to the two reward conditions. Further-

Table 4. Speak & Spell Study: Children's Self-Reported Rating Differences
(Posttest minus Pretest) on Various Educational Activities

| | Group[a] | |
Item	Speak & Spell (N = 60)	Comparison (N = 39)
Spelling	+1.22*	−.13
Reading	+0.51*	−.02
Arithmetic	0.00	−.05
Games	0.06	−.07
Word games	0.47*	+.03
Arithmetic games	0.37*	−.03

[a]A positive value indicates an increase in self-reported liking between the pre- and
posttest assessment.
*$p < .05$.

more, within each reward condition subjects were assigned to one of three
activity conditions to examine the generality of potential reward effects. One-
third of the children were allowed to play the game ("Say it" or "Spell it") they
had originally selected, one-third were required to play the game they did not
select, whereas the final group was told to play with either game. In all conditions
the experimenter observed and recorded the children's performance on Speak &
Spell activities.

Our results indicate that a brief exposure to the microelectronic learning aid of
Speak & Spell was sufficient to have a differential impact on children's rating of
various educational activities. The rating changes between the pre- and posttests
are presented in Table 4. The rating differences for the children with Speak & Spell
exposure showed reliable increases in their self-reported liking of spelling and
reading, whereas no change was observed in their rating of interest in arithmetic.
Children also showed positive rating changes in their interest in playing of word
and arithmetic games, whereas game playing in general was not associated with a
rating change due to a ceiling effect. An additional sample of 39 boys and girls
from third-grade classes served as a comparison group. These children were
administered the rating questions twice. The interval between the two tests was 2
weeks, approximating the pretest/posttest interval for the Speak & Spell group.
The rating differences for this comparison group are also presented in Table 4. In
contrast to the Speak & Spell group, no changes in children's self-reported liking of
the different activities was observed. The absence of rating differences was not due
to a ceiling effect, with the exception of the item concerning game playing. Thus,
our findings indicate that a brief exposure to Speak & Spell can enhance children's
self-reported liking of specific educational activities, such as spelling and reading,
and certain learning games. A potential implication of this finding is that Speak &
Spell, and perhaps devices like it, can be used to help develop children's interest in
specific subject areas. However, the long-term impact of such exposure is not
known and will require examination in future work.

The experimental manipulations of reward (present vs. absent) and activity condition (same game vs. different game vs. free play) was assessed using analysis of variance. Recall that subjects were asked to rate the fun level of Speak & Spell prior to and at the conclusion of their individual session. This rating measure can be viewed as an attitudinal index of intrinsic interest in the Speak & Spell task. Analysis with time of rating included as a repeated measures factor indicated that subjects initially rated Speak & Spell high in enjoyment ($M = 5.83$ of a possible 6.0) and these high ratings were not altered meaningfully by the experimental manipulations (all $p > .05$). Three spelling performance measures were also evaluated: (1) percentage of words spelled correctly on the first complete trial ($M = 78\%$); (2) percentage of words spelled correctly across trials ($M = 76\%$); and (3) total number of trials completed ($M = 2.50$). Analyses indicated that the experimental factors did not affect these measures of performance reliably ($p > .05$).

The absence of reward condition effects on the self-rating question and performance measures contrast with some previous findings which indicate that "external reward" may serve to undermine activities that are high in intrinsic motivation. Arnold (1976) suggests, however, that activities which are *extremely* high in intrinsic motivation, like computer games, may not be as vulnerable as other tasks to the negative effects of external reward. Children in our study viewed the games on Speak & Spell as highly desirable. Thus, the absence of a reward effect may not be surprising. Furthermore, this finding suggests that whether we introduce children to Speak & Spell with supervision and rewards or informally, their desire to play and to learn from the learning aid will probably not be adversely affected. Admittedly, children's exposure to the different reward conditions was quite limited in this preliminary study. Longer exposure to the different reward conditions and examination of factors known to affect children's intrinsic interest in activities (see Condry, 1977; Lepper, 1982) are currently being examined with Speak & Spell in a follow-up study.

SUMMARY AND CONCLUSIONS

The preceding vignettes provide some examples of personal computers in language and reading research. Because personal computers can be adapted by the computer program used to perform different functions, they will become a utility in the research enterprise. For example, the first vignette demonstrated how a personal computer was programmed to function as a precision dual-task instrument in the study of language laterality, whereas in the second vignette the personal computer was used both as a "treatment" and in the coding of behavioral events from videotapes of parent–child reading activities. Furthermore, powerful statistical software available for personal computers allows the user to perform on a personal computer complex analyses such as multivariate analysis of variance and regression (see Callamaras, 1983; Lachenbrach, 1983).

Thus, applications for personal computers will be found in all phases of the researcher's activities.

Personal computers and allied technology, such as hand-held learning aids, will prompt not only new approaches to studying basic processes, as in the first vignette, but also more applied questions concerning their impact on children's reading and language development. Two examples of the kinds of relatively applied studies prompted by these new research questions—parent–child early reading activities and motivational and learning aspects of a hand-held spelling aid—were illustrated in this chapter. Other topics which are beginning to be explored include reading instruction (Lesgold, 1983; Shelton & Kleinman, 1983), writing skill development (Miller, 1979; Owens, 1984; Watt, 1984), reading comprehension (Waern & Rollenhagen, 1983) and instructional courseware development (Walker & Hess, 1983).

Whatever roles we select for personal computers in our research, this technology promises to facilitate the completion of our studies, alter the focus of some of our research questions, and create new research opportunities at both the basic and applied levels.

ACKNOWLEDGMENTS

The preparation of this chapter was facilitated by various grants from the California State University, Fullerton. Appreciation is expressed to Annette Gilbert for her efficient and timely word processing.

Vignette No. 1: This research was supported in part by a Small College Faculty Opportunity award from the National Science Foundation to D. W. Kee (funded under BNS-821739 to J. B. Hellige). Kathy Brown collected the data for this project and her children Jennifer and Michael provided the Atari computer used. The contribution of the Brown family is deeply appreciated. The children in the study were part of A. W. Gottfried's longitudinal study of early development supported by the Thrasher Research Fund. Appreciation is also expressed to Kay Bathurst for her contribution to this project.

Vignette No. 2: This research was partially supported by an equipment grant from the Atari Institute for Educational Action Research to D. W. Kee and P. E. Worden. Melanie Ingle and Joy Miyaoka provided invaluable help with the data collection and analysis. Special thanks to Brent, Brian, David, Genevieve, Gregory, Kelly, Lauren, Lori, Ricia, Ryan, and their mothers for participating in this project. Finaly, author D. W. Kee's son Matthew provided inspiration for this project by his early enjoyment of "My First Alphabet" software on a personal computer.

Vignette No. 3: This study was supported in part by an equipment grant from Texas Instruments Incorporated to D. W. Kee and C. Beauvais. C. Beauvais directed the data collection conducted by Andrea Whittaker and Kathy Brownell, and their invaluable assistance is gratefully acknowledged. Appreciation is also extended to the children and staff of the participating elementary schools in Orange County, California.

REFERENCES

Allen, J. (1980). *The happy golden ABC*. Racine, WI: Golden Press.

Arnold, H.J. (1976). Effects of performance feedback and extrinsic reward upon high intrinsic motivation. *Organizational Behavior and Human Performance*, *17*, 275-288.

Bathurst, K., & Kee, D.W. (1983). *Asymmetry and visuospatial asymmetry in left handers*. A paper presented at the American Psychological Association, Anaheim, CA, August.

Bryden, M.P. (1982). *Laterality: Functional asymmetry in the intact brain*. New York: Academic Press.

Callamaras, P. (1983). Statistical software. *Popular Computing*, *2*, 206-220.

Cochrane-Smith, M. (1983). Reading stories to children: A review/critique. In B.A. Hutson (Ed.), *Advances in reading/language research* (Vol. 2). Greenwich, CT: JAI Press, pp. 197-229.

Green, J.L., & Smith, D. (1983). Teaching and learning as linguistic processes: The emerging picture. In B.A. Hutson (Ed.), *Advances in reading language research* (Vol. 2). Greenwich, CT: JAI Press, pp. 273-349.

Condry, J. (1977). Exercise of exploration: Self-initiated versus other-initiation learning. *Journal of Personality and Social Psychology*, *35*, 459-477.

Eastman, P.D. (1974). *The alphabet book*. New York: Random House.

Gottfried, A.E. (1983). Research in review: Development of intrinsic motivation in young children. *Young Children, November*, 64-73.

Gottfried. A.W., & Bathurst, K. (1983). Hand preference across time is related to intelligence in young girls, not boys. *Science*, *221*, 1074-1076.

Guinagh, B.J., & Jester, R.E. (1972). How parents read to children. *Theory Into Practice*, *11*, 171-177.

Kee, D.W. (1981). *Implications of hand held electronic games and microcomputers for informal learning*. Washington, D.C.: A paper commissioned by the Home Community and Work Division, National Institute of Education.

Kee, D.W. (1984). Comments on Hughes and Sussman's time-sharing study of cerebral laterality in language-disordered and normal children. *Brain and Language*, *22*, 354-356.

Kee, D.W., Bathurst, K., & Hellige, J.B. (1983). Lateralized interference of repetitive finger tapping: Influence of family handedness, cognitive load, and verbal production. *Neuropsychologia*, *21*, 617-624.

Kee, D.W., Bathurst, K., & Hellige, J.B. (1984). Lateralized interference in finger tapping: Assessment of block design activities. *Neuropsychologia*, *22*, 197-203.

Kee, D.W., Hellige, J.B., & Bathurst, K. (1982). *Cerebral lateralization: Assessment of concurrent cognitive and manual task activities*. A paper presented at the annual meeting of the Psychonomic Society, Minneapolis, MN, November.

Kee, D.W., Morris, K., Bathurst, K., & Hellige, J.B. (in press). Lateralized interference in finger tapping: Comparisons of rate and variability measures under speed and consistency tapping instructions. *Brain and Cognition*.

Kinsbourne, M., & Hiscock, M. (1983). Asymmetries of dual task performance. In J.B. Hellige (Ed.), *Cerebral hemispheric asymmetry: Methods, theory, and application*. New York: Praeger, pp. 255-334.

Lachenbrach, P.A. (1983). Statistical programs for microcomputers. *Byte*, *8*, 560-570.

Laosa, L.M. (1982). School, occupation, culture, and family: The impact of parental schooling on the parent-child relationship. *Journal of Educational Psychology*, *74*, 791-827.

Lepper, M.R. (1982). *Microcomputers in education: Motivation and social issues*. Paper presented at the annual meeting of the American Psychological Association, Washington, DC, August.

Lepper, M.R., & Greene, D. (1979). *The hidden costs of reward*. Morristown, NJ: Erlbaum.

Lesgold, A.M. (1983). A rationale for computer-based reading instruction. In A.C. Wilkinson (Ed.), *Classroom computers in cognitive science*. New York: Academic Press.

Masur, E.F. (1982). Cognitive content of parents' speech to preschoolers. *Merrill-Palmer Quarterly*, *28*, 471-484.

Mendoza, O.A.P. (1983). *Joint mother-infant picture-book reading*. Unpublished master's thesis, University of Illinois at Urbana-Champaign.

Miller, G.A. (1979). *Automated dictionaries, reading and writing*. Chairman's Report of a Conference on Educational Uses of Word Processors with Dictionaries. National Institute of Education, December.

Ninio, A. (1983). Joint book reading as a multiple vocabulary acquisition device. *Developmental Psychology*, *19*, 445-451.

Ninio, A., & Bruner, J.S. (1978). The achievement and antecedents of labeling. *Journal of Child Language*, *5*, 1-15.

Owens, P. (1984). Creative writing with computers. *Popular Computing*, 3, 128-132.

Ownby, R. (1985). The neuropsychology of reading ability and disability: Pieces of the puzzle. In B.A. Hutson (Ed.), *Advances in reading/language research* (Vol. 3). Greenwich, CT: JAI Press, pp. 119-149.

Porac, C., & Coren, C. (1981). *Lateral preferences and human behavior*. New York: Springer-Verlag.

Rubin, A., & Bruce, B.D. (1985). Reading and writing with a microcomputer. In B.A. Hutson (Ed.), *Advances in reading/language research* (Vol. 3). Greenwich, CT: JAI Press, pp. 97-117.

Shelton, J.B., & Kleiman, G.M. (1983). Computers and teaching children to read. *Compute*, *5*, 132-136.

Waern, Y., & Rollenhagen, C. (1983). Reading texts from visual display units. *International Journal of Man-Machine Studies*, *18*, 441-465.

Walker, D.F., & Hess, R.D. (1983). *Instructional software*. Belmont, CA: Wadsworth, Inc.

Watt, D. (1984). Tools for writing: Computers are changing the way tots and technicians are learning to write. *Popular Computing*, 3, 75-78.

Williams, G. (1957). *The big golden animal ABC*. Racine, WI: Golden Press.

RESEARCH ON TEACHER–PUPIL INTERACTIONS DURING ORAL READING INSTRUCTION

Jerome A. Niles

INTRODUCTION

Oral reading plays a significant role in the acquisition of literacy for most children in the United States. This instructional activity is widely accepted as an integral part of most schoolwide programs (Howlett & Weintraub, 1979). The heaviest emphasis on instructional oral reading occurs in grades one through three and decreases in the later elementary school years. The continued popularity of oral reading as an instructional activity in the acquisition of literacy is somewhat surprising given some of the extensive attacks on its pedagogical usefulness (cf. Artley, 1972).

Hoffman (1981) described some of the factors which have allowed oral reading to survive as well as why it has been heavily criticized. For example, oral reading provides a structured setting for the teacher to closely monitor students' reading

Advances in Reading/Language Research, Volume 3, pages 207-226.
ISBN: 0-89232-389-2

performance and growth. On the other hand, such a setting can inhibit the number of reading opportunities for some learners (Allington, 1983).

Although few areas in education have attracted more research interest than the acquisition of literacy, relatively few studies have focused specifically on the teacher-pupil interaction during oral reading activity. Numerous studies have been and will continue to be conducted to explain the acquisition of the complex cognitive skill of reading. Researching such a skill requires particularly clever researchers because reading is a covert activity that is conducted in private, "behind the eye" (Goodman, 1970). The primary evidence one has of skill acquisition is the end product that may be conveyed in various forms, such as word pronunciations, responses to comprehension questions, retellings, and filling in cloze blanks.

While this relatively invisible acquisition process is troublesome for reading researchers, it is especially problematic for teachers of reading and those who research the teaching/learning process in reading. When teaching an observable skill, the teacher has the advantage of being able to describe the subroutines of the skill, demonstrate the skill for the learner, and provide demonstrative feedback to the learner based on the learner's performance of the skill. Thus, in swimming, teachers may provide specific information to their learners on the angle at which their arms enter the water or the size of the leg kicks. Teachers of reading, on the other hand, decide what to tell their learners based on what they think should be happening cognitively for the reader or based on inferences from products provided by readers. For a beginning reader, oral reading is one of the most common products from which a teacher may infer processes. The inferences that are drawn help answer the instructional questions of "how is the learner doing?" and "what can I do to help?" One of the major sources of assistance a teacher can give, when helping a learner acquire a complex, unobservable, cognitive skill such as reading, is to provide feedback if and when a learner needs it (Smith, 1975).

The purpose of this chapter is to examine the pupil-teacher interactions which occur as the result of unexpected responses or miscues made by readers during oral reading and the corresponding response decisions made by the teacher. These teacher responses are defined as feedback.

THE FEEDBACK PROCESS

The importance of feedback in the learning process has been well documented (cf. Kulhavy, 1977). Learners who undertake an action and receive information about their efforts usually do better than those who do not have some form of subsequent information available to them. While this generalization can be offered with some degree of comfort, the specification of such associated factors as the type of feedback information, the frequency with which feedback needs to be administered, the timing of the feedback, who can most effectively provide the feedback, and how individual learner differences interact with aspects of the feedback process are far less well understood for the acquisition of literacy.

Feedback, like any widely used term, is represented by a large if not fuzzy set of meanings. For this chapter it is defined as a source of information, external to the stimulus, which aids learners in the solution of a problem (Bourne, 1966). This information, which is provided subsequent to processing, draws the learner's attention to the accuracy of the response and may contain augmenting information. In the case of an incorrect answer the augmenting information might represent the correct answer or attempt to lead learners to the correct answer with the intent of indicating how they should respond in the future. Anderson, Brophy, and Evertson (1979) designate providing the correct response as *terminal feedback* and providing cues to the correct answer as *sustaining feedback*.

Teachers generally provide feedback to learners because they believe that knowledge of results will yield improved performance. However, to produce better performance three conditions must be present: the learner must be motivated, the knowledge of results must be informative, and the learner must be told what to do to correct the error (McKeachie, 1974).

As was mentioned, a learner must be motivated for knowledge of results to improve performance. Thus, teachers face the task of motivating learners as well as providing them with informative feedback (terminal and sustaining). Often teachers will combine informative feedback with affective feedback or praise which conveys the teacher's surprise, delight, or excitement regarding the learner's performance (Brophy, 1981). Although the affective dimension of feedback is certainly important in the learning process, it is beyond the scope of this chapter. The primary purpose of this review will be limited to the informational aspects of the feedback process during oral reading and some of the teacher and learner behaviors that are related to the interactive nature of the process.

FEEDBACK VIEWED AS DECISION MAKING

Teacher feedback behavior during oral reading can be explained from a decision-making perspective. To do so, one must first examine the instructional intentions of teachers and learners. Oral reading can serve a number of instructional purposes. For example, a teacher might use oral reading as an assessment and evaluation tool for monitoring the acquisition process, for a practice activity, or for a direct instructional activity to convey knowledge about the application of a given skill or a subskill. For beginning readers, oral reading is an opportunity to perform the major purpose of reading, constructing meaning. Also, they may have the opportunity to refine or extend their word recognition knowledge by testing hypotheses about relatively unfamiliar words.

Thus, during the oral reading activity there are three major processes potentially occurring simultaneously: teaching, learning, and reading. Because each major process is itself interactive, the potential for higher order interactions between teachers, learners, and text is almost assured. Admittedly, such a portrayal of the oral reading event is overwhelming but it is necessary. For teachers and researchers to understand the process of feedback during oral reading, we need to acknowledge the simultaneity of the three interactions and the effects that changes within each interaction can have on another interaction and the final outcomes of the instructional event. None of the studies reviewed here attempted to deal with all of the interactions. However, their contributions help explain critical pieces of the instructional activity and will allow for the design of more comprehensive studies.

To date, efforts to study teacher feedback during oral reading have focused primarily on describing teacher behaviors, the effects of feedback on reading behavior, and training teachers to administer feedback effectively. It would be possible to organize a review in terms of these three areas, but the hope here is to examine not only what is known but what should be. For that reason, this review will be organized around the decisions that teachers make about providing feedback during oral reading.

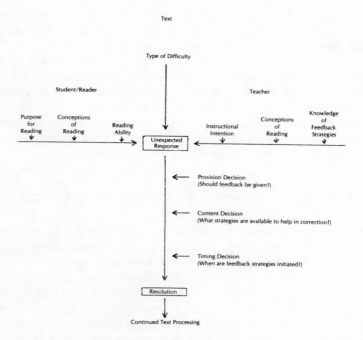

Figure 1.   Framework for analyzing teacher–pupil interactions during oral reading instruction.

Because of the numerous possible variations in oral reading feedback situations, Figure 1 is presented to help describe a set of typical behaviors of a reader and teacher. It is not intended to be an inclusive model but rather a point of departure for discussion. The framework uses a decision-making notion (cf. Shavelson & Stern, 1981) as the explanatory vehicle. It portrays the interactions between and among text, reader, and teacher as a series of decisions which are affected by teacher, learner, text, and classroom context variables. Teacher variables include such points as knowledge of feedback strategies, conceptions of reading, and purpose or intention. Reader variables may include reading ability, conceptions of reading, and purpose. Type and difficulty are the principle text variables, and type of setting, group or tutoring, as well as general classroom environmental features, form the context variables.

While reading orally most readers normally make some unexpected responses. Once the miscue is made it sets in motion a potential teacher–student interaction which is driven and modified by variables such as those mentioned above. First, the teacher must decide whether or not to respond to the miscue and provide feedback. Next, if feedback is to be provided, the teacher must decide on the informational content of the feedback, i.e., will the response be an indication of inaccuracy or will it contain augmenting information such as the correct response (terminal feedback) or cues for the correct response (sustaining feedback)? Finally, the teacher must decide on the best time to deliver the feedback, immediately or at some subsequent point or time. After this student–teacher interaction some resolution is attained and text processing continues. Temporally, this process may last a second or it may be drawn out to 30 seconds or longer (Hoffman, 1982).

Instructional Contexts and Feedback Decisions

The findings of the studies reviewed in this chapter must be tempered with the factor of instructional context. A number of studies on oral reading have been done in group settings under typical classroom circumstances and others have been conducted in one-to-one tutoring. In addition, the length of time of treatment has varied in experimental studies. The major concern regarding these context differences is the amount of feedback any one reader receives. For example, a reader in a classroom group setting will not have the intensive feedback interactions that a reader will receive on a one-to-one basis. In a group during a half hour oral reading period readers may spend between 50 and 60% of their time reading and many receive feedback about 10% of the time. In a group of five that is about 3 minutes of reading time per child (Hoffman, & Clements, 1981). A child in a tutoring setting may read for as much as 10–15 minutes. Assuming similar error rates, the individually tutored child will have three to five times as many feedback opportunities as the child in a group.

At this point it is impossible to determine how much feedback administered over what period of time is required to produce an intended effect for an individual reader. Moreover, it is not known how much transfer there is to one member of a group from the feedback received by another. These are important questions which will ultimately demand answers.

Similarly, we do not know the interactive effects of several different training strategies. We know, for example, that reader strategies are affected by instruction (Barr, 1974/75). However, in a number of the studies reviewed there is serious confounding of various oral reading feedback strategies in lessons. These were usually heavily decoding-oriented, based on the perceived instructional needs of the readers, but the exact nature and mix of feedback was not always described. It seems likely that the instructional needs of the reader, the selected feedback strategy, and the overall instructional plan interact to produce differential reading behaviors.

Feedback Decision Choices

Figure 2 schematically displays a teacher's decisions about giving feedback following a student's miscues during oral reading: (1) whether to provide feedback, (2) form and content of feedback, and (3) timing of feedback. This representation is intended to frame teacher decisions in some reasonable sequence for discussion purposes only. In practice, teachers may change the order of the decisions or default on various decisions for any number of reasons.

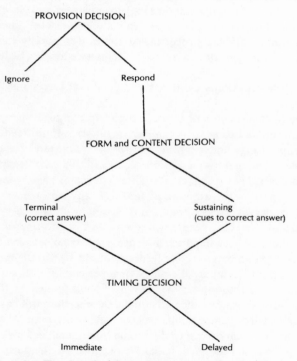

Figure 2.   Teacher decisions about responding to miscues.

This decision scheme will be used to present much of the pertinent literature concerning feedback during oral reading. Generally, I have included extended discussions of studies under the decision category in which I feel they have made their major contribution. However, in some cases an investigation will fall into more than one decision category.

Provision Decision

The provision choice ("Should I provide feedback?") is the critical or highest order decision in the feedback process. If the answer is no, then the process is completed. If it is yes, then the teacher proceeds to subsequent decision making.

The "no" argument for not providing students with feedback is that it interrupts fluent processing of language, interferes with comprehension, and impedes the development of vital self-correction strategies (Smith, 1975). The "yes" argument is embedded in the direct-instruction model because it calls for immediate corrective feedback to improve word recognition accuracy, which is expected to lead to good comprehension (Engelmann, 1969).

Teachers seem to be in the middle of the two positions. In classroom settings, second-grade teachers gave feedback to their oral readers 65% of the time and no feedback 35% of the time (Hoffman & Clements, 1981). A group of studies represents these two polarities of the provision argument and measures the effects on readers' word recognition and comprehension performances.

Pehrsson (1974) had 25 fifth graders read orally from different 200-word sixth-grade passages under one of three conditions: (1) comprehension, in which the readers received no help but were directed to read for meaning; (2) correction, in which readers were asked to correct each unexpected response and told to pay attention to words; and (3) unaided, in which readers were not assisted but were directed to pay close attention to words. The dependent measures were comprehension as measured by an RMI format (Goodman & Burke, 1972), rate of reading, and number of errors. Main effects were evident across all conditions for each dependent variable. (No rate was recorded for the correct condition.) Specifically, the comprehension condition (reading only) was superior to the correction condition and the word attention condition.

Pehrsson (1974) contended that a meaning orientation was beneficial to both comprehension and word recognition as measured by the number of errors. The study also reflected the ability of at least some readers to provide their own feedback effectively. However, the superior performance in comprehension is not unusually surprising given the directions for the three conditions and the methods of comprehension testing. Overtly directing readers' attention to one level of information (word) and then testing at another raises the possibility of confounding in transfer from processing to testing (Stein, 1978), which can be spuriously interpreted within a levels of processing framework (Craik & Lockhart, 1972). Moreover, the dependent measure of number of errors can be quite misleading without a qualitative analysis. While an RMI procedure was used, the reporting of results did not include adequate information about the qualitative findings. In contrast, in a similar investigation, Niles, Graham, and Winstead (1977) found that there was no difference in the number of errors made in a teacher correction condition compared with a no-correction condition.

Niles et al. (1977) compared fourth-grade readers' performance under a correction condition in which the teacher used graphic and sound prompts and an uninterrupted condition whereby no feedback was given. Unlike the subjects in Pehrsson (1974), both groups were told that they would be asked to tell about what they read. Also, treatment was conducted on four consecutive days for 15 minutes per day. A qualitative analysis of the miscues made on the fifth day using RMI procedures (Goodman & Burke, 1972) showed higher graphic and sound similarity scores for the readers who received graphophonic (letter-to-sound) prompts such as "sound it out" and a higher proportion of meaning-preserving responses for the readers who did not receive teacher feedback. The uninterrupted readers also produced higher retelling scores.

The results of this study (Niles et al., 1977) indicated that at least some readers can effectively provide their own feedback and that consistent feedback behavior by the teacher can yield a qualitatively predictable pattern of reader behavior. However, the range of teacher feedback behavior examined by Niles et al. (1977) and Pehrsson (1974) was limited and the range of reading ability was narrow. The single type of feedback information used directed the readers' attention to only one available due source, graphophonic. Also, there is evidence that good and poor readers may not use information cues in text similarly (cf. Weber, 1970). Thus an interaction might be predicted between ability and the type of information contained in the sustaining feedback.

A number of ethnographic investigations have verified differential treatment for good and poor readers. The studies have found over and over again that poor or low group readers were interrupted (provided feedback) more than their good counterparts on similar error patterns. Moreover, poor readers received greater instruction on pronunciation and single-word decoding (cf. Collins, 1981; Cook-Gumperz, Gumperz, & Simons, 1981).

Allington (1980) specifically examined the differential instruction proposition over 20 teachers and 147 good and 120 poor first- and second-grade readers. The teachers and readers were taped during their normal group oral reading activities. The transcripts were analyzed for the selection (response vs. no response), timing (point of feedback), and content of the prompt (graphemes, phonemes, semantic/syntactic, teacher pronunciation, and other). Based on proportion scores for errors made, because good readers read with 99% accuracy and poor readers 96%, the poor readers received far more feedback than good readers—74 to 31%, respectively. Even for semantically unacceptable responses, the poor readers received more feedback than good readers—76 to 54%, respectively. Only 20% of the time when poor readers made an inappropriate semantic response were they allowed to read on, compared with 52% for good readers. The pattern for the content of the response for poor readers was teacher pronouncing the word 50%, graphemic 28%, and semantic 8%. For good readers it was 38%, 18%, and 32%, respectively.

The teachers in the Allington (1980) study seem to be indicating that they are willing to accept that their good readers know what they are doing and need less assistance but that poor readers' errors, even when equated for quality, need the teacher's attention, through feedback, to improve learning. This behavior would seem to coincide with statements by teachers who indicated they would temper their conceptualizations about reading based on the reading ability of their students (Bawden, Burke, & Duffy, 1979).

Pany, McCoy, and Peters (1981) examined teacher feedback behavior effects on poor readers' performance. They conducted a constructive replication of the Niles et al. study (1977) using remedial students. They used two age levels (primary and intermediate), extended the treatment time to 10 days, and measured comprehension with story retelling and comprehension questions. Pany et al. (1981) failed to replicate Niles et al. (1977) in all but one instance. The story retellings of the no-correction primary readers were significantly better than those of the corrective feedback primary readers. However, the major conclusion was that corrective feedback may not necessarily be a hindrance to effective comprehension processing. Similarly, students who were not interrupted were generally not impeded in their reading by the lack of feedback. Pany et al. (1981) added several new dimensions to the study of teacher feedback effects. Their discussion raised the possibility of text type, expository and narrative, as a variable for consideration, as well as how much feedback might affect comprehension. Neither of these variables was controlled by Niles et al. (1977). Moreover, the extensions to poor readers, the increase in treatment time, and the multiple measures of comprehension are all important contributions to this study. Yet the findings of the study must be interpreted in light of the participants' instructional program. From the description given, a large portion of the program was devoted to the development of decoding skills (phonics, isolated word recognition, and spelling). It is possible that this heavy instructional emphasis on decoding could have interacted with the comprehension and word recognition purposes during oral reading and acted to override any feedback effects, i.e., readers who received a consistently large dose of graphophonic instruction may have reacted differently to graphophonic feedback than readers who were in a more balanced program.

Focused interviews with teachers (Hoffman & Kugle, 1981) suggest that reader ability is also a factor in the decision about providing feedback. Teachers commented that a student's reading ability definitely affects their decision to intercede. For example, with a poor reader a teacher might let a significant miscue pass if the student had already been interrupted frequently. Conversely, with a good reader, a teacher might interrupt on a non-meaning-change miscue because the teacher "hadn't said anything for a while." Although these comments do not systematically describe teacher's provision behavior, they do reflect the fact that poor readers are making significantly more errors than good readers (Hoffman, 1982) and that teachers are responding differentially.

Thus, teachers in general do not provide feedback for all unexpected responses. However, they do give proportionately more feedback to poor readers than to good readers. While there are broad outlines of the effects of feedback on comprehension and word recognition, the studies on selection (the decision to provide or not to provide feedback) have raised many issues. Some of the more important are the following:

1. What effects might text type have on the feedback process?
2. How much feedback is required by a learner to manifest an effect on reading performance?
3. Are there interactive effects between the overall instructional program and specific teacher feedback patterns?
4. Are there differential feedback needs for beginning, poor, and proficient readers?

Form and Content Decision

Once teachers decide to provide feedback to a reader they also must decide what form and content the feedback should take. The second-grade students in the Hoffman and Clements study (1981) were prompted 64% of the time while reading. Fifty percent of the feedback was terminal (the teacher pronounced the word), 14% was sustaining feedback (the reader was given clues to the word's pronunciation), and 35% of the time teachers ignored the miscue and provided no feedback. Allington's (1980) primary-grade teachers were somewhat less likely to supply a word (approximately 20%) and more likely to ignore a response (about 54% for the combined sample); they supplied sustaining feedback 20% of the time. In addition, these teachers used an accuracy prompt of "no" 8% of the time. (The figures of Allington's participants are my estimates based on combining the low and high groups because he presented the findings by ability groups.) Both investigations (Allington, 1980, and Hoffman & Clements, 1981) found differential feedback patterns for high- and low-ability students regarding the content of the feedback. This issue will be addressed later.

It is clear that teachers can and do vary the form and content of their feedback. Terry and Cohen (1977) actually trained participating teachers to vary their feedback, first in provision (correcting only meaning change miscues) and then in the specific content of feedback (structural analysis, attention, word families, phonics, or context). The purpose of the study was to examine prompting differences by teachers and performance differences by high and low readers. Since most teachers have not received training on the development and application of a repertoire of feedback strategies (Hoffman & Kugle, 1983), this study adds an interesting and valuable feature to the literature.

Unfortunately, several design flaws reduce somewhat the usefulness of their findings. The sample selection was generated by students reading between one and two levels below grade level. It seems awkward to label the stratification of the sample high and low readers. In fact, four of the nine "low readers" were less than one grade equivalent year below eight of the "high readers." Also, based on more recent work (Hoffman & Clements, 1981), it seems that a number of sustaining prompts in the Terry and Cohen study (1977) are of the same content category, i.e., letter names, spelling isolated sounds, sound out, word families, and phonics are graphophonic feedback whereas word meaning and context are contextual. Structural analysis (the teacher tells the readers one or more syllables of the text word) might be described as a form of partial word supply or combined contextual and partial word supply, which would frequently render the same results as the typical terminal feedback response (teacher supplying the correct word).

If the findings of Terry and Cohen (1977) are collapsed across high and low groups to eliminate the rather questionable sample stratification and condensed into the subcategories of graphophonic, attention, context (sustaining), and word supply (terminal), we see that the tutors did differentiate the content of their prompts, including 54% sustaining feedback and 20% terminal. These findings were higher than Allington's overall findings but closer to his low readers' feedback pattern. Moreover, 24% of the feedback was graphophonic, 12% was attentional, and 16% was contextual. Because of the overlap in grouping, it is impossible to explain this differentiation adequately. However, the major finding of this study is important in that it demonstrated that teachers will differentiate their feedback strategies if given some preparation. It is even more interesting that these teachers were using, with these poor readers, far more sustaining feedback than was found in the normal classroom settings of other such studies (Allington, 1980; Hoffman & Clements, 1981). Whether the increase in sustaining behavior was a result of the training, the instructional context, and/or the ability of the readers remains an open question. The stability of the sustaining behavior by teachers also needs to be tested.

Niles (1979) systematically varied the content of sustaining teacher feedback for average third-grade readers. He used graphophonic feedback, contextual or semantic feedback, global sentence-repeat feedback, and no-feedback conditions. Treatment and testing were conducted over a 5-day period and delivered on an individual basis. The results revealed that readers who received graphophonic feedback were more likely to produce responses that changed the author's intended meaning than readers who received contextual feedback. However, the content of sustaining feedback did not affect the readers' use of graphophonic information or their ability to recall what they had read, i.e., readers who received sustaining feedback, graphophonic or contextual, produced similar quality miscues when compared on the graphophonic criterion. Also, neither type of sustaining feedback affected the overall free recall of the participants. These two findings are in contrast to those in Niles et al. (1977). Although readers who received different forms and content of sustaining feedback did not manifest any significant difference in their comprehension as measured by free recall and literal level questions, an important finding of this study was the verification that consistent teacher feedback behavior can produce predictable changes in student reading performance. In this case, if teachers consistently directed readers' attention to contextual or semantic information through semantic feedback, the readers produced higher quality meaning miscues.

The fact that graphophonic feedback did not influence readers similarly does not preclude the explanation that teachers' feedback focuses reader attention on various levels of information. What must be considered is the baseline performance of readers regarding their predisposition to the various levels of information. Reading differences in attention to information sources have been documented based on developmental levels (cf. Goodman & Burke, 1973) as well as by ability (Pflaum, Pascarella, Bostwick, & Auer, 1980). Niles (1979) did not account for these potential individual differences by obtaining a pretreatment measure of readers' use of the various levels of information. Average third graders might still be in the code emphasis stage of instruction. Thus the intervention of graphophonic feedback may not affect beginning readers as much as a semantic feedback because their attention is already intensively directed to the graphic cue source. This explanation may also hold for poor readers' performance.

It would seem that to measure teacher feedback effects researchers are going to have to demonstrate change in reader behavior more clearly than they have to this point. To design such studies they will need to account for entering behavior more adequately.

As with the initial decision about provision, it is apparent from the descriptions provided by Allington (1980) and Hoffman and Clements (1981) that teachers differentiate the content of their prompts based on a reader's ability. Allington's (1980) poor readers were more likely to receive a graphophonic prompt and less likely to receive a contextual prompt than were good readers. Also poor readers were more likely to have a miscue pronounced for them by the teacher; this finding was also reported by Hoffman and Clements (1981). Given these teacher preferences for content of feedback related to reader ability, the interaction questions assume additional importance.

Descriptive studies (Allington, 1980; Hoffman & Clements, 1981) have given us some insight into the substance of behavior for teachers and children during oral reading. These studies indicate that teachers do differentiate the content of their prompts, and one of the major factors in this differentiation is the reader's ability. A second set of studies (Terry & Cohen, 1977; Niles, 1979; Hoffman, Kastler, O'Neal & Daly, 1982) has attempted to examine the effects of differentiated feedback prompting on reader performance. These studies have several things in common. First, they were conducted under clinical conditions, with one-to-one tutoring, and second, they attempted to examine effects created by consistent teacher administration of feedback prompts. Teachers can influence reader behavior with their feedback but the exact nature of the influence has not been adequately described because of confounding methodological factors.

Findings from these studies raise some interesting questions:

1. How would training in feedback strategies affect teachers' classroom behavior?
2. Are findings from clinical studies at all applicable to classroom settings?
   a. Is it possible for classroom teachers to administer feedback in consistent patterns?
   b. Would consistent feedback patterns in a classroom setting yield predictable miscue profiles for readers?
3. Can any long-term achievement effects be generated for poor readers by altering the content of the classroom teachers' feedback to approximate the feedback provided to good readers?

Timing Decision

Once teachers determine the content of the feedback, they must decide when to administer it. (It is also possible that at times they decide when, then what.) Descriptions of feedback in classroom settings indicate that teachers tend to provide information at the point of error or in less than 3 seconds after the miscue has been made (Allington, 1980; Hoffman & Clements, 1981). The conventional laws of learning would seem to support such behavior. However, a reconceptualization of learning principles from a cognitive perspective argues against the overgeneralization of the acceptance of the immediacy principles for teacher feedback in oral reading (McKeachie, 1974). While the question of timing is an open one, it is clear that variations in timing of feedback by teachers affect reader performance.

McNaughton and Glynn (1981) examined the influence of timing of feedback on oral reading performance. Their operational definition of immediately was within 5 seconds and for delay was a teacher response at phrase or sentence boundary. The findings revealed that readers were less accurate and self-corrected a smaller percentage of miscues under the immediate correction condition. Also, readers were more likely to exhibit these same characteristics when reading independently. McNaughton and Glynn (1981) commented that the immediate interruptions by the teacher interfere with the normal monitoring activities of a reader and impede the development of the important skill of self-correction. In a further examination of the timing data, McNaughton (1981) analyzed miscues from the independent reading sample in the earlier investigation. The second-year students were prompted in an immediate or delayed manner on the treatment day and then read independently on the following day. This cycle occurred four times. The readers who received immediate correction were less likely to offer a response on troublesome text words and less likely to self-correct miscues which were semantically unacceptable, syntactically unacceptable, and graphically dissimilar.

An important elaboration in the McNaughton and Glynn study (1981) is the emphasis on transfer of effects of teacher feedback. They measured reading performance on alternate days and found that readers' performance manifested effects from the previous day's instruction without the corresponding feedback from the teacher. Few studies have included or demonstrated this transfer effect.

Reading ability and content and timing of feedback are surely interactive. One of the most comprehensive studies in teacher feedback in oral reading was conducted by Hoffman and his colleagues (Hoffman, Clements, O'Neal, Nash, & Kastler, 1982). They varied content of feedback (terminal, graphophonic sustaining, and contextual sustaining), timing (immediate and delayed), and reading ability (high and low). Participants read two passages under their assigned conditions. Feedback was given on eight targeted difficult words per passage which appeared twice per passage. The results indicated that differences in feedback can affect reading performance. The lower ability readers in the immediate graphophonic condition tended to manifest more hesitations in their reading behavior than higher ability readers. This tendency to hesitate in the immediate condition is similar to the nonresponse behavior that McNaughton (1981) found for his immediately prompted readers. The effects of timing are also evident for poor readers when combined with content; the immediate contextual prompt was followed by more mispronunciations. It is possible that the immediate correction for low readers does not allow them the processing time necessary to apply critical strategies (Hoffman, O'Neal, & Clements, 1981; McNaughton, 1981; and Allington, 1980). Thus the low readers are either hesitant to respond or quickly produce an arbitrary response, perhaps because they feel help is coming anyway.

Delayed contextual prompting, on the other hand, had a significant positive effect on readers' identification of their own miscues. Also, delayed feedback enabled readers in all prompting conditions to identify the target word on its second occurrence more frequently than readers who received immediate feedback.

The timing studies share one major limitation, as do all the attempts to study feedback behavior experimentally: they were conducted in a tutorial or individual instructional setting. Whether these effects would hold under normal classroom conditions is open to question.

Timing does appear to play an important role in teacher feedback behavior, particularly for poor readers. Descriptive studies reveal that teachers tend to provide more immediate feedback for poor readers (Allington, 1980; Hoffman & Clements, 1981). Interviews indicate that teachers want to reduce frustration for poorer readers. Also, teachers with a stronger decoding orientation in reading seem to prompt more immediately (Hoffman & Kugle, 1981). The initial work on timing of feedback is promising but will require elaboration. Some major questions which remain unanswered are similar to the content decision questions:

1. Does or can the timing of feedback have an effect on readers in a classroom setting?
2. How consistent does a timing pattern have to be to generate an effect?
3. Can a delayed timing pattern affect the long-term development pattern of a beginning reader's self-correction strategy?
4. What is the relationship between delayed feedback and the acquisition of new sight vocabulary?

METHODOLOGY ISSUES

The case has been made that to study feedback satisfactorily a system must be used which accounts for both teacher and reader behavior. Brady and Lynch (1976a) developed an instrument which describes and categorizes reader responses and concomitant teacher feedback behavior. Brady and Lynch see feedback in oral reading as a means of improving word recognition. Moreover, the Brady and Lynch conceptualization views the end goal of teacher feedback (prompting) as no prompting at all. In other words, they see the teacher goal as guiding readers through the use of judicious feedback to develop independent feedback processes by effectively using all three cue systems (graphophonic, syntactic, and semantic). While they state that their purpose is word recognition, the description indicates that the overall objective of teacher feedback is to produce effective self-correcting strategies characteristic of mature readers.

Their descriptive data indicate that teachers (1) tend to correct all miscues, regardless of appropriateness, (2) utilize almost no meaning prompts, and (3) prompt with clues that are unsuccessful in developing independent decoding. Their correction finding tends to conflict with Allington's (1980) results for good readers. Brady and Lynch (1976a) do not report student ability, so it is impossible to draw any generalizations about this difference. The Brady and Lynch teachers were like Allington's (1980) in that they produced few meaning prompts.

From the observation of teachers and review of the literature, Brady and Lynch (1976b) developed a nine-category observation instrument to analyze both reader and teacher behavior (Oral Reading Observation Schedule). In general, the instrument indicates whether or not the miscue changes meaning and how the pupil responds to prompts (reader behavior), and whether the teacher provides look or sound prompts, provides meaning prompts, or supplies the word (teacher behavior). Interestingly, category 7 on the instrument is labeled feedback and management, which implies that Brady and Lynch do not consider the teacher prompts as a form of feedback. Apparently they feel that feedback consists of either knowledge of results only (correct or incorrect) or nonacademic reminders. This conception does not conform to the definition in this chapter of feedback as external information provided to the learner which increases the probability of a correct response in the future. Nonetheless their findings and instrument are relevant to this discussion.

The purpose of the Oral Reading Observation Schedule (OROS) is to determine whether teachers are using effective prompts and whether readers are assimilating these prompts as part of their own reading strategies. Apparently, Brady and Lynch are suggesting that the acquisition of appropriate self-feedback (self-correction) procedures by the reader can be assisted through the thoughtful systematic application of feedback strategies during oral reading. Investigations conducted by Biemiller (1970), Weber (1970), and Goodman (1973), for example, suggest that readers do indeed progress developmentally in their acquisition and use of self-feedback strategies.

This notion of teaching acquisition of self-feedback procedures is provocative in the manner in which it treats the two general purposes for oral reading, improved word recognition and practicing skilled reading behavior in an integrated format. Most investigations to date (cf. Jenkins & Larson, 1978; Niles, 1979) have examined these issues independently. Currently, extensive testing of the Brady and Lynch notion is unavailable.

A more sophisticated and sensitive instrument, FORMAS, has been developed by Hoffman and Baker (1981). The FORMAS is similar to the OROS in that it measures and categorizes teacher and student behavior simultaneously. The FORMAS improves on the OROS by more clearly defining the teacher feedback categories under the three dimensions used in this chapter: provision, content, and timing. In addition, the FORMAS allows for qualitative analysis of student miscues, recognition of related reactions of students, and classification of the final resolution. The instrument has been used extensively in a program of research by its developer (Hoffman, 1982) as well as by others (Johnston & Afflerback, 1983).

The OROS and the FORMAS are useful tools for studying the feedback process in oral reading from both teacher and student perspectives. Yet we must be concerned with the limitations of the qualitative analysis of miscues when trying to draw instructional implications from studies which use such analysis (Leu, 1982). Oral reading is not an end product of reading instruction for beginning readers. Rather, it is an instructional event along the way to developing proficient reading.

While the development of instrumentation has helped in the study of teacher feedback behavior, the interactive nature of the activity has presented difficult design problems. Most of the evidence we have compiled on feedback in oral reading is descriptive and correlational (Hoffman, 1982). The few attempts at establishing causal links have been modest (e.g., Hoffman, 1982; Niles, 1980). However, results of these studies have provided the basis for more productive studies.

Johnston and Afflerback (1983) offer a promising way to study specific intervention effects and student behavioral change during oral reading using a single-subject, multiple-baseline design. The advantage of such a design for studying teachers and pupils in instructional settings is that the behavior of teachers, after planned interventions, can be charted and analyzed over time. Moreover, the concomitant behavior of students can also be carefully monitored and causally linked to changes in teacher performance.

Although this methodology may be used for any student–teacher instructional sequence, Johnson and Afflerback tested its usefulness by examining teachers' timing decisions and student performance during oral reading in a remedial program. Using direct and indirect methods of instructional intervention with the tutors, they found that they were able to trace observable changes in tutor feedback behavior for timing related to interventions. Similarly, they observed concomitant changes in the reading behavior of the pupils. For example, one of the tutors was giving immediate feedback to a student in the first several sessions. The tutor's pupil was producing almost no self-corrections. After session 2, the instructor suggested that the tutor allow more "think time" for the student. During session 3, the tutor did change behavior and supplied delayed feedback; the student's behavior also changed as self-corrections increased and hesitation errors decreased.

The single-subject design is attractive because it can account for the reader's entering behavior. This consideration has been noticeably absent from prior research and needs to be addressed if useful and verifiable instructional interventions for both students and teachers are going to emerge from feedback research during oral reading. The OROS and the FORMAS are instruments which are designed to accommodate this requirement.

SUMMARY AND OVERALL CONCLUSIONS

Oral reading is ubiquitous as an instructional activity in beginning reading instruction. Descriptive studies have shown that teachers do provide feedback to readers during oral reading and that teachers differentiate their behavior based on a reader's ability. It is clear that instructional decisions by the teacher regarding whether feedback is needed, what the content of the feedback should be, and when it should be delivered have effects on the reading behavior of students. The specific effects of teacher feedback have yet to be documented because of the failure of existing research to account for such variables as present instructional program of participants, adequate qualitative description of reading ability of participants, and sufficient control of text type and difficulty. Yet even imperfect studies can contribute to knowledge if we interpret them with full understanding of their strengths and weaknesses. We must depend most heavily on the findings a given study is best designed to test and qualify other findings appropriately in terms of studies that have more fully explored other relevant factors. Each study can contribute to the total picture. Patterns that converge though drawn from different sources are most convincing.

At this point it would seem that enough evidence is available from descriptive and quasi-experimental studies to encourage us to move ahead in our efforts to examine teacher feedback behavior during oral reading. Research in teacher effectiveness has demonstrated that specific teacher behaviors will create predictable patterns of learner responses. While the complexities of the teaching, learning, and reading processes prevent any simplistic causal explanations of teacher–pupil effects, we now know enough to design intervention studies that can control for individual differences and context variables and systematically vary the amount, content, and timing of teacher feedback. Single-subject design studies, experimental studies, and naturalistic classroom studies can all provide the opportunities we need to construct a useful model for teacher behavior during the critical instructional interactions in oral reading. Because of the numerous possible teacher feedback decisions available, we must avoid the temptation to make the model prescriptive (Doyle, 1978). The model needs to structure vital information about learners, contexts, strategies, and effects in a form which enables teachers to use the information rationally in the planning, delivery, and evaluation of their instruction. The creation of such a model will not be an easy task, yet the payoff will surely be worth the effort.

REFERENCES

Allington, R.L. (1983). The reading instruction provided readers of differing abilities. *Elementary School Journal*, *93*(5), 548-559.
Allington, R.L. (1980). Teacher interruption behaviors during primary grade oral reading. *Journal of Educational Psychology*, *72*, 371-377.
Anderson, L., Evertson, C., & Brophy, J. (1979). An experimental study of effective teaching in first grade reading groups. *Elementary School Journal*, *79*, 193-222.
Artley, A.S. (1972). Oral reading as a communication process. *Reading Teacher*, *36*, 46-51.
Barr, R. (1974/75). The effect of instruction on pupil reading strategies. *Reading Research Quarterly*, *4*, 555-582.
Bawden, R., Burke, S., & Duffy, G. (1979). *Teacher conceptions of reading and their influence on instruction* (Report No. 47). East Lansing, MI: Institute for Research on Teaching.
Biemiller, A.J. (1970). The development of the use of graphic and contextual information as children learn to read. *Reading Research Quarterly*, *6*(4), 75-96.
Bourne, L.E. (1966). *Human conceptual behavior*. Boston: Allyn & Bacon.
Brady, M., & Lynch, W. (1976a, April). *Observing reading teachers: A critique of systems and the development of an instrument specific to teaching word recognition*. Paper presented at American Educational Research Association, San Francisco.

Brady, M., & Lynch, W. (1976b).*Oral reading observation system: Observer's training manual.* Bloomington, IN: Center for Innovation in Teaching the Handicapped.

Brophy, J. (1981). Teacher praise: A functional analysis. *Review of Educational Research, 51*, (1), 5-32.

Carroll, J.B., & Chall, J. (1975). *Toward a literate society: The report of the committee on reading of the National Academy of Education.* New York: McGraw-Hill.

Craik, F., & Lockhart, R. (1972). Levels of processing: A framework for memory research. *Journal of Learning Verbal Behavior, 11*, 671-684.

Collins, J. (1981). Differential treatment in reading instruction. In J. Cook-Gumperz, J. Gumperz, & H. Simons, *School-home ethnography project* (NIE G-780082). Washington, D.C.: National Institute of Education. (Final Report)

Cook-Gumperz, J., Gumperz, J., & Simons, H.D. (1981). *School-home ethnography project* (NIE G-78-0082). Washington, D.C.: Institute of Education. (Final Report).

Doyle, W. (1978). Paradigms for research in teacher effectiveness. In L.S. Shulman (Ed.), *Review of research in education* (Vol. 5). Itasca: IL: F. E. Peacock, 5, 163-198.

Engelmann, S. (1969). *Preventing failure in the primary grades.* New York: Simon & Schuster.

Goodman, K. (1970). Behind the eye: What happens in reading. In K. Goodman & O. Niles (Eds.), *Reading: Process and programs.* Urbana, IL: National Council for Teachers of English, pp. 3-38.

Goodman, K.S., & Burke, C.L. (1973 April). *Theoretically based studies of patterns of miscues in oral reading performance.* (U.S.O.E. Project No. 90375) Washington, D.C.: U.S. Department of Health Education and Welfare.

Goodman, Y, & Burke, C. (1972). *Reading Miscue Inventory Manual.* New York: Macmillan.

Harste, J.C., & Burke, C. (1977). A new hypothesis for reading teacher research: Both the teaching and learning of reading are theoretically based. In P. David Pearson (Ed.), *Reading: Theory, research and practice.* Twenty-sixth Yearbook of the National Reading Conference, Clemson, SC: The National Reading Conference.

Hoffman, J.V. (1979). On providing feedback to reading miscues. *Reading World*, May, 342-350.

Hoffman, J.V. (1982). Feedback to oral reading miscues. (NIE 6-80-0030) Washington, D.C.: National Institute of Education. (Final Report).

Hoffman, J.V. (1981). Is there a legitimate place for oral reading instruction in the developmental reading program? *Elementary School Journal, 81*(5), 305-317.

Hoffman, J.V., & Baker, C. (1981). Characterizing teacher feedback to student miscues during oral reading instruction. *The Reading Teacher, 34*, 907-913.

Hoffman, J.V., & Clements, R.O. (1981, May). *A descriptive study of the characteristics of miscue focused verbal interactions between teacher and students during guided oral reading.* Paper presented at the annual meeting of the International Reading Association. New Orleans.

Hoffman, J.V., Clements, R.O., O'Neal, S.F., Nash, M.F., Kastler, L., & Segel, K.W. (1983, April). *Guided oral reading and miscue focused verbal feedback in second grade classrooms.* Paper presented at the annual conference of the American Educational Research Association, New York.

Hoffman, J.V., & Kugel, C. (1983). A study of theoretical orientation to reading and its relationship to teacher verbal feedback during reading instruction. *Journal of Classroom Interaction, 18*(1), 2-7.

Howlett, N., & Weintraub, S. (1979). Instructional procedures. In R.C. Calfee & P. Drum (Eds.), *An analytical study of compensatory reading programs.* Newark, DE: International Reading Association.

Jenkins, J., & Larson, K. (1978). *Evaluating error correction procedures for oral reading.* (Technical Report No. 55). Champaign, IL: Center for the Study of Reading, University of Illinois at Champaign-Urbana.

Johnston, P., & Afflerback, P. (1983) Measuring teacher and student change in a remedial clinic. In J. Niles & L. Harris (Eds.), *Searches for meaning in reading language processing and*

226 JEROME A. NILES

instruction. Thirty-second Yearbook of the National Reading Conference. Rochester, NY: The National Reading Conference.

Kulhavy, R.W. (1977). Feedback in written instruction. *Review of Educational Research, 47*, 211-232.

Leu, D. (1982). Oral reading analysis: A critical review of research and application. *Reading Research Quarterly, 17*(3), 420-437.

Kulhavy, R.W., & Anderson, R.C. (1972). Delayed retention effect with multiple choice tests. *Journal of Educational Psychology, 63*, 505-512.

McKeachie, W. (1974). Decline and fall of the laws of learning. *Educational Researcher, 3*, 7-11.

McNaughton, S. (1981). The influence of immediate teacher corrections on self-correction and proficient reading. *Journal of Reading Behavior, 8*(4), 367-371.

McNaughton, S. & Glynn S. (1981). Delayed versus immediate attention to oral reading errors: Effects on accuracy and self-correction. *Educational Psychology, 1*, 57-65.

Niles, J. (1979). The effects of selected teacher prompting strategies on oral reading performance. In A. Moe & M. Kamil (Eds.), *Perspectives on reading research and instruction*, Twenty-Ninth Yearbook of National Reading Conference.

Niles, J.A. (1980, December). *Effects of teacher feedback on beginning readers' oral reading behavior*. Paper presented at the annual meeting of the National Reading Conference, San Diego.

Niles, J.A., Graham, R.T., & Winstead, J.C. (1977). Effects of teachers' response strategies on children's oral reading performance: Case of interference? *Reading in Virginia, 5*, 25-28.

Pany, D., McCoy, K., & Peters, E. (1981). Effects of corrective feedback on comprehension skills of remedial students. *Journal of Reading Behavior, 74*, 99-105.

Pehrsson, D. (1974). Are you a helper Mr. Gelpher? *Journal of Reading, 19*(8), 617-621.

Pflaum, S.W., Pascarella, E.T., Boswick, M., & Auer, C. (1980). The influence of pupil behaviors and pupil status factors on teacher behaviors during oral reading lessons. *Journal of Educational Research, 74*, 99-105.

Shavelson, R.M., & Stern, P.S. (1981). Research on teachers' pedagogical thoughts, judgments, decisions, and behavior. *Review of Educational Research, 51*, 455-498.

Smith, F. (1975). *Comprehension and learning*. New York: Holt, Rinehart & Winston.

Stein, B. (1978). Depth of processing reexamined: The effects of the precision of encoding and text appropriateness. *Journal of Verbal Learning and Verbal Behavior, 17*, 165-174.

Terry, P.R., & Cohen, D. (1977, May). *The effect of different teacher prompting techniques on pupil success in decoding for high and low level readers during oral reading*. Paper presented at the annual meeting of the International Reading Association, Miami.

Weber, R.M. (1970). A linguistic analysis of first grade errors. *Reading Research Quarterly, 5*, 428-451.

Weinstein, R.S. (1976). Reading group membership in first grade: Teacher behaviors and pupil experiences over time. *Journal of Educational Psychology, 68*, 103-116.

INDEX

Ability
   language, reading achievements
      and, initial, individual differ-
      ences in, in peer-directed read-
      ing groups, 87-94
   reading, and disability, neuropsy-
      chology of, 119-124
Acquisition, spelling quality and,
      48-51
Addressing real audiences, use of
      microcomputer in, 106-107
Adult comprehension of expository
      prose, review of issues and
      findings on, 10-15
American educational research, ver-
      sus European, 151-164
Analytic/speculative emphasis,
      empirical versus, in American
      versus European research,
      153-155
Anatomy, brain, 121-124
Asymmetry, language, dual-task
      studies of, personal computer
      for, 184-189
Attentional processes, 140-141

Audiences, real, addressing of, use of
      microcomputer in, 106-107
Automaticity
   in spelling and awareness, 68-70
   preliminary studies of, 63-65
Average readers, dyslexic and, differ-
      ences between, 132-134
Awareness, automaticity and, in spell-
      ing, 68-70

Books
   versus computers, joint parent-
      child reading with, 189-199
   behavioral analyses of, 195-199
Brain anatomy, 121-124

Categorization, 172-174
Cerebral dominance, and dyslexia,
      125-127
Children, use of requests and
      responses by, recent research
      on, 80-82
Communication triangle, components
      of, 170
Communications, human, model of
      processes in, 172

viewed as decision making, 209-221
Form and content decision, on feed-
back, in oral reading, 216-219
Frontal lobe, 123

Game, language, hand-held microelectronic, learning and motivational aspects of, 199-202
Generalization probes, in spelling,
55-63

Hand-held microelectronic language
game, learning and motivational aspects of, 199-202
Human communication, model of
processes in, 172
Hypothesis testing versus illuminative
emphasis, in American versus
European research, 155-160

Illuminative emphasis, hypothesis
testing versus, in American
versus European research,
155-160
Independent variables
affecting comprehension, 10-13,
30-33
measurement of, 13-15
Individual differences
in initial reading achievements and
language ability, in peer-
directed reading groups, 87-94
instructional pragmatism and, in
spelling, 51-54
Instruction, reading, oral, teacher-
pupil interactions during,
research on, 207-224 (*see also*
Feedback)
Instructional contexts, and feedback
decisions, 211-212
Instructional pragmatism, and individual differences, in spelling,
51-54

Integration, of reading and writing,
use of microcomputer in,
101-105
Interactions, teacher-pupil, during
oral reading instruction,
research on, 207-224 (*see also*
Feedback)
Interest
definition of, 11
measurement of, 13-14
and prior knowledge, 12-13
and readability, in relation to
comprehension, study of,
15-35
readability and, 12
analysis of, 22-23

Joint parent-child reading, with
books versus computers,
189-199

Knowledge, prior (*see* Prior
knowledge)

Language ability, reading achievement and, initial, individual
differences in, in peer-directed
reading groups, 87-94
Language asymmetry, dual-task studies of, personal computer for,
184-189
Language function, in dyslexia,
127-132
Language game, hand-held microelectronic, learning and motivational aspects of, 199-202
Language research, and reading
research
personal computers in, 183-203
viewing and reviewing, 1-7
Learning aspects, and motivational,
of hand-held microelectronic
language game, 199-202

Research Annuals and Monographs in Series
in the
BEHAVIORAL SCIENCES

Research Annuals

Advances in Adolescent Mental Health
Edited by Ronald, A. Feldman and Arlene R. Stiffman, *Center for Adolescent Mental Health, Washington University*

Advances in Behavioral Assessment of Children and Families
Edited by Ron Prinz, *Department of Psychology, University of South Carolina*

Advances in Behavioral Medicine
Edited by Edward S. Katkin, *Department of Psychology, State University of New York at Buffalo* and Stephen B. Manuck, *Department of Psychology, University of Pittsburgh*

Advances in Business Marketing
Edited by Arch G. Woodside, *College of Business Administration, University of South Carolina*

Advances in Descriptive Psychology
Edited by Keith E. Davis, *Department of Psychology, University of South Carolina* and Thomas O. Mitchell, *Department of Psychology, Southern Illinois University*

Advances in Developmental and Behavioral Pediatrics
Edited by Mark Wolraich, *Department of Pediatrics, University of Iowa* and Donald K. Routh, *Department of Psychology, University of Iowa*

Advances in Early Education and Day Care
Edited by Sally J. Kilmer, *Department of Home Economics, Bowling Green State University*

Advances in Family Intervention, Assessment and Theory
Edited by John P. Vincent, *Department of Psychology, University of Houston*

Advances in Health Education and Promotion
Edited by William B. Ward, *School of Public Health, University of South Carolina*

Advances in Human Psychopharmacology
Edited by Graham D. Burrows, *Department of Psychiatry, University of Melbourne* and John S. Werry, *Department of Psychiatry, University of Auckland*

Advances in Law and Child Development
Edited by Robert L. Sprague, *Institute for Child Behavior and Development, University of Illinois*

Advances in Learning and Behavioral Disabilities
Edited by Kenneth D. Gadow, *Office of Special Education, State University of New York, Stony Brook*

Advances in Marketing and Public Policy
Edited by Paul N. Bloom, *Department of Marketing, University of Maryland*

Advances in Mental Retardation and Developmental Disabilities
Edited by Stephen E. Breuning, Director of Psychological Services and Behavioral Treatment Polk Center, Johnny L. Matson, *Department of Learning and Development, Northern Illinois University,* and Rowland P. Barrett, *Section on Psychiatry and Human Behavior, Brown University Program in Medicine*

Advances in Motivation and Achievement
Edited by Martin L. Maehr, *Institute for Child Behavior and Development, University of Illinois*

Advances in Nonprofit Marketing
Edited by Russell W. Belk, *Department of Marketing, University of Utah*

Advances in Psychophysiology
Edited by Patrick K. Ackles, *Institute for the Study of Developmental Disabilities, University of Illinois at Chicago,* Richard Jennings, *Western Psychiatric Institute and Clinic, University of Pittsburgh School of Medicine* and Michael G.H. Coles, *Department of Psychology, University of Illinois*